WACO-McLENN
1717
WACO TX 76701

M000222716

To Walter Mouat Johnson (1925–2015) – who gave me all he had;
and who knew exactly how to step up and how to step back

'Too many organizations hold in their collective minds a Hollywood notion of how change happens: A charismatic leader arrives, announces a plan, and delivers change through force of personality. In her wise and provocative book, Elsbeth Johnson exposes that myth and offers a more strategic and realistic approach – one in which leaders step back and give their team greater autonomy. This is an exciting new view of the strategic change process and one that will reap benefits for C-suite executives and line managers alike.'

Daniel Pink, author of Drive *and* When

'As leaders, we all grapple with how to execute strategy and lead change in a way that gets it done, but without us having to be involved in the detail. That's what Elsbeth Johnson's new "Step Up, Step Back" approach offers. This is a great book – full of both rigorous research and practical examples.'

Ronan Harris, MD of Google, UK and Ireland

'*Step Up, Step Back* is a terrific treatment of the structural and behavioural challenges that face managers trying to bring about a major strategic organizational change. Comprehensive of the many – often unrecognized – phases and stages involved in such change efforts, Elsbeth Johnson takes aim at the Great Leader myth so often given credit for bringing about needed change and instructively focuses much of her attention on those charged with implementing the change. By drawing our attention from the leaders to the led, by pushing out the time frame required for significant change to spread throughout an organization, and by focusing on those who ultimately have the power to sustain an initiative and make it stick, Johnson develops a most practical yet theoretically and empirically informed framework for bringing about successful organizational change – a framework that extends well beyond current approaches. This is a stimulating, sharply written "how to" book that offers critical lessons for change agents everywhere.'

John Van Maanen, Erwin Schell Professor Emeritus,
Sloan School of Management, MIT

'It's one of the most fundamental challenges facing any executive: How do you make your big strategic change program stick? Based on many years of research and consulting, Elsbeth Johnson's important book gives us a fresh and highly *personal* perspective on this old problem – it's about knowing when you should step up, and when you should step back. Every leader – regardless of their level of seniority – should read this book.'

Julian Birkinshaw, Professor and Deputy Dean,
London Business School

'You can't police sustained change. Elsbeth Johnson's book *Step Up, Step Back* offers a new, much-needed approach to change – where employees are fully empowered to deliver.'

Dan Cable, Professor of Organizational Behaviour,
London Business School, and author of Alive at Work

'To those of us who lead, getting change to become permanent has always been a challenge. With *Step Up, Step Back*, Elsbeth Johnson provides a better way to lead, which both implements and sustains change. Johnson takes us through the Four Delusions of Leadership to a place where our understanding of leadership is refreshed, restored, and renewed. This is a must-read for anyone who dedicates their life to creating positive change in organizations.'

Thomas A. Kolditz, Director, Doerr Institute,
Rice University and author of In Extremis Leadership

Step Up, Step Back

How to *Really* Deliver Strategic Change in Your Organization

Elsbeth Johnson, PhD.

BLOOMSBURY BUSINESS

LONDON • OXFORD • NEW YORK • NEW DELHI • SYDNEY

BLOOMSBURY BUSINESS
Bloomsbury Publishing Plc
50 Bedford Square, London, WC1B 3DP, UK

BLOOMSBURY, BLOOMSBURY BUSINESS and the Diana logo are
trademarks of Bloomsbury Publishing Plc

First published in Great Britain 2020

Bloomsbury Publishing Plc does not have any control over, or responsibility for,
any third-party websites referred to or in this book. All internet addresses given
in this book were correct at the time of going to press. The author and publisher
regret any inconvenience caused if addresses have changed or sites have ceased
to exist, but can accept no responsibility for any such changes

A catalogue record for this book is available from the British Library

Library of Congress Cataloguing-in-Publication data has been applied for

ISBN: 978-1-4729-7064-0; eBook: 978-1-4729-7066-4

2 4 6 8 10 9 7 5 3 1

Typeset by Deanta Global Publishing Services, Chennai, India
Printed and bound in Great Britain by CPI Group (UK) Ltd, Croydon CR0 4YY

To find out more about our authors and books visit www.bloomsbury.com
and sign up for our newsletters

Contents

Why this book is needed

I was looking out at New York's East River when the man I had come to see that morning walked into the room. It was my second meeting that day and it was with the company's CEO. (The names in this story have been changed to protect the innocent, but the story is real.)

Charming, smart and an industry veteran, Tom had been running the company for nearly two years. He'd called because he wanted my help. The new strategy he'd started to put in place just over a year ago was running out of steam and he was frustrated.

> I feel like we're really getting bogged down. And I don't know why. I mean, people seemed really up for this a year ago – and really clear about what needed to get done. Now the people we tasked with delivering the change are coming to me for – well, for everything. Every Senior Team meeting we have, it's not so much a report on progress, as a list of things that haven't worked and a list of questions for me and the team about what they should do instead. They don't seem to know what to do. I feel like I'm getting dragged into the weeds of this thing when I need to be leading the whole business. This isn't my job. So, what's going wrong here?

It was a good question. Especially, since in my first meeting that morning, on the same floor of the same building (albeit in a smaller room, without the river view), a woman called Sue had told me the other side of this story. Sue was one of Tom's key change-leaders. Two levels below him, she reported to Rich, the COO. Sue had asked to see me because she also needed help. The new strategy, whose implementation she'd been asked to lead just over a year ago, was running into real difficulties and she was frustrated.

> It's suddenly all really hard. Everybody in the team seems to have way too much on. They're asking me what they should be prioritizing and I don't really know. Actually, I don't really know what *I* should be prioritizing. So, I'm having to go upstairs *a lot* – to ask Rich and, in some cases, Tom. Checking in with them, getting a steer. Pretty much asking them to decide on what we should be doing. Actually, it increasingly feels like it's not really me running this thing. I feel more like a mail-box. Rich and Tom are making most of the decisions and I'm just passing them on.

My immediate reaction was to wonder why Tom and Sue hadn't had this conversation with each other; but, equally, I knew how it often takes talking to a relative stranger for issues like these to be expressed. At least now the problem was on the table. Even better, Tom and Sue had parallel concerns about essentially the same issue: both worried that they weren't exercising their proper roles and that the new strategy was suffering as a result. And so, given what Sue had told me, for the rest of my meeting with Tom, we talked about what he needed to do to enable Sue and her team to implement the new strategy without his ongoing involvement. What was that going to take? What had Tom failed to do so far that was holding Sue back, and meaning that he was getting pulled into the detail? What specifically was it that Sue should be asking Tom for, to enable her to exercise the autonomy she had? What could Tom do now to help Sue – and to help himself – deliver the new strategy the business needed?

The advice I gave him that morning – and that helped him do just that – is what this book is about.

Why strategic change is harder than it needs to be

Change comes in all shapes and sizes – and for a myriad of different reasons: because growth has petered out and you need to re-invigorate innovation within the business; because consumers' preferences are changing and you need to change with them; or perhaps even because the once-prized culture of your firm has become a liability that's holding you back. Whatever the reason, one thing is common: when a business needs to implement change – be it in culture, strategy or focus – that's the time when its senior leaders and most trusted managers should be most valuable to the organization, because it's a time when the stakes are high.

But while the stakes are high for leaders and managers, the odds are against them. The fact is that many change efforts fail.[1] And even if they don't completely fail, most change efforts are harder than they need to be.

Why is this? Well, it's usually not because the change that was attempted was a bad idea – not at all. Most change efforts fail because something gets lost in translation between the people who ask for the change (in this book, I'll call them 'leaders') and the people who are tasked with delivering it (I'll call them 'managers'). Sometimes, it's because the signals leaders are sending aren't clear enough at the start of the change, so managers don't know what they're aiming for. Sometimes it's because a leader sends very clear signals (perhaps through what they say) to go in one direction, but then sends equally clear but conflicting signals (perhaps through what they measure or what they give resources to) that suggest another direction is what's wanted. So, managers, trying to do their best, are confused – not knowing which direction to go in. And sometimes it's because the signals leaders send aren't clear enough for long enough; and so change starts to happen but isn't given the time it needs to stick.

Either way, managers can't make their own decisions about how best to deliver the change and so, likely as not, either the change that was asked for doesn't happen, or leaders are pulled into delivering the change – a job that managers ought to be doing.

The result is bad for the organization, bad for managers and bad for leaders. The organization suffers because it doesn't get the benefits of the new strategy or change – or at least not as quickly as shareholders would like. It's bad for managers because it saps their authority. Unsure about what leaders really want, they go back again and again to clarify and check that they're on the right track – or, worse, end up doing the wrong thing. But it's also bad for leaders, whose time is sucked up by this need to re-clarify and re-confirm; by these micro questions managers feel compelled to pull them into, which they'd much rather not be involved in – but which managers aren't able or willing to solve on their own.

Imagine instead a world where, as a leader, the change you want gets delivered as you intend, and without you having to be involved in every detail. A world where, as a manager, you understand the change that leaders want so that you can fully use the autonomy you have to deliver it. And where, as an organization, you can build a track record of successful, sustainable change that galvanizes people rather than frustrates them.

Based on the findings of my new empirical research, this book gives leaders a roadmap for leading change in this way, and managers a toolkit to know what to ask for. This roadmap shows how, by delivering on **four specific 'asks'** at **three critical points**, leaders can get the change they want – and in a way that sticks.

But leading change in this way requires leaders to do things differently. They actually need to **step up and do more** than they typically do in the early stages of the change, including being much clearer and more prescriptive about what outcomes they want from it. And then, in the later stages of the change, leaders need to **step back and do less** than they often do, again in specific ways and at specific times, to help managers embed and sustain the improvements that are starting to come through.

The 'Hollywood' version of leading change: charisma is all you need

Leading change in this way requires leaders to 'unlearn' much of what they have been told about how to lead change. Specifically, it requires leaders to move away from what I call the 'Hollywood' version of leadership that has dominated research and teaching in this area for the last 30 years. In this 'Hollywood' movie, a new leader comes in to rescue a failing company, turning it around with a mixture of charm, inspiration and sheer force of will. He's a charismatic, rock-star leader, inspiring people towards a more successful future. But there are a few problems with the 'Hollywood' version of how to lead change.

The first problem is that this 'Hollywood' version is written predominantly from the leader's point of view – he's definitely the main character. And that's because too much of the research that's made it into books and research papers to date has focused on asking leaders and CEOs how they led change. Far too little has focused on asking the people whom leaders tasked with getting the change done what *they* experienced, and what made life easy or hard for them.[2]

The second problem with this 'Hollywood' version is that while it tells us what happens at the start of the change, it doesn't have much to say about how change is *sustained*. This movie just doesn't last that long. And that's because much of the research on leading change only investigates how change gets *started*. What about what it takes to make change *stick*? How is change sustained beyond the initial few months – and how does it survive when the leader leaves?

By designing research to deal with these two problems, I have unearthed a different version of how to lead strategic change. When we talk to the led, rather than the leaders and when we study what happened over a longer time frame what we hear is that having a charismatic leader inspiring people towards a more successful future is an important *part of* how to lead change, but it's a long way from the whole story. Instead, the most successful change-leaders also honour the much less glamorous work of deciding on new structures, new roles and new metrics so that the future they've laid out is grounded in the reality of their business – and therefore more likely to happen. And that while leaders may need to step up and do more of this kind of work in the early days of the change, once the change is taking root, they then need to step back and do much less than they might expect, so that their people can get on and deliver it. And *that's* what enables the change to survive not only in the longer term, but to survive even a leader's departure.

The result is a win for the organization – the change happens and it sticks. But it also makes working life much more engaging and enjoyable for both leaders and the people they're leading. The prize for the managers is huge – to get more done, with less effort and frustration; to have real, meaningful autonomy within the business and more satisfaction as a result; and, by taking on more responsibility, to learn how to become better leaders themselves.

For leaders, though, the prize is arguably even greater. To step out of the day-to-day management of activities and instead to use their time and effort for the true work of leadership: to think about the strategic rather than the tactical; to focus on the future rather than the present; to lead rather than do. And ultimately to build a legacy – within the managers who will succeed them, and for the organization which they are stewarding – that outlives their own personal involvement.

The genesis of this book

This book is based on the case studies I first investigated for my doctoral research – begun nearly 10 years ago now. But I came to academia late: I had done 15 years in banking and strategy by the time I started a PhD. I like to think this meant I chose a research question – 'How and why is strategic change more successful in some companies than others?' – that had a more practical application than is often the case. But the rigour required for a PhD would mean the research and analysis required to answer this question would take years.

The research itself, begun in 2010, took seven months of field work: I conducted hundreds of interviews with leaders and managers about what helped and hindered them to deliver strategic change successfully. The analysis of these interviews, and the development of a new theory for how to lead change, took another two and a half years.

The first product of this research was a prize-winning PhD. But by the time I finished the doctorate, I was already working again – as both a teacher and an adviser.

It was the Nobel Prize-winning physicist Richard Feynman who said: 'You have to understand something really well if you want to teach it to somebody else.' For many years I taught the concepts that are now in this book as part of The Sloan and EMBA Programmes at London Business School and on my Organizational Theory course at the London School of Economics. I use it now as the basis for the 'Leading Change' class I teach at the Sloan School of Management at MIT. The kind of questions you get from the quality of students I've been lucky enough to teach at LBS, the LSE and MIT mean you really have to understand your research. This has prompted me, on a number of occasions over the years, to return to the data and look again at how certain parts of it were coded and interpreted to see whether the model could be made clearer. Although the model itself didn't change, this process of going back to the data and how it was interpreted definitely helped me hone and refine the language I use to explain it. (I'll explain more about my research methods in Chapter 2.)

By 2012, I was also working with leaders and senior managers to teach and coach them on how to lead change. I have now worked with more than 2,000 such leaders, including participants in executive education programmes at London Business School and Duke CE, in a range of companies and sectors, across five continents. These workshops and speaking engagements have given me the opportunity to test and use the research in a range of different contexts, from relatively young organizations facing their first growth challenges to older, bigger companies trying to navigate a new path in a fundamentally different world. That the ideas in this book, and the core dimensions of my approach, resonated with all of these leaders has given me confidence that it works in most companies, regardless of size, age or geography – and that it will probably work in yours too.

Many of these leaders were also already familiar with the well-known, established approaches to leading change. Thanks to their questions about how and why my approach goes against much of the existing advice that's already out there, I am now much clearer about the ways in which my approach is *different* – in particular, in its advice that leaders be far more prescriptive about the non-negotiables of the new strategy or change right at the start. It was also during a Q&A session on one of these programmes that I first advised a leader that he needed to 'step up and then step back' if he was to clearly set the parameters of the change and then let others deliver it. Very quickly this 'step up, then step back' phrase became the most succinct way I had to describe the new approach I was advocating.

Over the past three years, I have focused on what this approach means for leaders *in practice*. My consulting business helps clients decide on their strategy but then, using the 'Step Up, Step Back' approach, work out how best to implement it. Being an adviser is a more involved and more detailed endeavour than being a speaker or even an educator. It requires you to really engage with the specific strategy being implemented, to roll your sleeves up and help. You get to see and hear the feedback the organization is giving you – whether from the corner office or the front line – on how the implementation is faring. This detailed feedback, from hundreds of the leaders and managers with whom I've now worked, has not only helped validate this new approach, but has also helped frame the more practical advice that you'll find in this book, including the tips for leaders and managers that you'll see at the end of each chapter.

It was also clear from this work that clients use the 'Step Up, Step Back' approach not only to implement long-term, strategic *change* initiatives but also to help plan and execute *strategy*. The application makes sense, of course – all new strategies imply change of some kind, either in what the business is doing or in how it is doing it. In this respect, Strategy = Change. So, while technically the original research had produced a model to help implement *change*, I now use it just as frequently for what might be termed '*strategy execution*'. And so, throughout the book, wherever I refer to this being an approach for leading strategic change, you can read it as 'an approach for implementing a new strategy or change'.

Who can benefit from this book?

The first intended audience for this book are leaders who want to have their strategies and change programmes successfully implemented – and who want to empower their people to make this happen. This book offers you a new approach, one that says successful change (and empowered managers) only comes as a consequence of you being really prescriptive in the early stages of a change and then gradually less involved – but still consistent – in its later stages.

My extensive work with leaders tells me there is a clear need for a different approach to leading change and executing strategy. Not only because too many strategy and change efforts still fail but also because, in an attempt to be the exception, too many leaders find themselves *policing* their organizations when they should be *leading* them.

The second audience are managers who want to successfully implement change and need real autonomy to do so. All too often, managers are officially given the mandate they need but don't feel able to fully use it. Because just having the authority to make the decision isn't enough. What specifically should they be asking leaders for, if they want real autonomy? This book tells them what they really ought to expect from leaders, and when.

In my 30s, as a senior middle manager in a large organization, I was a member of this second group – and did *not* know what to ask my leaders for. I wish I'd had this research during those years because not knowing what to ask for cost me time and effort – and made achievements harder to grind out than they ought to have been.

The ultimate beneficiaries of this book, though, will be the organizations of which these leaders and managers are part, and the investors who fund them, because change can now be delivered faster and more effectively than before; by leaders and managers who are less frustrated by the place in which they work and so more likely to create something of lasting value, for their shareholders, for themselves and for each other.

Roadmap for the book

This book won't help you decide what your new strategy should be. There are a lot of good strategy books out there – and a lot of smart strategy consultants – who can help you with that. What this book *will* do is help you understand how to implement whatever new strategy you decide on. It will show you what you need to put in place, and when, in order to have that strategy or change implemented. Because whatever new strategy you decided on – and however you decided on it, whether top-down or through a more participatory process – delivering a new strategy or change needs certain elements in place, at specific times, in order to stand a chance of being delivered.

To this, I would add two claims. I believe this approach will help you not only implement the change you want, but will do so in a way that means it is sustained. I also believe it will do so in a way where managers are the ones implementing and sustaining the change, without the need for ongoing support from leaders.

Here's how the book unfolds. In Chapter 1, I present the problems with the current advice on how to lead strategic change. Let's be honest, this is not a greenfield site – there's a lot of advice already out there. But much of that advice isn't producing the outcomes leaders, managers or their organizations want. Why has so much of the research to date produced inadequate answers for leaders? What delusions do we often see leaders succumb to? And what biases would any new approach to leading change need to overcome to be capable of producing better-quality advice for leaders?

Chapter 2 sets out how my research seeks to provide better advice for leaders of strategic change. It's in this chapter that you'll find the methodology behind the research, including how the cases were chosen, how the data was captured and analyzed and how this methodology helped counter the biases we identified in Chapter 1. You'll also find a summary of the four cases that were studied in detail. We'll discuss what's different about this research and why it has produced a very different understanding of how and why change happens – and therefore very different advice for leaders about what they should do and when.

Chapter 3 gives you an outline of the resulting approach. Here, you'll find a high-level view of the advice, including the four critical 'asks' of leaders and when each of these is necessary. The first two of these 'asks' (Clarity and Alignment) require leaders to do **more** than they might typically do in the initial stages of a change: this is where leaders need to 'step up'. The second two 'asks' (Focus and Consistency) require leaders to do **less** than they might typically do, during the later stages of a change. This is where leaders need to 'step back' so that the change that has started can be sustained, and so that managers can continue to deliver it without ongoing leader involvement.

The next four chapters take you through each of these four leader 'asks' in detail, with a chapter on each one, so that you can understand what each of these requires from leaders – and when. Each chapter includes stories from the four main case studies, as well as additional examples – I call them 'Practice Spotlights' – to help you see how other organizations have delivered on each element. There are also 'Science Spotlights' included in each chapter: these give you more detail on the empirical research, from myself and others, that backs up the claims I make. And each chapter ends with some Tips and Watch-outs for both leaders and managers, to act as a summary of the chapter's key points.

Chapter 4 covers the first 'ask' – Clarity. This is what you need to achieve within the first few months of the change. But what specifically do leaders need to be clear about? And what do they need to watch out for so that Clarity isn't compromised? As you'll discover in this chapter, there are four Elements you need to have in place in order for managers to have Clarity – the chapter takes you through each one.

Chapter 5 is about the second 'ask' – Alignment. This is the focus for the whole of the first year of the new strategy or change. It also has four Elements that leaders need to put in place and, although it might be tempting to only do some of these, all are needed if you're to set the change up to succeed.

Chapters 6 and 7 are about the two second-year 'asks' – Focus and Consistency. Chapter 6 describes what Focus requires from leaders. We learn why slack and patience are critical if managers are to be able to focus on the long-term, strategic change – and what leaders can do to help foster these two concepts. As we'll see, this is the stage at which leaders first need to 'step back' – we'll also see how this will require leaders to overcome some of their deep-seated delusions that may otherwise derail or corrupt the change just as it is starting to deliver. Chapter 7 tackles the fourth and final 'ask' – that of Consistency.

I explain why this might be the most difficult 'ask' of all for leaders to deliver on, but why it is critical if the change is to be successful and also sustainable.

Chapter 8 is all about what this gives you – the concept of 'meaningful' autonomy. This is what enables managers to deliver the change in a way that leaders intended and without the need for ongoing input from them. This is also what enables the organization to get the change it needs in the most effective and efficient way possible. I explain the two Elements that make autonomy 'meaningful' rather than 'meaningless' for managers. And we take a final look back at the stories the managers in the four cases told themselves as the change unfolded.

The final chapter of the book sets out the philosophy of leading strategic change on which this new approach is based. It mirrors Chapter 1, by returning to the leadership delusions I introduced there. But while Chapter 1 just described these delusions – so we could understand why a new approach was needed – Chapter 9 offers some advice on how to counter them. What different attitudes ought leaders to be adopting, and how differently might they need to view the 'work' of leadership, so that strategic change is no harder than it needs to be?

At all times in this book, I have my two audiences in mind – both leaders who have unique positions of power and leverage within the firm and need to know how to use these to best effect; and managers, who are tasked with delivering the change and need to be able to use the authority that their roles give them to best effect. Although their roles are different, all of my work with them suggests that their aims are the same – not only to implement the strategic change their firm needs, but also to use their time and energy in ways that have the greatest impact and make their roles as personally meaningful as possible. That means more time spent on the interesting work and less time being frustrated. More time spent fixing the fundamentals and less time fire-fighting the symptoms. And more time thinking and learning and less time box-ticking and reporting. That's my wish for all of you – whether leader or manager – who read, and use, this book.

Elsbeth Johnson, PhD
Founder, SystemShift
Senior Lecturer, MIT Sloan School of Management; and Visiting Fellow, The London School of Economics and Political Science

CHAPTER ONE

The Problem

*What's wrong with the current advice about
how to lead strategic change*

In this chapter, I set out what's wrong with the current advice being given to leaders about how to lead change. And when I say 'change', I mean big, strategic, long-term change – the kind where you're changing what the company does (its strategy or orientation) and/or how it does it (its culture or capabilities). So we're not talking here about small or incremental change. You should be doing that ordinarily, as part of your everyday job. And in order to effect small or incremental change, you likely won't need the kind or extent of help that I'm setting out here in this book – which is distinctly aimed at big, strategic, long-term change.

The existing advice about how to lead this type of change is based on, I argue, the wrong kind of research. As a result, we have, all too often, received only a partial view of what goes on during the long and sometimes tortuous process of putting in place a new strategy or change.

The 'Hollywood' version of how to lead change

Over the years, a clichéd, and now stereotypical, version of leadership has become established. We see it everywhere – from *The West Wing* and *The Apprentice* to CEO memoirs and MBA case studies. In this version of leadership, the story goes something like this. The business has lost its way and it needs a new strategy. Tweaking or tinkering won't do – this will take fundamental change to the business and what it does.

The shareholders believe they need a new leader in place – often from outside the organization – to make this happen. They choose a guy called, say, Steve. Steve has a credible background in leading strategic change and, from the first few weeks of him being in the role, there are quite a few things that people like.

The first is that Steve is charismatic. This means the people around him want to follow him, and he's clearly building up personal loyalty from his new team. People talk about how impressive and compelling he is in conversations and presentations. He has real gravitas and yet at the same time is a real people person. He remembers your name and asks after your kids. He's a nice guy one-on-one and yet, when he's in front of the room, he's a rock star – he's got charisma and he knows how to use it.

Second, Steve has set out a pretty inspiring picture of what the future could look like for the business and the people who work in it. It feels exciting again. And doable. He's held a series of town halls to explain the new strategy and how important it is to do this now. And he's explained how he's personally, 100 per cent committed to it. People want to come to work again and that's a big improvement.

Third, Steve is always saying that it's up to everyone – but especially those lower down the organization – how it gets delivered. This sounds great. He's asking people to be creative and take risks. And it really feels like people will be empowered to do what they believe will work. Steve knows that empowered employees who own how the strategy gets delivered are more likely to make that strategy successful. People start to feel like grown-ups again and that feels pretty good.

And finally, Steve tells folks that he will always be there for them, to help and support them. People believe him: they feel he genuinely cares about them and that he'll support them as the new strategy plays out. And so they start showing more initiative and taking more responsibility.

The four attributes that Steve is displaying are known as 'transformational leadership' (described in more detail in the Science

Spotlight below). The result of leading in this way is that – at least in the short term – Steve becomes a bit of a hero for the people who work for him. Leading this way seems to come easily to Steve – he's a natural. Meanwhile, things improve, the change yields some impressive early results and people start to feel better about the business they work for.

Science Spotlight: Transformational vs. Transactional Leadership

In the leadership literature, the four attributes that Steve displays are known respectively as:

1) **'idealized influence'**, sometimes also called 'charisma'. This is the ability to be focused on people, whether one-on-one or an audience of thousands;

2) **'inspirational motivation'**, the ability to paint a fabulous story of the future that people can believe in;

3) **'intellectual stimulation'**, the ability to make others feel they have a critical contribution to make and that this is an endeavour they want to be part of; and;

4) **'individualized consideration'**, the ability to make others feel that you genuinely care about them and their future, and that you will be there to support them.

Together, these four attributes make up what we call 'transformational leadership'. The classic definition of this kind of leadership is:

'when leaders broaden and elevate the interests of their employees, when they generate awareness and acceptance of the purposes and mission of the group, and then they stir their employees to look beyond their own self-interest for the good of the group.'[1]

Transformational leadership is often conflated with 'charismatic' leadership because of the dominance given to charisma within the measurement of this type of leadership. Many scholars have argued that charismatic leaders have a particularly strong impact on employee motivation because such leaders tend to focus on creating 'faith in a better future' and 'unconditional commitment' rather than relying on 'proximal, specific goals' such as KPIs (Key Performance Indicators) or rewards.[2]

Transformational leadership became popular in the 1980s and has dominated leadership research ever since.[3] This may have been helped by the fact that one of the founders of the concept, Bernard Bass, became editor of one of the most prominent academic journals in the field (*The Leadership Quarterly*) and oversaw the publication of hundreds of articles on this subject.[4] The result is that transformational leadership is now all but accepted as the only kind of leadership to which leaders should aspire.

It has become particularly popular as the leadership of choice in times of strategic change, with several authors – notably Harvard Business School's John Kotter – arguing that you need transformational leadership for transformational change.[5] The result of this kind of leadership, we have been told, is that people will be more inspired and motivated, they will feel more empowered and therefore they will be more able to go out and get on with the new strategy or change.

You'll notice that within the job description of a 'transformational leader' there is no mention of KPIs and metrics, or roles and rewards. That's because leadership that uses these kinds of instruments is known as 'transactional leadership' and is the opposite of transformational leadership. Indeed, while 'transformational leadership' is the type of leadership to which, we're told, all leaders should aspire, 'transactional leadership' is very much its poor relation.

'Transactional' leadership happens when leaders:

> 'engage in a transaction with their employees: they explain what is required of them and what compensation they will receive if they fulfil these requirements ... [They clarify] th[e] promise and reward for good performance, [and the] threat and discipline for poor performance ...'[6]

This kind of leadership has been described as 'dull and mechanical'.[7] It involves leaders being prescriptive about roles and metrics, measuring what employees are doing and making pay and promotion dependent on performance (what's known as 'contingent reward'). As a result, *at least when done on its own* with none of the attributes of transformational leadership, 'transactional leadership' is claimed to make people less motivated, less inspired and less able to go out and get on with the new strategy or change. They remain dependent on leaders for detailed guidance and take less responsibility themselves. Indeed, as Bass once claimed: 'transactional leadership is a prescription for mediocrity'.[8]

But there are at least three major flaws in this split between transformational and transactional leadership – and, in particular, with the love affair some have developed with transformational leadership. First, the privileging of transformational leadership has meant that too little effort has been put into researching the effectiveness of *transactional* leadership. And so an inadequate empirical understanding of how leaders *actually* lead change (which, were it to be studied, may actually include some transactional elements) has become a prescription for how leaders *should* lead change – resulting in the mantra of 'transformational leadership is enough'.

Second, hardly any research has been done on how we might combine transformational *and* transactional leadership in the efforts of leading change[9] – because, again, all the interest has focused on proving how effective transformational leadership is all on its own. And third, it turns out that transformational, or charismatic, leadership actually has some downsides.

These downsides are fairly well established in other bodies of literature (for example, in psychology and behavioural science) – just not in the literature about how to lead change.[10] The main downside of working for a charismatic leader is that you can become dependent on them – you get sufficiently hooked on their seemingly unique ability to paint a picture of the future and to point you in the right direction that you no longer feel able to do this for yourself, or for those who work for you. If you're a manager, becoming dependent on senior leaders is quite an imposition on your own autonomy within an organization, as well as on your ability to grow within it.

So perhaps this transformational leadership isn't all it's cracked up to be? Perhaps even if leaders manage to achieve all four attributes of transformational leadership, they might not be doing enough to lead the organization through a successful change and, critically, to empower the people below them to implement it? Perhaps transactional leadership might also be valuable in leading change – and especially in making that change sustainable?

The problem with the story about Steve is not the things that it describes him doing. These are all good things and, to be honest, all good leaders should be striving to do them regularly. The problem with this story is *the things it leaves out* – in other words, the *other* things that Steve ought to be doing *as well as* these four 'rock star' attributes. Because, while these four attributes are *part of* what it takes to lead change well, *they are not enough*. As my research shows, leaders also need to work on the structural elements of the change. They need to consider the roles and rewards, the KPIs and metrics, by which their organization runs. Only when they give time and attention to these structural – more transactional – elements of the firm, will the change get delivered and sustained.

All too often, the result of using *only* the old clichéd, charismatic leadership is that the change doesn't stick. The initial improvements, kicked off by charismatic leadership, don't continue; the more fundamental change that was promised doesn't materialize and managers respond by starting to question what they should be doing – and having to involve Steve in more and more of the decisions they ought to be making themselves.

So why is it that leaders continue to believe (and be told) that charismatic – so-called 'transformational' – leadership is all it takes when it comes to leading change?

I believe a major reason is because leaders fall prey to what I call the **Four Delusions of Leadership**. Most of the leaders I have worked with believe in at least one of these delusions. Yet they serve to limit leaders' thinking about the true nature of their role as leaders – and therefore the work that leaders need to do, especially during times of strategic change.

The Four Delusions of Leadership that underpin much of what we still believe about how to lead change

Having worked with leaders now for many years, as they decide on and then try to deliver change; having seen what they struggle with and what holds them back, it is clear to me that even good leaders, through no fault of their own, labour under some unhelpful delusions about what 'good' looks like when it comes to leading change. It's time we called out these leadership delusions that continue to limit leaders' thinking about the work they need to do. In my experience, there are four – and they can lead even good leaders astray.

1. The Magic Delusion
The Magic Delusion is the belief that the secret to making change happen lies in the personal magic of the leader – their charisma and their ability to charm and inspire followers. The Magic Delusion has

led to what some scholars have called 'the ideology of "leaderism"'.[11] I have heard leaders, beholden to the Magic Delusion, say:

> 'I can get this organization to do this – this is what I'm here for. I mean, it's what leaders *do*, right?'

> 'I know it's going to be hard, and it's maybe not going to make that much sense initially, but I can make the case. Let's put some town halls in, let's talk to the next two levels down. They'll go with me on this.'

> 'We need to keep it high-level at this stage. Don't let's get bogged down in too much detail. We've got to lead them up to the top of the hill so they can see where we're going.'

There are three main problems with this Delusion. The first is that leaders believe that charismatic leadership is enough and that they need do nothing else – when actually, as we will see, sustainable change requires more than this, including some elements of the so-called 'transactional leadership' we mentioned earlier.

The second problem with believing in the Magic Delusion is the disproportionate strain it puts on leaders. Under this Delusion, leaders are the only source of 'magic' for organizations, so they need to keep providing it. Not many leaders who believe in the Magic Delusion ever wean their organizations off their magic – perhaps in part because they don't really want to. The Magic Delusion therefore makes leaders' lives harder than they need to be.

And this leads to the third problem. Which is that, because magic only comes from one source and continues to be needed for the duration of the change,[12] leaders often just get tired. They reduce the amount of time and effort they devote personally to the change. Coupled with the fact that many will leave within two to three years of the start of a change (the average tenure of a CEO globally is now only around five years),[13] this leaves the organization – and especially the managers tasked with delivering the change – in a precarious position. How can the change continue without the leader's magic? What do they have to fall back on when the source of that magic is gone?

2. The Activity Delusion

The second Delusion is the Activity Delusion. This is the idea that leading change is all about getting activities going as quickly as possible, thereby creating early momentum for the change through that very familiar phrase 'quick wins'. In businesses where the Activity Delusion is rife, we hear statements (from either leaders or indeed from the managers they influence) such as:

> 'We just need to get some stuff happening. We need to get some scores on the doors.'

> 'Yeah, I'm not sure what all these projects will roll up to. But it's important to get moving and I've got a good hunch about what's first off the block.'

> 'Let's not spend too much time over-thinking this at this stage – I mean, we know what this needs to look like, right?'

The problem is that the business might *not* know exactly what is needed, or what the ultimate goal should be. Moreover, the business is likely to already have myriad targets and deliverables to which it's already committed – most new strategies are implemented not on greenfield sites, but on already crowded landscapes. Given this context, rushing into action when the new outcome you're targeting isn't yet clear is a recipe for, at best, wasted effort. And tempting though it is to prove the value of the change by getting some 'quick wins' up and running, the 'quick wins' that are chosen in organizations that succumb to the Activity Delusion are, all too often, wasteful or downright dangerous.

The wasteful ones are often existing projects that have simply been repurposed for the 'new' change effort; or pet-projects that a manager has always fancied doing and which she can now re-badge as 'change' in order to get them funded. Either way, they are often not the best way to start the kind of fundamental change which is being asked for.

The dangerous ones are where managers choose quick, cosmetic projects that make the numbers look better in the short term, but achieve little or no fundamental change in the nature of the business or what it can do. These are 'lipstick on the pig' – as one of the managers whom I interviewed for this research memorably put it. And, as we will see from the case studies in this book, they can do long-term harm to the business and the change it is attempting. Yet the persistence of the Activity Delusion enables both leaders and managers to believe that this is still a sensible way to spend the early months of the change.

3. The Drama Delusion

The third Delusion is the Drama Delusion. This one is closely related to both the Activity and the Magic Delusions – often because the same leaders seem to suffer from both of them – but the Drama Delusion is separate.[14]

Whereas the Magic Delusion is about believing that your own personal charisma can push the change forward, and the Activity Delusion is about just getting projects started as quickly as possible, whatever their long-term value, the Drama Delusion believes that change is inherently fast, exciting, action-packed and risky. It requires constant newness to be worthy of the name. And, therefore, in order to lead change, leaders need to engage in lots of visible activities, and take sometimes quite risky, big-bet decisions, with the aim of delivering fast results.

These are often the same leaders, by the way, who have waited for the fabled 'burning platform' before embarking on the change. So their delusion that change has to be fast, exciting, action-packed and risky seems real – but only because, by waiting too long, they have closed down the options they may once have had for slower, duller, less eventful and much less risky change. The kind of change that would have been easier to manage and more likely to work.

But, because they failed to change sooner, their change now *has to be* fast, risky and dramatic – because they no longer have time for anything else. And so their Drama Delusion becomes a self-fulfilling prophecy.

For these folks, fast, exciting, action-packed and risky is the essence of what change is and, therefore, these words also describe how it should be led. As a result, Drama-deluded leaders say things like:

'Change is the only constant now – so we need to get used to it. We need to *embrace* it!'

'We need to dial up the pace on this. This change simply *cannot* take this long.'

'You know, I worry about wrapping too much process around this new way of doing things. We don't want to make this too bureaucratic. Process and bureaucracy were what got us here in the first place.'

There are two problems with this Delusion. The first is that Drama-deluded leaders expect – and also signal – that a new strategy or change should happen quickly; they have little patience for change that takes too long. This means they often ignore or even avoid altogether the elements of the change programme that will take the most time – even when these are usually the ones that will have the most fundamental and longest-lasting impact.

The second problem here is a more existential one. Until and unless this new way of doing things becomes just 'the way we do things', the change won't stick. In other words, if change doesn't become routine – albeit a new 'routine' – then it will have failed. That sounds sensible when we state it in those terms. But leaders who believe that change inherently entails – even requires – drama, tend to eschew the use of routines to help the change bed down. They often conflate routine with bureaucracy and use the word 'process' as a pejorative term. The result is that they pay too little attention to the new processes and routines that could help support and embed the change, thereby denying their organizations the full benefit of some of the most important change tools they have.

4. The Agency Delusion

The fourth and final Delusion that infects leaders is the Agency Delusion. This is where leaders believe that it is people alone who make change happen, with no help required from the structure of the organization.

It's worth clarifying what 'agency' means here. Agency is the capacity of individuals to make decisions and then enact those decisions. It is the manifestation of free will. People who believe in the endogenous power of agency believe that individuals alone can shape the outcomes of their lives. In contrast, we can think of 'structure' as being those exogenous factors that could influence someone's life – such as their social class, their gender or ethnicity, or where they were born. People who believe more in the influence of structure than in the pure power of agency argue that these structural elements enable or constrain the individual agent's ability to make, and enact, their decisions – however good those decisions are, and however much effort the individual puts in.[15] People who believe more in the pure power of agency, and less in the enabling or constraining impact of structures, are more likely to fall for the Agency Delusion.[16]

In some ways, this fourth and final Delusion is just a larger version of the Magic Delusion. But the Agency Delusion deserves to be seen as separate because the full pervasive extent of the damage it can do to organizations is much greater than merely having a bit too much charisma floating around. Because whereas the Magic Delusion can be cured by leaders saying, 'Of course, it's not just about *me*, it's about *everyone* in the organization', or, even better, 'Sure, it's not just about me and how charismatic I am: it's also about all the mundane stuff that we need to fix', that still isn't quite enough to optimize the organization. To do that, leaders need to admit that sustainable change isn't created just by the effort and willpower of *people*, but rather by people using their efforts to change the *structures* of the organization. The structures that people create then either enable or constrain the change that individuals wanted to enact.[17] But leaders beholden to the Agency Delusion don't really believe this. Which is why such leaders still say things like:

'This is all about effort and willpower. We just need to keep going and we'll get there.'

'Yeah, the issue here is just plain old resistance to change. These folks don't want to change.'

'What we need to do is get this through the permafrost of the organization. We all know who we're talking about here.'

Now while I have heard these phrases said by leaders throughout a change effort, they are especially common when the change is running into difficulties. These leaders are focusing on *people* as the source of resistance, rather than on the structure to which these people are responding.

So what do we mean by 'structure' in the context of an organization? Well, for these purposes, the structures of the organization are all the bits that aren't dependent on *new, conscious effort* by particular individuals to make them happen. Some of these elements are what we might call 'hard' structure – things like processes and standard procedures, KPIs and metrics, decision-rights and reporting-lines, MIS and dashboards.[18] The other parts of an organization's 'structure' are what we might call 'soft' or even 'social' structure – things like its routines, habits and behaviours – all of which accumulate to become the settled practice of 'how things are done around here';[19] in other words, its culture. Whether 'soft' or 'hard' structure, these are all established ways of doing things that don't require someone to make a new, wilful decision every morning in order to make them happen – they just happen.[20] That's what structure does for you.

The problem with the Agency Delusion is that leaders believe that it's all down to agency – individuals exercising their will – to make change happen. As a result, they become blind to the power of structural change to help them achieve their goals. And for as long as leaders believe in the Agency Delusion, they won't feel the full urgency of using their positional power to make structural changes because they will always be able to fall back on their latent belief that, 'I'll fix it' or 'so-and-so will fix it'. In other words, they will revert to a purely personal (or 'agentic') fix for what may well be a structural problem. The result is a change effort that is harder work than it needs to be and, typically, doesn't last as long as it should.

All four of these Delusions play into, and reinforce, the idea that transformational leadership is the only kind of leadership we need to make change happen. Equally, all Four Delusions devalue transactional leadership and the role it could play in effecting and sustaining strategic change. The result is that these Four Delusions perpetuate the 'Hollywood' version of leading change. So why has this vicious circle not yet been broken?

Why the 'Hollywood' version of leadership – and the Four Delusions – persists

If these Four Delusions, and the 'Hollywood' version of leadership that they support, are so dangerous for organizations and the people who work in them, why do they persist?

As an academic who researches and teaches leadership and change, this next part is hard to admit. But I think one of the main reasons these Four Delusions not only continue, but have become so influential in our models of leadership – especially in what we think we know about how to lead change – is because the research that most academics produce doesn't really offer us an alternative view.

When I talk to leaders about why they continue to believe (or at least act as if they believe) in these Four Delusions, and therefore why they don't bother with the less glamorous, more structural aspects of implementing change, using what the literature would term more 'transactional' leadership efforts, one main reason emerges. Which is that these leaders have been told not to focus on this part of leadership too much – and told often by well-known academics in journals and books, and by lecturers on MBA courses. The danger, they have been advised, is that if they are overly prescriptive about what they want followers to do, or about their new roles in the change or the measures by which they should calibrate its success, they will limit employees' empowerment. Therefore, they believe that good leaders – which they all want to be – ought to leave managers to decide what to do and how to measure it.

But, wait. This hasn't actually been working for these change-leaders. So why hasn't the advice coming from academics changed, in the face of disappointing results? Why hasn't empirical research *rewritten* the existing advice on how to lead change?

The underlying reason for *that* seems to be that the type of research being done on strategic change is often flawed. Not because it contains mistakes – academics aren't making stuff up or reporting erroneous data. Most academics are honest, hard-working people who just want to progress in their careers. The problem is *how* they progress.

Most academics get promoted and eventually get tenure (which basically means they can't be fired) by publishing several articles a year in respected, peer-reviewed journals. The 'revise-and-resubmit' process of getting published is laborious, often taking up to a year for each article. That means that academics need to scope and complete their research, and then write it up and get it out for publication as quickly as possible. And that means that they often scope research projects where the actual research part is quite short in duration. In fact, most studies of 'long-term' change or strategy execution that are published in academic journals study implementation periods which are shorter than 12 months.[21] Yes, really. Less than 12 months. Now, in the real world, that's not most people's definition of 'long-term' change. But it's what gets studied because it's what gets published quickly – and that's what helps academics build a tenure-track career.

This design flaw – too-short periods of time spent actually studying change in real life – means that most published academic empirical research suffers from some major failings, or biases. It's these biases in how the research is designed that limit what the resulting findings are capable of telling us. We can group these biases into three categories.

The three major biases in much of the empirical research on leading change

Bias No. 1: The Early-Stage Bias

This bias means that most of the studies which look at how to deliver change only investigate what happens in the very early stages of a change – usually the first three to six months. Anyone who has ever worked on a strategic change knows that, while this is no doubt a critical time in the change, it is not the only important time. In fact, it's really only the first mile or two of the marathon.

Yet this is where most existing models focus. Set out in the table opposite are four well-known models of how to lead change. The paucity of intelligence about what goes on in the later stages of strategic change is clear to see. As shown in black, the majority of the steps in these models tell us how to kick the change off. There are very few stages that relate to how change might be sustained (shown in lighter grey). In fact, in three out of the four models, there is only a single, all-encompassing stage which relates to how to sustain the change.

Figure 1.1: Summary of four normative models of change[22]

Morris & Raben's 12-stage plan for large scale change, 1992	Kanter, Stein & Jick's 'Ten Commandments for Implementing Change', 1992	Cummings & Worley's 5-step process for effective change management, 1993	Kotter's 8 stages, 1995 & 1996
1. Surface dissatisfaction with the present state	1. Analyse the organisation and its need for change	1. Motivating change	1. Establish a sense of urgency
2. Promote participation in change	2. Create a shared vision and common direction	2. Creating a vision	2. Form a guiding coalition
3. Give rewards for supporting change	3. Separate from the past	3. Developing political support	3. Develop a vision
4. Provide time and opportunity to disengage from the present state	4. Create a sense of urgency	4. Managing the transition	4. Communicate the vision
5. Develop and communicate a clear image of the future	5. Support a strong leader role	5. Sustaining momentum	5. Empower others to act on the vision
6. Use multiple/consistent leverage points	6. Line up political sponsorship		6. Generate short term wins
7. Develop organisational arrangements for the transition	7. Craft an implementation plan		7. Consolidate gains and produce more change
8. Build in feedback mechanisms	8. Develop enabling structures		8. Anchor new approaches in the culture
9. Assure the support of key power groups	9. Communicate, involve people and be honest		
10. Use leader behaviour to generate energy in support of change	10. Reinforce and institutionalize change		
11. Use symbols and language			
12. Build in stability			

By asking about and observing *only these very first months* of what might be a three- to four-year change programme, researchers can't hope to understand all the aspects of the change – especially those elements that pertain to how that change is sustained, rather than simply how it is initiated.

What we know from the few longer-term studies that *have* been published[23] is that it's the *non-'Hollywood' elements* of leading change – the benefits of focusing on the seemingly mundane details such as KPIs or budgets to help support the change – that really come into their own in the later stages. Equally, the cost of *not* focusing on these less glamorous details early on only really becomes apparent as the change matures. But in order to see either of these impacts you have to be watching. Whereas most researchers have packed up, gone home and probably published by the time these long-dated effects start to emerge – meaning the Early-Stage Bias continues to go unchallenged in their research.

Bias No. 2: The Agentic Bias

The Agentic Bias means that too much of the research focuses solely or mainly on agents (i.e. people) and what they did during the change, rather than asking about, and therefore revealing insights about, how the non-agentic elements of an organization may have helped or hindered the change effort. And those 'non-agentic' elements are things like org charts and rewards, roles and decision-rights, KPIs and metrics, budgets and resourcing.

The Agentic Bias may be due in part to the Early-Stage Bias we've already talked about – because the early stages of the change (which are often the only parts of the change to be studied) usually disproportionately feature people (especially CEOs or other senior leaders) as the agents of change at this stage. That's because in the early stages of a change, people *have to be* disproportionately involved if the change is to be kicked off successfully. But the result of the Agentic Bias is that much of the research is insufficiently focused on the *structural* aspects of the organization – its KPIs, its rewards, its IT, its dashboards, its culture – and how these might help or hinder the change effort.

In practice, researchers ask people (and, it has to be said, they often ask *leaders*) what they *did* during the change, framing questions in terms of actions and behaviours. Rarely do studies on how change is led focus on the structural changes that leaders make (or fail to make). And because of the Four Delusions we talked about earlier, unless researchers specifically *ask* leaders for details about such endeavours, many leaders may not think to mention it, so it never makes it into the research write-up.[24] Instead, responding to questions about what they did, leaders reply that they performed a myriad of interesting, notable, charismatic actions. And of course they did – those recollections are not untrue. Nor are they unimportant. Indeed, many of those activities may have been useful to the change and supportive to their followers. But that probably wasn't *all* they were doing.

Because some of these leaders – and I would argue the most effective ones – were also starting to change the systems and structures of their organizations. But without research that allows us to identify these elements, it is easy to underplay their importance. Equally, some leaders were *not* spending time or effort on structural elements;

and without research that specifically explores the role played by this kind of structural endeavour, it is easy to underplay the impact of *not* making structural changes. As a result, it is much easier to conclude that a failed change is due to its leaders' communications or behaviour – rather than its leaders' failure to change the structure.

Of course, the Agentic Bias doesn't just mean we over-focus on the role played by *leaders*, but rather that we over-focus on the role played by *people* in general. Some studies also ask those lower down the organization what impact this 'leadership' had on them. This at least balances out the *leader*-bias which may be thought of as a sub-set of the overall Agentic Bias. But it doesn't overcome it, because questions framed as 'What activities did you do?' or 'What did you say?' are still inherently biased in favour of agentic, as opposed to structural, solutions to the problem of how to lead change – regardless of whether these questions are asked of leaders or followers.

Instead, we need to re-frame how we study change by actively seeking information on these structural aspects. By deliberately adding into our study questions such as 'What work was being done on metrics at this stage?' – to complement the usual 'Tell me about what you were doing at this stage?' – we can bring the organization's systems and structures much more clearly into focus and, as a result, stand more of a chance of understanding the balance between agency and structure that successful, sustainable change might require.[25]

Bias No. 3: The Event Bias

The third bias that we see in much of the empirical research on change can be termed the Event Bias. The Event Bias means scholars have focused too much of their investigation on the big *events* that happened during a change, and not enough on the *processes* by which these events occurred. Examples might include the change-programme launch event, or the specific projects or 'quick wins' being worked on. These events become the phenomena that are studied, rather than how and why these events contributed to the change itself.

This is of course exacerbated by the Early-Stage Bias we've already mentioned, since the majority of such 'events' happen in the change's early stages. But even if we extend the period being studied, researchers still tend to ask for, and record, information about *events* that occurred, when what we really need to do is explore the *processes* by which leadership endeavours (whether actions or inactions, whether focused on people or structures) are linked causally to certain outcomes over time.

No one's saying that the events of a change programme aren't important, but they are not the *only* important part of a successful change. And when we consider, in particular, what might make change become embedded in a business, they are probably not the *most important* part either. But because of the Event Bias in much of the research, often leaders think of a change programme, or a strategy execution, as simply a series of events. This in turn feeds their Activity and Drama Delusions about how they ought to lead.

Moreover, the artefacts and tools that many organizations use to monitor change reinforce this 'event' focus. The 'boxes and arrows' diagrams and GANTT charts, by which many initiatives are managed, are good examples. The boxes and arrows diagram is potentially incredibly useful to help us understand the *process* by which change is happening, but only if we focus on the arrows as well as the boxes. All too often I see people focus far too much on the boxes ('What's going on here?') and not enough on the arrows ('How is this happening?' or 'Why does this box cause this other box?' or even 'Hang on, why is this *not* happening the way we thought it would?').

Notice that investigating process rather than events requires researchers to use different words: we now need to ask 'How?' and 'Why?' rather than simply 'What happened?'[26] It's these 'How' and 'Why' questions that also need to be asked much more often by leaders, if the organizations they lead are to start developing a better understanding of how and why their own change efforts succeed or fail. And sadly, the Event Bias in much of the research means that they are given little encouragement to do so.

Because of these three major biases – the Early-Stage Bias that tells us little or nothing about how to sustain change; the Agentic Bias that tells us little or nothing about the use of structure during change; and the Event Bias that tells us little or nothing about the process of how and why change succeeds – it is little wonder that leaders don't find ready answers to their questions about how to lead change in the existing research. And, therefore, why so many then fall back on the Four Delusions of Leadership which tell them that they simply need to be more charismatic, focus on activities, make it faster and more exciting and work harder. The truth is we have short-changed leaders in the advice we've given them. And that means we've also short-changed their organizations and all the other people who work in them.

So now we know the problems with the current advice we give leaders – the Four Delusions of Leadership, fostered by the three biases present in much of the existing research, that in turn perpetuate the 'Hollywood' version of leadership. The next chapter will describe the research on which this book is based – research that, because of how it was designed, mitigates the three biases we have talked about here. Because of this, it offers us a different story about what's going on during a long-term, strategic change – and therefore the possibility of properly understanding what managers need from leaders during such a time.

CHAPTER TWO

The Research

*Why asking different questions, of different people,
reveals the truth about strategic change*

We know now that there are certain biases in the existing research. These have fostered Delusions about how to lead change that, in turn, have given rise to the 'Hollywood' version of what leadership means. So, to counter these Delusions and produce better advice for leaders, we need research that overcomes these biases. In this chapter, I'll describe the research this book is based on and how its design mitigates the three main biases we talked about in Chapter 1, helping us develop a much better understanding of what's really going on during long-term, strategic change.

If you feel less need to understand how this research was conducted, and are instead eager to discover what it produced, you can skip most of this chapter. You do need to know about the cases, though. These are covered in the next few pages: in the **Background to the research**, **Which of the 16 business units to study?** and the **Summaries of the four cases** sections. Once you've read these sections, you're ready to dive into Chapter 3.

Background to the research

The businesses I chose to study for this research were all business units within the same company. They all operated in the same sector and used the same business model. And they were all tasked with implementing the same new strategy. The implementation had begun in each business unit at exactly the same time and had been completed – whether successfully or not – nearly four years later.

The company in question had 16 business units – therefore, I had 16 potential research sites from which to choose. These business units were large businesses in their own right, each with its own local CEO and Senior Leadership Team, but they all reported up to the Group CEO on their progress. The target outcome of the new strategy was to make their businesses more customer-focused and, as a result, to improve customer retention. This would have a direct impact on margin, by reducing their marketing and customer service costs as a proportion of each dollar of revenue.

Which of the 16 business units to study?

Which of the 16 business units within this single organization, tasked with implementing the same new strategy, would be best to study? Given the depth of the research I needed to do within each one to properly answer questions of 'how' and 'why' change happens over the full duration of the change, I recognized that studying all 16 would be impossible – at least not without compromising the depth and richness of the data captured about each one. It's also established practice in this kind of research to be selective about which cases to study – this is known as 'theoretical sampling' and the idea is to choose the cases that will best illuminate the phenomena you want to understand.[1]

I was trying to understand and explain *differences* in how successfully the same new strategy was implemented. So first of all, I needed to define success. Well, actually I didn't. Success had already been defined for the new strategy by the business itself: it was defined as reducing the number of customers leaving the business – what they referred to as 'customer attrition'. So this is the definition of success that I adopted when assessing how successful each of these business units had been: had they reduced customer attrition, or, measured in the opposite way, had they increased their rate of customers retained, each year?[2]

Each business unit had agreed a different *target level* for this common metric. They had come up with these targets themselves and each target level reflected the specific nature of the market the particular business unit operated in (its maturity, the level of competition, the state of regulation and consumer awareness) and what the business unit thought was reasonable, given its starting position. These targets, therefore, were not imposed by a crazy, out-of-touch Head Office: rather, they were the targets each business unit believed were reasonable for it to achieve. By having each business unit choose its own target and then try to achieve it, this was arguably a truer test of the business's ability to successfully implement change.

Another benefit with this research site was that all of the businesses had regularly tracked their progress against their target metric, so I had quarterly data on how they had progressed for the full four years of the change. I graphed this data to better understand the progress of each business unit over time. Looking at the 16 progress graphs, it was easy to see big differences across the businesses and this helped me choose the four business units to study. (The Progress Graphs for the four business units I chose are shown in Diagram 2.1. Each one shows how customer retention [the line, measured on the Y-axis] progressed over time [the X-axis] against their agreed target [the grey horizontal line].)

Diagram 2.1: The Progress Graphs: Business unit progress in closing the gap between their actual and target customer retention rates

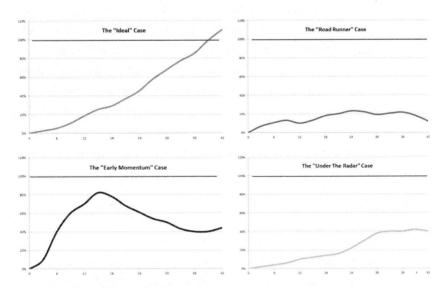

Using this definition of success, and the progress graphs, I first chose:

1) **The business unit with the greatest success according to this measure** – because I was interested in how and why successful change happens. In this case, the change started slowly but progressed steadily and this progress was sustained. I later called this **the 'Ideal' Case** because in many ways its leaders and managers did just about everything right. Its progress graph is shown in the top left-hand graph above. I wondered why this case had started off slowly, but then been able to maintain such steady progress over the full three and a half years of the change.

To contrast with this 'Ideal' Case, I then chose:

2) **The business unit with the least success** – because I was equally interested in how and why change doesn't happen.[3] In this case, the business made some progress – but the least

progress relative to the other 15 business units. And the progress it did make was erratic: after a period of gains there would be a period of worsening numbers. But it never gave up and so progress bumped along, as its progress graph (the top right-hand graph) shows. I later termed this **the 'Road Runner' Case**, because the manager in this case said she often felt like Wile E. Coyote in the Road Runner cartoons – she'd be running flat out chasing the goal and then suddenly she'd realize there was nothing solid underneath her to support the change she was striving for. So how had leaders contributed to this situation? And why was this case so different in outcomes from the Ideal Case?

And then, to help understand some other features I noticed in the progress graphs, I added into the study:

3) **The business unit with the greatest success in the early stages of the change, even though this success wasn't sustained** – because I thought that might tell an interesting story about how and why success starts off well but isn't sustained. I called this the **'Early Momentum' Case** and it's clear from its progress graph (shown in the bottom left-hand graph) why it earned this name. Progress here was spectacular in the early days (far more impressive, in fact, than in the 'Ideal' Case) but then fell away. Why was progress so much better than the Ideal Case initially? And why was it not then sustained?

And finally, I decided to also study:

4) **A business unit that was very much the middle of the road when it came to success.** I later termed this the **'Under The Radar' Case** because that's how one of the managers described how this change was done. As can be seen from its progress graph (the bottom right-hand graph), its results were on an upward trajectory over the four years, but never gained the

traction that we see in the Ideal Case. After a comparable start, there was then a period of slow improvement before results flattened out. What explained why this case started so slowly? And why was this (albeit lower) level of success nevertheless then sustained, so that it ended up at roughly the same level as the Early Momentum Case?

The organizational scientist Professor Stephen Barley once noted that 'difference is the root of all interest'[4] – and so it is here. As you can see when we view their progress data together (see Diagram 2.2 below), these four cases produced very different outcomes over the three and a half years of the change:

Diagram 2.2: Progress over three and a half years

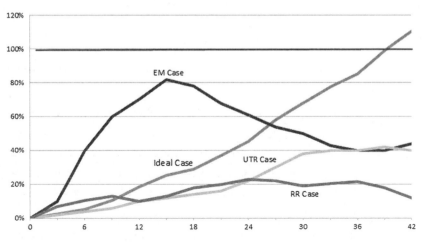

So, what caused these very different outcomes? What were leaders doing differently across these four cases? Did it matter when certain leadership actions were taken? And what did it feel like for the managers involved in trying to deliver the change? These are the questions I'll answer in detail in Chapters 4–8. But to make it easier to navigate these chapters, it's worth giving you the key features of each case before we move on.

Summaries of the four cases

The Ideal Case

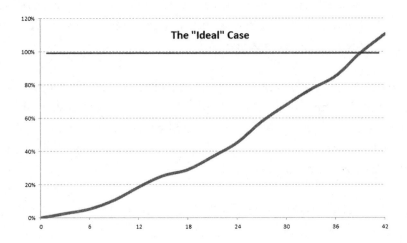

- Started slow – notably much slower than the Early Momentum Case
- Chose to work mainly on data and systems in the early days with not many 'quick wins'
- Also spent time in the early days agreeing target outcomes and metrics
- After a slow start, it maintained steady upward progress towards its target. It never slipped back. In fact, its progress almost became exponential in the later stages of the change
- This was despite the fact that the CEO – an inspirational leader whom managers loved and who'd kicked off the change – left the business at the beginning of Year 3
- Managers in this case reported feeling motivated by the work they were doing and were rarely stressed or frustrated.

The Early Momentum Case

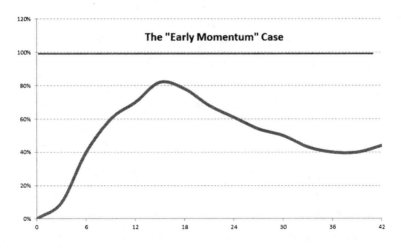

- Made stellar early progress – and notably much greater early progress than the Ideal Case
- Chose mainly 'quick wins' in the early days, with much less early work on data or systems
- Spent some time in the early days agreeing target outcomes and metrics – although less than in the Ideal Case
- After this stellar start, progress peaked around 18 months in. From there, it was a downward trajectory
- It was only in Year 2 that this business started working on data and systems. This meant managers' workloads increased dramatically at this point
- By Year 3, another new strategy was introduced by the CEO, causing doubt among managers about what the priority was
- This CEO was an inspirational leader whom managers loved. She stayed with the business for the duration of the change and was heavily involved in it from start to finish
- Managers in this case reported feeling motivated by the work they were doing and were rarely stressed. They were frustrated by the drop in progress during Year 2, however, and confused about what they should prioritize.

The Under The Radar Case

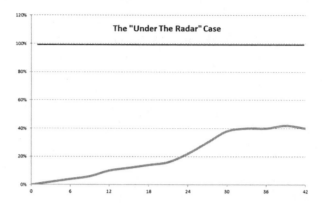

- Started slow – comparable to the Ideal Case in the early days
- Chose mainly 'quick wins' in the early days, with much less early work on data or systems
- Spent less time than either the Ideal or Early Momentum Cases considering target outcomes or metrics in the early days
- Termed the 'Under The Radar' Case because this was how the CEO wanted the change done. Knowing not all of his senior team supported the new strategy, he chose to delay the fight about this and instead kick off the change (which he personally believed in) in a low-key way so as not to 'scare the horses'
- One consequence of this 'under the radar' approach was that budget was always an issue in this case
- After a slow start, this business maintained steady, upward progress towards its target. It never slipped back
- But its progress never became exponential, as in the Ideal Case. In fact, progress plateaued around Year 3, well short of the target
- This CEO was an inspirational leader whom managers loved. He stayed with the business for the duration of the change and was heavily involved in it from start to finish
- Managers in this case reported feeling motivated by the work they were doing, but also stressed. They were overworked and, although personally supported by the CEO, felt frustrated at the lack of resources and the lack of support from the rest of the business.

The Road Runner Case

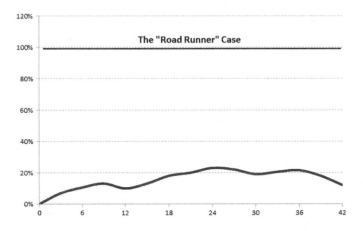

- Made significant early progress – second only to the Early Momentum Case – thanks to choosing only 'quick wins' in the early days and by starting to work on these activities immediately
- This case spent virtually no time considering target outcomes or metrics, and did no early work on data or systems
- Progress was patchy and temporary: after a period of gains there would be a period of worsening numbers
- This case never gave up, but kept working on the initiatives they had agreed on
- The CEO was an inspirational leader whom managers loved. While still with the business, he was heavily involved in the change and a major source of personal support for the change team
- Termed the 'Road Runner' Case because the Head of Change said she often felt out on a limb with nothing to support her. This worsened after the CEO, who had kicked off the change, left the business in Year 3
- Relying largely on personal support from the CEO and the goodwill and dedication of the change-team, progress was hard won for this case. Managers reported feeling motivated by the work they were doing but remembered being frequently stressed and frustrated.

Overcoming the Three Biases in existing change research

The structure of the cases and the research design I chose had several clear advantages for studying how and why change can be successful – and, specifically, for addressing the three biases I identified in Chapter 1.

1. Overcoming the Early-Stage Bias

To overcome this bias, you need to study (i.e. ask people about) the later stages of the change, i.e. the second, third and fourth years – what one paper memorably described as the 'death valley' of change initiatives.[5] Because that's often how long strategic change takes. And because CEOs will often have changed during this time,[6] that necessitates talking to a wider and probably a less senior group of people – because they will be the ones who are still around in the later years of a long-term strategic change.

The fact that the change being studied here was already complete meant two things. First, I was able to study *the whole* of the change, without having to wait for it to mature. As a result I was able to collect as much data about the later stages of the change as its early stages. The second benefit was that the results were already in – therefore, I already knew which business unit had done a better job in implementing the new strategy and which had disappointed.[7] That meant I didn't have to place a bet on which business units to study and thereby possibly miss important insights had I chosen the wrong ones.

These kinds of case studies are known as longitudinal, *historical* cases (see the Science Spotlight below) and are recognized as being particularly helpful in unearthing the reasons how and why some things work in organizations while others don't.[8] This is because people can think back over the full duration of the change (not just its early stages) and, with the benefit of hindsight, see linkages between actions (or inactions) and outcomes over time.[9]

There is, however, one caveat to this kind of research: it is valid *as long as* the actions, behaviours or events being recalled are still sufficiently recent that people's recollection of them hasn't faded, and the materials being used to substantiate their recollections (the strategy documents, slide decks, diaries and announcements from the time) are all still available to be studied.[10] Helpfully, this was the case here – the change was sufficiently recent to be recalled easily by the people I spoke to; they also still had all of the key documents from the time.

All of which should help mitigate the Early-Stage Bias and therefore enable me to say something about what helps *sustain* change, rather than merely what helps *start* it.

Science Spotlight: Longitudinal, Historical Cases

Longitudinal studies mean we study events and outcomes *over time*. This is in contrast to what we call *cross-sectional* studies, which investigate only a small snapshot of an event, i.e. how one variable relates to another at a single point of time. From 'snapshot' studies, we can claim correlation ('We believe that Steve's leadership behaviours of X are related to outcome Y'), but we can make no claim as to causality, i.e. we don't know whether these leadership behaviours caused outcome Y, nor do we understand *how* or *why* this relationship might have come about. A cross-sectional study is like a 'snapshot' of a phenomenon, in that, although X and Y are both present in the same frame, we don't know how either of them got there, nor whether one caused the other.

In contrast, a longitudinal study is more like a *movie* of a phenomenon, so we can see how things play out over time. Such studies often try to explain the *process* by which change occurs – i.e. not just *what* happens but also *how and why* things happen as they do. Indeed, as process scholars such as Andrew Pettigrew and Ann Langley point out, because process occurs over time, *process can only be understood over time*.[11] This means that longitudinal studies give us the opportunity to suggest *causality* between actions and outcomes – for example, 'if Steve does X, then because of X, Y appears to occur'.

And actually 'appears to occur' is about as far as we can go as researchers. This is because even if you know the likely direction of causation (because by studying the phenomena over time, you've established that X happened before Y), nevertheless causality can never be claimed with any certainty. That's because in any situation that involves humans, different combinations of 'inputs' will produce different outcomes, depending on the specific context they're in. Real life – which is what we study here – is never as clean or deterministic as it might appear to be, if all you study are people in behavioural labs or in theoretical settings.

So that's longitudinal studies. Longitudinal, *historical* case studies are so-called because they are longitudinal studies of events or phenomena that have already occurred – rather than those that are still on-going or occurring in real time. The big advantage with longitudinal, historical cases is, pretty obviously, that the phenomena are already finished and so we can take a view about whether these phenomena were successful or not. As Jeffrey Fear put it:

Because a historical perspective is necessarily retrospective, the researcher has access to information that contemporaries did not have about the future and can judge outcomes or the long-term consequences of (quiet) choices for their significance – a luxury theorists studying organizations in the present cannot have.[12]

The one big watch-out when doing longitudinal, *historical* case studies is that these events didn't occur so long ago that people can't accurately recall what happened, or who was involved or what they said. As with all histories, we also need to have access not only to secondary sources (e.g. people's recollections of events) but also to primary sources (e.g. the artefacts such as press releases, photos, diaries, presentations and the like) that were created at the time. These need to have been preserved so that the researcher can get at least copies of these artefacts; we also need to establish that these surviving artefacts are properly representative of what took place and don't themselves create a bias in the data we're analyzing.[13]

The historian Geoffrey Elton drew an important distinction regarding *which* data to select as being important in a historical study. He distinguished between what he called 'the legitimate activity of selecting the meaningful [data]... [and] the idle activity of forgetting the inconvenient' (2002: 39) – i.e. the quotes that don't fit with your emerging theory of how or why change happens. Nothing in my years of training on social science methodologies helped quite as much in this study as Elton's distinction. And, in many ways, the skills and mindset the researcher needs to investigate such cases are those of an historian.[14]

2. Overcoming the Agentic Bias

If we are to better understand the role played by agency, versus the role played by structure, during strategic change, then we need to include specific questions about both agency *and* structure in our data collection. In other words, we need to ask people not only about what they were saying and doing, but also specifically about the structural changes they were making. We also need to be able to show the linkages between making structural changes (or indeed failing to do so) and how the change turned out.

So, in this research, I encouraged all the people I spoke to, whether leaders or managers, to talk about the *structural* elements of the change and how they thought these had either helped or hindered their progress. This meant that, alongside the typical questions about what they were saying and doing as individuals,

I added into the conversations specific questions that asked about KPIs and metrics, budgets and resourcing. These questions acted as prompts to help them recall the structural elements of their work, elements that may otherwise have gone unmentioned, and therefore unrecorded.

Another feature of this research design helped unearth insights about the importance of the structural elements of a change. I talked not only to leaders about what they had done, but also to managers about what they had needed. In fact, the vast majority of the interviews I did for this study were with the middle managers tasked with delivering the change. And, as we'll see, the managers in these businesses talked much more frequently about structural aspects than did their leaders – even though it was leaders who'd made most of the structural changes being discussed. It was as if the structural aspects of the change didn't make it onto the leaders' radar, whereas for managers, these structural aspects were recalled as being very important to them, and to the success of the change.

Studying the change for its full duration also helps mitigate the bias towards agency. The reason is that structural changes (for example, changes to IT or HR systems, to KPIs or dashboards) take much longer to enact than agentic change, such as leaders changing what they're saying or how they're acting. Moreover, even after these structural changes have been made, it takes much longer before we see their impacts emerge. Put simply, the feedback loop on structural changes is much longer than the feedback loop on agentic changes. As a result, it is only when we study organizations over years rather than months that we can properly understand the role which structures and systems play in long-term change.

3. Overcoming the Event Bias

To combat the Event Bias, researchers need to focus much more on the *process* by which change happens and much less on the events contained in the change. They do this not just by choosing the best possible research sites – for example, a change which has already occurred where the process can be studied in its entirety – but also by specifically asking questions about 'how' and 'why' (rather than just 'what happened').

Framing the research to focus more on the *process* by which change occurs has other implications. In particular, if you want to understand how and why certain change processes have been more successful than others, it really helps if (a) you can study change processes that have recently happened and (b) the organizations studied are as comparable to each other as possible.[15] This is exactly what I had the opportunity to do here: to study comparable business units (they were part of the same company, in the same sector and all tasked with implementing the same new strategy) whose change had been recently completed – whether successfully or not.

Because all the business units studied were in the same company, in the same sector, and used the same business model, we could eliminate exogenous reasons such as 'well, it's harder to change in this sector and easier in that other sector' as a possible explanation for different levels of success. And the fact that all the business units were targeting the same change meant we could eliminate another possible excuse, namely that 'it was a different type of change that was asked for in company A compared with company B' and so that explains why A was more successful than B. Those kinds of exogenous excuses couldn't be made here. Which meant I had a better chance at unearthing the endogenous (i.e. *process*-related) reasons why the change worked better in some of the business units than others – things like how well leaders led the change or how different stages of the change were sequenced and managed.

And to ensure that I was getting to the heart of the *process* by which the new strategy was implemented – rather than just a recollection of the events that occurred at the time – I adopted an historian's methodology to investigate these cases. An historian pays keen attention to when, and the sequence in which, things occur. This careful sequencing of events over time, and the collection of data about the possible linkages between actions and outcomes, mapped against the progress each case was making, is the critical first step in us being able to say anything about the *process* by which change occurs.

The research design

This research aimed to build a new theory of how and why long-term, strategic change can be delivered and sustained. When you're using research to generate a new theory, rather than to prove an existing one, this is known as inductive research. And when done using case studies, it is known as the inductive case study method. This method has important implications for how the research is conducted; and, when done properly, can be a major source of new insight into how and why things happen as they do.[16] (For more on this, see the Science Spotlight below.)

Throughout this chapter, I have argued that it's because of how this research was designed that I have been able to overcome the three biases we see in most of the existing research on how to lead change; by designing research that allowed me to hear different stories and, from this different data, to discern a different way to lead change. What this means in practice is not just choosing the right sites for the research, but also collecting and analyzing the data in the right way.

Science Spotlight: the Inductive Case Study Method

Inductive research is the kind of research you do when you want to explore and understand a phenomenon. It's the kind of research you do when you don't yet have a strong idea of what the answer might be. In fact, you might not even be sure you know the question you should be asking. And you certainly don't have anything as firm as a hypothesis or a proposition to test. It is the opposite of what we call *deductive* research, which is the kind of research you can do if you have some ideas (or hypotheses) about what the answer might be and you want to test whether these are supported by actual data.

Deductive research has dominated scientific research for much of the past 300 years. Perhaps it is no surprise then, that when the nascent field of organizational 'science' – starting in the 1920s and developing in the 1950s and 60s – was looking to establish itself as a robust discipline capable of producing rigorous research findings, it relied (initially at least) on deductive methodologies. Of course, some scholars would argue that even the use of the term 'science' here is spurious. But, as the sociologist and Stanford Professor James March noted, just as economists had 'physics envy' and responded by making economics more mathematical, management theorists suffered from 'economics envy' and responded by using deductive methodologies to make their new field more 'scientific'.[17]

But unlike the established sciences that studied objective and external phenomena, such as chemical substances or physical movement, the units of analysis being studied in organizational science involved people. People are not inert objects. As one scholar has put it: 'The vagaries of human behaviour make it very difficult to model as a pure science.'[18] Because people's behaviour changes depending on the context they find themselves in: they behave differently on their own vis-à-vis in groups and differently with different groups of people. Indeed, the behaviour of these 'study-objects' (to use deductive language), i.e. people, can itself be changed just by the involvement of the researcher. All of which means that a deductive research methodology – whereby a researcher accumulates sufficient knowledge about a field to be able to come up with some preliminary ideas (hypotheses) and then tests these against the actual observed behaviour of the people in question – is often a flawed way to study collective human endeavours, such as organizations.

Equally concerning is the potential bias that humans code into deductive research when studying other humans. Humans are a varied species, after all. What if the researcher doesn't know these particular people well enough to know what he should ask them? What if he asks them the wrong questions? Or leads the witnesses by asking closed, overly prescriptive questions? More fundamentally, what if the group of people the researcher chooses to talk to isn't even the right group to be studying at all? Any one of these flaws in a deductive research design could mean that the story that these people really want to tell remains untold, and so the real reasons that explain a phenomenon remain undiscovered. Which explains why studying human behaviour using inductive methodologies is usually a better bet.

There are two big differences between inductive and deductive research in practice. The first difference happens before we do the research. We are seeking to produce a new theory, rather than prove an existing one. This means inductive researchers need to spend time understanding the phenomenon first – rather than time reading up on the existing literature, largely because there may not *be* existing salient literature on the phenomenon. If there was, there would be no need for a new theory.[19]

The second big difference happens during the research itself. We are seeking to *explore* the phenomenon, rather than prove a hypothesis about it, so we use different methods to collect the data and analyze it. For example, we use open questions (rather than what has been termed 'leading the witness questions')[20] and what we call semi-structured conversations to ask our informants about what they might want to tell us. 'Semi-structured' because of course we have an idea, going into these conversations, of the sort of intel we want to learn from talking to someone but we can't *know* precisely what the conversation will yield because we haven't talked to them yet and we need to leave enough space in the conversation so they can take us in a different direction, and tell us a different story, if that's what they want to talk about.[21]

Whereas an inductive interview is only partly structured, leaving plenty of space for the informant to shape the conversation, a deductive research interview can sound a lot like a verbalized survey questionnaire. In other words, you have a pre-agreed survey that you'd like to take the interviewee through and whereas you could have had them do it online, you've decided to talk them through it. Equally, if it wasn't you talking them through it, it could be a bot, because you won't change the questions, or the flow of the interview, regardless of what they say back to you.

And, in inductive research, to make sure we maintain the validity of our informants' story, we try to use their own words and phrases wherever possible when we are analyzing and presenting the data. The test is always 'would the informant recognize the interpretations I am coming to?' so that the story remains theirs and not the researcher's.

In this kind of analysis, the researcher goes from specific quotes recorded from the people they spoke to (the 'data') to their interpretation of what this means. We do this by grouping the data into increasingly large and more abstract 'buckets'.[22] These buckets become the dimensions of the theory that seeks to explain the phenomenon you're studying. Thus, in an inductive study, the direction is from specific data to generalized dimensions that generate a new theory. Whereas in a deductive study the direction is the opposite – you start with hypotheses based on existing theory and go to specific data that will either prove or refute these hypotheses.

One final point. Notice the difference in the language we use here. In the deductive methods, we call the people from whom we collect data our 'respondents' because we've decided what to ask them and they are merely responding to our questions. They are dancing to the researcher's tune. In inductive methods, we call the people from whom we collect data 'informants' because they are informing our view about what is really going on and talking about what they feel is important about a phenomenon. They are telling us what tune we should be listening to. And that perfectly captures why it is *this* kind of research, done in this way, that is much more likely to unearth the real reasons why people do certain things and not others, and why certain actions and behaviours work and others don't.

1. Collecting data

In this kind of research (an inductive case study design), the first step in collecting the data is to work out who to speak to – rather than worrying too much about what we might find. Having chosen the four business units that I wanted to study, I needed to decide who within these businesses could tell me most about what had happened in them so that I could understand why the results were so different. For each of the four cases, this meant I spoke to:

- the CEO – to get their take on events;
- the senior manager tasked by the CEO with delivering the new strategy – usually called the 'Head of Change'; and
- all of their direct reports who were on the change team.

For each case, I spoke to between 15 and 20 informants across these three different levels. And critically, I spoke to each of them on at least three separate occasions. This helped me build trust with each informant, giving me a better chance of getting them to tell me the real story of what went on.[23]

2. Analyzing the data

As the renowned qualitative researcher Professor Ann Langley has noted: 'Process data are messy.'[24] You start with a 'shapeless mass'[25] of data – i.e. hundreds of pages of transcribed interviews – and, by repeatedly reading it, writing notes on it, interpreting it (or 'coding' it), first one way and then another, you gradually work out a plausible story that explains why people said what they did about the phenomena you're studying.

When the interviews were all taped and transcribed, the result was over 2,500 pages of data. These were first time-coded, i.e. the quotes, stories and documents from all the different informants were grouped into the 14 separate quarters over which the change lasted. This gave me a sense of what had happened when, in each case. Then I mapped these quotes onto the progress charts so I could start to see possible linkages between what leaders and managers were doing and the outcomes being produced (i.e. the rate of customer retention). The time-lags involved and the exact combination of causality would never be precise, but I now had a sense of the sequence and that offered at least the possibility of saying something about which actions or behaviours could be linked to which outcomes.

In each case, I started by using the informants' own words to classify their quotes and then, as patterns gradually emerged across the four cases, I used more generic terms to describe what they were talking about. Gradually, this process (which took over two months to complete) produced five 'buckets' into which I could put all of the informants' data, at different times across the three-and-a-half-year change. Each of these 'buckets' of data was bracketed by a start and end date, denoting the time during the change when informants were remembering the importance of a particular concept.[26] These time-bracketed 'buckets' of data suggested that:

- in **the first three months** of the change, informants needed **Clarity** from leaders;
- in **the first twelve months** of the change, informants needed **Alignment** around the change that had been asked for;
- in **the next two to three years** of the change, informants needed both **Focus** in how they worked and **Consistency** in what leaders asked for and did;

- and taken together, these four Elements determined how much **Autonomy** managers felt they had, and in particular whether they experienced this autonomy as being meaningful or meaningless. Autonomy was meaningful if managers were able and happy to take action on their own. But it was meaningless if, regardless of the authority they had been given, managers were not able or happy to exercise it because of a failure by leaders in one or more of the first four dimensions.

These 'buckets', and the labels I gave them, became the five dimensions of the new approach I set out in this book – and which explains how and why change was led more successfully in some cases than in others. It's this design – i.e. how the four cases were chosen, and then the way in which the data was collected and analyzed – that means I can claim that this new approach can help leaders not only know **what** to do, but also **when** to do it.

My approach is different – largely because, as I have set out in this chapter, it specifically deals with the three main biases we see in much of the existing research. Because of that, it allows us to hear different stories – stories not of what leaders did, but of what managers needed. The results this research produced are outlined in the next chapter and then explained in more detail in Chapters 4–7.

CHAPTER THREE

The Result

A new approach to leading strategic change

This chapter gives you an outline of my new approach to leading strategic change – an approach that helps leaders achieve the change they want, by truly empowering their people to deliver; and that helps managers achieve real autonomy, because they'll now know what to ask for from leaders.

The headline of this new approach is this: leaders first need to '**step up**' and do more than they might typically do – in specific ways and at specific times – during the early stages of the change. And then they need to '**step back**' and do less than they might typically do – again in specific ways and at specific times – in the later stages of the change. This chapter gives you the highlights of what leaders need to do (and when) – and therefore also of what managers need to ask for. The four chapters that follow take you through each of the stages in more detail.

A new, 'anti-Hollywood' approach to leading change

This new approach to leading change may, at times, seem counter-intuitive. Some of the advice here goes completely against that of the existing consensus. This may mean we need to 'unlearn' some of the established, common folklore of what we think we know about how to lead change. But the prize, for leaders, managers and their organizations, is huge.

Remember that the main sources for this new research were not leaders, but managers, i.e. those actually tasked with delivering the change. The resulting framework therefore tells us what managers genuinely need from leaders, rather than just what leaders think they ought to do. I think of this new approach as an 'anti-Hollywood' version, because it challenges many of the assumptions of the old 'Hollywood' version and exposes how inadequate it is.

The framework has five dimensions. The first four describe what managers need from leaders in order to deliver the change without having to revert to them for help or direction. I call these the four 'asks' leaders need to deliver on. The fifth dimension is the *result* – what is gained by managers if leaders deliver on the four 'asks'. And while what is gained is initially most significant for managers, it is also of enormous benefit to leaders and their organizations.

How and when leaders need to Step Up

In the early stages of any change, leaders need to do more than they might typically do – and, critically, do *different types of work* than they might typically do.

1) **The first 'ask' from leaders is Clarity. This is the first way in which leaders need to step up** – in other words, do more than they might typically do to kick-off the change. Clarity takes around **three months** to get right – and although that might sound like a long time for those still addicted to the Activity and Drama Delusions, trust me, it isn't. You have a lot to do in this time and some of it is hard.

What does it take to provide Clarity for managers? There are four Elements leaders need to get right:

- first, leaders need to talk about the change as being something they believe is right and to which they are **personally committed**;
- second, they need to create a credible narrative for the change, by explaining **why this change is needed and why now**, and by

explaining how this new strategy relates to previous strategies. This helps managers decide what they should keep and what they should ditch from their existing work. You can think of these first two Elements of Clarity as coming straight from the 'transformational' leaders handbook;

- third, leaders need to talk about what will change as a result of the new strategy. This means they need to be clear about the **long-term outcomes** they want to see from the change, and these need to be big enough improvements over current performance so that people understand the extent of the change being undertaken. Leaders also need to be clear about any new behaviours they are expecting to see;
- fourth, leaders need to communicate the fact that, given the extent of the change, this is a **fundamental, rather than merely cosmetic, change**. While there may be some 'quick wins', much of the early work will be decidedly unglamorous. And while the leader won't be doing that work themselves, they care about it and they will give it – and the people doing it – their time and attention. You'll see that these second two Elements of Clarity look a lot more like 'transactional' leadership.

The Clarity stage in this framework requires a different type of effort from leaders than they may be used to. Of course, the old 'Hollywood' version of kicking off change requires time and effort from leaders too – these were high-activity, high-drama events, after all. But delivering Clarity requires leaders to spend their time and effort very differently – essentially, to spend it *thinking rather than just doing*. Thinking about the outcomes and how the change fits with what's gone before; thinking also about how they will explain this so that managers are sufficiently clear about what's wanted that *they* can start making decisions about how to deliver it.

This Clarity stage is the essential foundation on which the other three 'asks' are laid: without it, managers will flail around in these later stages, however hard-working and smart they are, and leaders will be sucked into the detail of the change as a result. It is at this Clarity stage that the hard work is needed from leaders – not later. *This* is when leaders first need to step up.

2) **The second 'ask' from leaders is Alignment. This is the second way in which leaders need to step up** – this time by making sure that all the signals, from leaders personally and the organization overall, support the change that's been asked for. Alignment needs to be delivered for managers **by the end of the first year of the change**, but as you'll see, you need to start work on it immediately – much earlier, and with much more focus, than is seen in your typical change effort.

In my framework, there are four Elements of Alignment leaders need to use:

- the first is by what leaders talk about, ask about and agitate for. Right from the first days of the change, managers will be looking for signals – and one of them is what leaders say. Once the formal announcement of the change is done, what is it that leaders are talking about? What does she ask about if you meet her in the lift on the way to lunch? What does she always mention or refer to, even in passing, every time you see her? What's the thing she's complaining about or agitating for? All these are ways leaders signal what they really care about. I call this **'Alignment by Conversations'** to help convey that the way leaders communicate is not just in formal set-piece speeches or announcements (though those are important) but also in day-to-day chats, emails and meetings. These are often the real leadership 'tells' that managers are looking at;
- the second way to drive Alignment as a leader is by what you do and how you use your time. I call this **'Alignment by Actions'** because it doesn't just mean 'walking the talk', i.e. behaving in the way that you've asked others to – though that is important; it also means that you've taken action to support the change. This could be freeing up time in your diary to make sure there's always

enough time to discuss progress and issues, or making decisions on the structures of the organization that will better support the new strategy. Actions speak louder than words;

- the third way to align the business around the change is to make sure it has the right people working on it, and sufficient budget to make it happen. I call this **'Alignment by Resourcing'** and it's important to recognize that this isn't just about money, it's about people too. Who are the best people to work on the change? Will they be dedicated resources or will they also be working on other things? How much budget do we need, given what we have to deliver, and how long will it take? This is about putting your money (and your people) where your mouth is. And because you've already agreed what outcomes to target and how long this will likely take – as part of the Clarity stage – it is now possible to make much better decisions about resources, even though it might still be hard to secure them;

- the fourth and final way leaders can align the business around the change they've asked for is through **'Alignment by Metrics'**. This speaks to the power of changing the data, metrics and KPIs of your organization to help signal the kind of organization you want. And because you know the outcome being targeted by the change – you will have thought that through as part of delivering Clarity – it is relatively easy to now work out what data you need to gauge progress, which metrics ought to be used to calibrate success and, therefore, how managers should be rewarded differently because of this new strategy. That said, this isn't really about money: it's about recognizing that high-performing managers really just want to deliver whatever target you give them. And so leaders need to make sure that it's the *right* set of targets – ones that support the new strategy, rather than work against it.

Now, the first two Alignment Elements here (by Conversations and by Actions) are examples of 'transformational' leadership. The second two (Alignment by Resourcing and by Metrics) look a lot more 'transactional' in their nature. To get all of these four Elements of Alignment working in favour of the change takes time and effort from leaders. As with the Clarity stage, this probably takes *more* time and effort from leaders at this stage than would be true in the old 'Hollywood' version of how to lead change, but it pays dividends. By making sure that all four of these signals are working *for* the change, rather than against it, you not only help managers understand and believe in the change, you also ensure that they have the resources, the data and the rewards to help them deliver it. So, step up and make sure that you don't send mixed signals at this time. That way, you'll set managers up to succeed and give the change the best possible chance of being delivered.

With the foundations of successful change now laid during this first year (the first three months to achieve Clarity, and the full twelve months to achieve Alignment), managers have enough context to be able to make their own decisions about what activities to work on and how to prioritize their time. Leaders had to step up to achieve this – doing more and often different work than they might typically do at this stage of a change. But it is this early investment that will, in the later stages, enable leaders to step back.

How and when leaders need to Step Back

In the later stages of the change (by which I mean from the start of the second year onwards), leaders need to do less than they typically do – though 'doing less' will still take effort and discipline. It won't, however, require any new decisions and it will take less time overall from leaders as the change progresses. (For more on this, see the Science Spotlight 'Leader Time Spent Differently', page 69). Leaders need to keep stepping back for the duration of the change, if they are to see it delivered by their managers, rather than by them.

3) **The third 'ask' from leaders is Focus. This is the first way in which leaders need to step back.** What I mean by Focus is the

ongoing process by which leaders, managers and the whole of the organization remain focused on the new strategy. This is what enables managers to keep on delivering. Focus matters because it ensures that the change isn't diluted over time. If you have insufficient Focus (and instead, you have too many other 'priorities' on your plate, or you don't give it the time and patience it needs), then the change can become just another initiative.

There are two Elements leaders need to get right to achieve Focus:

- first, they need to make sure that managers have enough 'slack'. In other words, managers should not be overwhelmed with work, but have time to think about and learn from what they are doing. This means they need to have enough resources to get the work done. But even with enough resources, managers can end up with too many projects on at any given time. Of course the managers themselves should be the ones choosing the projects to work on (they know the outcomes they need to hit, after all). But keen managers, empowered by all the 'stepping up' work leaders have already done to give them Clarity and Alignment, may now be tempted to take on too many initiatives in the hope of out-performing expectations. So a leader's job will also be to encourage managers to do less rather than more – to focus on fewer projects in order that the 'biggest bang for the buck' ones get the attention they need.

  The boon for managers of no longer drowning in activities is not just that the most important work gets more of their attention, though that is hugely valuable. It's also that they have time to stand back, think and reflect on how the work is going. Which initiatives are producing the best results and why? What isn't working so well, and why is that? Without time to reflect on these kinds of questions, managers won't be able to learn from and refine what they're working on. Without learning and refinement, they won't be able to produce better, less risky results as the change goes on.

- the second thing leaders need to do to enable managers to focus is to show **patience**. This doesn't mean leaders shouldn't show interest in the progress being made, or ask for regular updates. Rather, it means they understand that the extent of the change they've asked for will take time. This is a strategic change, after all, and they made clear at the very start (as part of giving Clarity) that this was a fundamental, and long-term, endeavour. They mustn't go back on that now.

If they do, managers may respond by choosing some cosmetic 'quick wins' to give the pace of change a bit of a spurt. But that's just a quick sugar-rush that has little lasting impact and can actually interrupt the real work of change that managers ought to be really getting into at this time (Year 2 onwards). So, leaders need to stay both patient and engaged for as long as the change takes.

4) **The fourth 'ask' from leaders is Consistency. This is the second way in which leaders need to step back.** Like Focus, leaders need to be Consistent from the beginning of Year 2 for as long as the change lasts. Consistency means that nothing happens that is incompatible with the new strategy or change that was asked for. In other words, leaders need to stick with the strategy until it is implemented. If they want a different strategy instead, then of course they can choose it. But they can't be inconsistent and expect managers to continue delivering the original strategy that they asked for.

There are again two Elements leaders need to get right to achieve Consistency at this stage:

- first, they need to **maintain all the changes** they made – personally and organizationally – during the first year. This means that they are still targeting the same outcomes, still talking about the change in the same way, still role-modelling it and still making time for it. And at the organizational level, they have maintained their commitment to resourcing it properly (both people and budget) and they haven't moved away from the revised KPIs and metrics that measure and reward the change that was asked for;

- second – and this may be the more difficult element of Consistency for leaders to deliver – they also need to stick to the same initial priority for the duration of the change. This means **no conflicting messages or new 'priorities'** being communicated while the original change continues. That's because, after the original change has been announced, every new initiative or strategy chosen – albeit for good reasons – introduces the potential for conflict in the organization. If some new initiatives *are* to be chosen, leaders must be sure that these don't conflict with the original change. They must also explain how any additional initiatives fit into the original change, rather than conflict with it.

This is because either the original change is still the best course of action, in which case, stick with it and don't deviate; or it isn't, in which case you actively need to make a fresh case for another, different change – requiring you to start over, with Clarity and Alignment, and fully aware that this will mean the original change won't get done.

Of particular importance for leaders at this stage is to make sure they aren't attracted to every shiny new idea they come across. This is sometimes a problem for leaders who are in this stepping-back phase, because they should find that they now have more time on their hands. However, this usually only happens when leaders *first* step away from the day-to-day (which managers are now taking care of) and before they've properly adjusted how they spend their time. We'll talk about what activities should take the place of the day-to-day when we discuss Consistency in more detail in Chapter 7. But one of the worst things leaders can do with this new-found time is scour the planet for the latest management fads being deployed in their sector, and then decide that these should be an 'additional priority' for managers to work on.[1]

This is where the strategic nature of the change becomes important. Obviously, were it a small, tactical or incremental change that was being attempted, the potential for conflict would be much less and the organization would have capacity to work on several change initiatives at the same time. But the nature of a *strategic* change – the implementation of a new strategy or a fundamental shift in capabilities or culture – means that you can only have one of these strategic changes happening at one time. That's just the nature of the beast.

Again, the Elements required for Focus and Consistency comprise *both* transformational *and* transactional leadership. And by delivering Focus and Consistency for the duration of the change, leaders continue to support their managers as *they* deliver the change. Ironically, this support for managers comes in the form of leaders stepping back. However, it is important to note that I am not suggesting that leaders should be stepping *out*. That would imply leaders disengaging from the change and not asking about it or showing they care about it. That would actually be the *opposite* of being consistent when, in fact, one critical aspect of Consistency is to maintain commitment to all the initial actions and behaviours that kicked off the change. So, stepping *back* does not mean stepping *out*. Rather, it means making sure you don't muddy the waters – or the managers' domain – by too many or conflicting demands; and that you stay engaged but patient for the long-term change that is underway.

Equally, leaders aren't expected here to give managers *unconditional* autonomy – managers still need to be delivering and learning from their work and leaders need to participate in holding them to account for that. Managers want autonomy, but they also still want leader involvement and input when they need it.[2] My argument is that they *ought not to* need it as often as they usually do – and it's leaders' responsibility to change that dynamic.

Science Spotlight: Leader Time Spent Differently

As part of this research, I asked leaders (in this case the CEOs of each of the four cases) to look back over their diaries and estimate how much time they spent working on the change programme as it progressed. I didn't necessarily expect that this would yield anything of interest – it was just a question I added into the interviews as another comparator between the cases. The results are shown in the graph below.

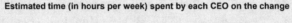

Estimated time (in hours per week) spent by each CEO on the change

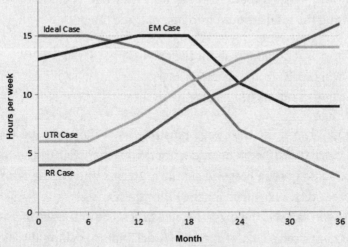

As you can see, having made a significant time investment during the first year of the change, the time spent by the CEO of the Ideal Case fell during the second year and then fell again during Year 3. In contrast, the time invested by the CEO in the

Early Momentum Case needed to increase during the second year, only falling during Year 3, but to a lesser extent than in the Ideal Case. And the time invested by the CEOs of the Under The Radar and Road Runner Cases actually increased over the three years – albeit from a much lower investment of time in the early days.

This graph perfectly illustrates the dynamic of stepping up and then stepping back. As seen in the Ideal Case, investing more time in the early days (and, as we will see in the following chapters, using this time to do specific things at specific times) meant that, in the later stages of the change, this CEO could afford to spend much less time on it. The opposite was also true: for those CEOs who hadn't stepped up enough in the early days, they weren't able to reap the longer-term benefits of being able to step back.

The differences in the *amounts* of time each CEO gave to the change were interesting, but so too was what they *did* with this time. I asked them to recall how they had spent their time, splitting the total amount into one of three categories:

1) time spent talking about the change
2) time spent thinking about it
3) time spent making decisions about it

The graphs on the next page illustrate what they told me – and this breakdown helps us understand why the CEO in the Ideal Case could gradually spend significantly less time on the change, whereas this wasn't true for the other three cases.

As you can see, the biggest single difference in the *use of leader time* is in how much of it these leaders spent making decisions about the change. In the Ideal Case, the proportion of their time (which, overall, was also falling, remember) spent on making decisions about the change had fallen dramatically by Year 3. And that's because, by the second and third years of the change,

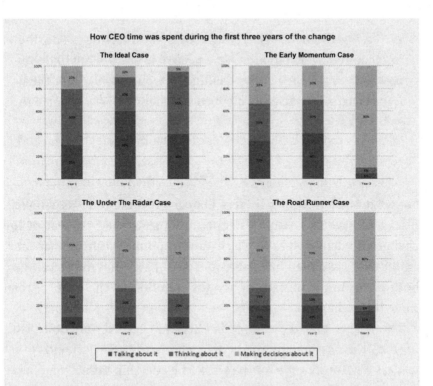

How CEO time was spent during the first three years of the change

the decisions about it were being taken by managers, not leaders. Whereas in the other three cases, their CEOs were spending an increasing proportion of their time making decisions about the change – because their managers didn't feel able or willing to do that on their own.

This situation was hard for the Early Momentum Case, where despite all their solid early work, leaders now needed to spend the vast majority of their (albeit reduced) time on making decisions about the change – arguably the least 'leaderly' use of time across the three categories. But the situation was doubly hard for the leaders of the Under The Radar and Road Runner Cases because not only were they now having to devote an increasing proportion of their time to making decisions about the change – rather than talking or thinking about it – but also the overall *amount* of their time taken up by the change was increasing dramatically. These leaders were having to do the job that managers ought to have been able and willing to do by now, but which they either couldn't or wouldn't. Because these leaders hadn't sufficiently stepped up, they weren't now able to step back.

The result

So, what is the result if leaders deliver on these four 'asks'? Well, if leaders have successfully stepped up during the first year of the change and delivered both Clarity and Alignment during that time, and if they have then been able to step back so that managers have both Focus and Consistency for the duration of the change, then three things happen.

The first is that the change is likely to succeed – a good result for the organization and the people who fund it. The second is that leaders have more time for the work of leadership rather than being sucked into the work of management. And third, managers will have **Autonomy** – the fifth dimension of my new framework for successfully leading change. Autonomy means that change succeeds without the ongoing need for leader input. The managers deliver it on their own, because they can.

But for this to be the case, autonomy has to be 'meaningful'. **'Meaningful' autonomy** is driven by two considerations:

- first, that it's **possible** for managers to exercise the autonomy that they theoretically have. This doesn't just mean they have the necessary authority to take decisions – though obviously that matters. It's more than that. For the exercise of autonomy to be *possible*, managers need to have the right resources (people as well as budget) and to have KPIs that support them in the choices they are making.

- but it's not enough that it's *possible* to exercise the autonomy you have. The second consideration that makes autonomy 'meaningful' is that managers feel **prepared** to exercise their autonomy and that means it mustn't feel personally risky for them to make a call on what to prioritize or how to act. They need to feel comfortable in doing this; they shouldn't feel they're having to go out on a limb or make a decision in the dark when choosing their priorities. If that's the case, then many managers *won't* exercise the autonomy they have – at least not without first checking in with leaders about what they really want. In my experience, if managers need extra input or 'cover' before they take a decision, and won't take it without that, then chances are the fault lies with leaders – because they haven't done a good enough job of delivering the first four dimensions of this approach.

And what is it that enables managers to feel like they're *prepared* to exercise their autonomy? *That* happens when all the leader's signals are pointing in the same direction. In other words, when the target outcome is clear, when the organization is properly aligned around the change (using all four sources of Alignment), when this has been maintained throughout the change; when managers have time to focus on delivering what they've been asked for, and when no new messages or conflicting new strategies have been announced in the meantime. All of that – the four dimensions of Clarity, Alignment, Focus and Consistency – is what makes managers comfortable to exercise their Autonomy.

To help us see how these five dimensions unfold over time, and also how interdependent they are on each other, see Diagram 3.1 overleaf. As this graphic shows, you need Clarity + Alignment by the end of Year 1. This is where leaders need to step up because getting to Clarity and Alignment takes, I would argue, more time and effort than many leaders typically devote to the early stages of a change. And if you get this first bit right, then having Clarity and Alignment will lay the foundation for you to then deliver Focus and Consistency – because

Diagram 3.1: How strategic change unfolds over time

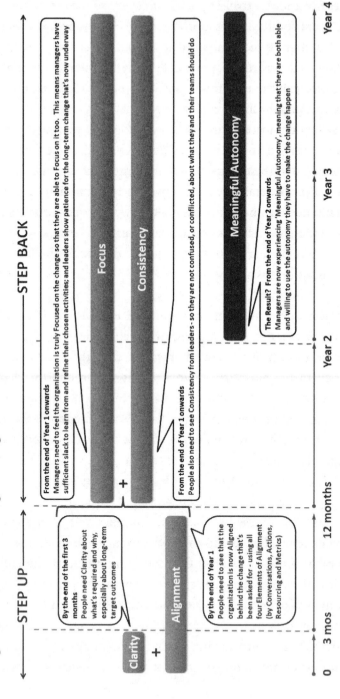

without Clarity and Alignment, how do you know what to Focus on, or be Consistent about? This is where leaders need to step back – to do less than they might typically do at this stage of the change, albeit that this 'stepping back' still takes effort and discipline – to *not* step in, to *not* change direction, to *not* add in too many new initiatives on top of the change you initially asked for.

For those leaders who are perhaps doubting that you need to step back between Years 1 to 2 – i.e. after you've established Clarity and Alignment but before seeing your managers truly exercising their autonomy – the evidence is clear that this is *definitely* where the stepping back needs to begin. It may not feel completely comfortable for either leaders or managers in this 'no-man's land', but this is precisely where managers will be looking to leaders most carefully to see whether they're serious about this change, whether they're going to stick with it or whether they might change their minds or add in some 'additional priorities' – a lovely oxymoron for stuff that will just mess up whatever good work has been done already.

If leaders deliver the four 'asks', by stepping up and then stepping back, managers have a chance. They will respond to the leader's efforts by exercising the autonomy they have – because having Clarity, Alignment, Focus and Consistency means managers feel able and prepared to take decisions on their own, without having to pull in leaders to help them.

An important caveat – organizations are human

Before we talk about this new framework in more detail, there is one important caveat to how it should be used. Put simply, there is no perfect answer that will work for every organization in every context. For that to be possible, your organization would need to be populated only by machines and robots, with no human element. Humans (because they have agency) add into the system an element that is unpredictable and variable. So, while I am confident that my framework for leading change is a *better* framework than that given by others – for all the reasons we talked about in Chapter 2 – the fact remains that, when it comes to organizations, no single approach can guarantee results in every setting. In fact, that's why leaders and managers still have jobs – because if we could come up with a fool-proof approach that could simply be programmed into every organization regardless of its context, we wouldn't need leaders and managers to judge how to lead and manage.

This means that, as a leader or a manager, you will need to look at the framework I set out in this book and think carefully about how this will work in your organization. Because while the *dimensions* and *sequence* of the change is clear, namely:

- you first need to get **Clarity** in order to know what to Align around, and Clarity takes **around three months** to establish;
- then getting the organization **Aligned** around the change you've asked for will take at least **a year**, given all the things you need to change;
- after that, **for the duration of the change**, it's all about being **Consistent** and allowing the organization to **Focus** on the change you've asked for.

Nevertheless, whether you are a manager or a leader, you will need to judge what each of these four 'asks' requires in your organization and the extent to which you've delivered on each of them by a certain time. Specifically on the *timing* of each of these four 'asks', you will still need to judge when exactly you've managed to put each one in place. This may mean that, for you, any one of the four stages may take a bit more (or a bit less) time than Diagram 3.1 on page 74 suggests. For example, in your particular business maybe getting everyone clear about what needs to change and what success looks like will take you four months rather than three. What we *do* know is that, if you take much longer than the time frames envisaged in this book (e.g. if it takes a lot longer than three months to establish Clarity about what the change means, or much longer than a year to Align the organization around the change that's been asked for), then you'll start to lose momentum and the change will be at risk. But only you can judge when you've achieved each of these stages in your business. (And, seriously, be grateful for that – because this is why, in a world of machine-learning-enabled AI, humans will still have a role.)

CHAPTER FOUR

Ask #1: Clarity

Communicate what you want

The first ask of leaders when kicking off a new strategy or change – and the first way in which leaders need to step up and do more – is for them to clearly tell the organization what they want.

Starting by explaining what the change should deliver and why it is needed sounds obvious, but too often gets short-changed by leaders too eager to 'just get on with it' – that unhelpful Activity Delusion I talked about in Chapter 1. The Activity Delusion may also explain why the *type* of Clarity given by leaders is very often 'what activities to work on', whereas the type of Clarity managers *need* is not what to work on, but rather what outcomes to produce.[1] It's *this type of Clarity* that managers need if they are to be the ones to decide what work to do. The leader's job, then, is to explain what they want in such a way that managers know *how to deliver it and can start acting accordingly.*

So how can leaders deliver on this first 'ask' and provide this type of Clarity? That's the subject of this chapter. As I outlined in Chapter 3 (see page 60), leaders must get four Elements right in order to deliver the level – and type – of Clarity needed right at the start of a change. Here, I will explain each of these four Elements in more detail, including, for each of them:

- why it's needed;
- what the Ideal Case got right at this stage;
- and what the other three cases (whether the Early Momentum Case, the Under The Radar Case or the Road Runner Case) failed to do.[2]

Some of the differences between the cases may appear subtle at this stage, but they turn out to have important implications for the change, and for those managing it, further down the track.

Peppered throughout this chapter are some 'Practice Spotlight' boxes – examples of how to do change well, taken from organizations with whom I have worked. These should give you some good, stealable ideas beyond those found in the Ideal Case.

Element 1 of Clarity: Make it personal

The first thing leaders need to do is to talk about why they believe this new strategy is the right thing to do, and also why it's something to which they are personally committed. Notice that this doesn't just require leaders to advocate for the change. That's an obvious point and most leaders will do this. But often leaders make the case for change by using purely rational arguments, or by calling on the authority of external advisers ('We asked McKinsey to look at this, and this is what they told us.'). While all good arguments are based on facts and can often be improved by having access to first-class advice, actually what makes advocacy powerful is that it's *personal*. Leaders who are most impactful in advocating for change are those who bring their own stories and a real sense of themselves to bear on why the new strategy is the right thing to do. (For a good example of this, see the Practice Spotlight: 'Making it Personal', on p. 81)

What the Ideal Case got right

As the managers from the 'Ideal' Case made clear:

> He [the CEO] absolutely believed in this. This was who he was – he was a real evangelist for this change. Every time he talked about the new strategy, he explained that this was why he was in this business, to make a difference to customers because of the products and services we offered. Doing that better meant delivering on our promise to them.

What the other cases got wrong

Actually, in this very first element, the other cases did nothing wrong. Their senior leaders were all making the case for the change in a way that was personal and authentic. When I spoke to each of the CEOs about why they had been so enthusiastic in how they kicked off the programme, they said this wasn't just because they genuinely believed in it (though that helped); it was also because all the leadership books they had read – and they'd read quite a few between them – stressed the importance of leaders kicking off a new strategy with enthusiasm and conviction. So that's what they did. These were good leaders, trying to do their best, trying to do what they'd been told they ought to do as leaders.

And why *did* they think they had to make it personal in this way? Maybe it's because this is the Element of Clarity most akin to the *transformational* type of leadership we discussed in Chapter 1 – inspiring followers and making them believe in a new strategy. It's a central tenet of the 'Hollywood' version of change leadership to which all these CEOs had been exposed and so it was something none of them had to think twice about doing. Which tells us that, whatever differences were later to emerge among these four cases, it wasn't an absence of transformational leadership at this early stage that could explain it. Instead, we'll need to go beyond Element 1 of Clarity if we are to uncover the reasons for the subsequent differences – because, right now, all four CEOs, in the Ideal Case, the Early Momentum Case, the Under The Radar Case and the Road Runner Case, as shown below – were ticking the first Clarity box.

	Ideal	EM	UTR	RR
Element 1: Make it personal Leaders need to talk about why they believe this new strategy is the right thing to do, and that it's something to which they are personally committed	☑	☑	☑	☑

Practice Spotlight: Making It Personal

The UK-based chip designer Arm Limited (previously, ARM Holdings) was acquired in 2016 by the Japanese technology conglomerate, SoftBank, for US$32bn. At more than 50x EBITDA, it was a huge deal. And it was a shock for many in the company, including the Cambridge-based engineers who had been so integral to Arm's growth over its 25-year history, and who would be critical to its future. SoftBank needed them to stay and be committed to working hard to deliver high growth.

When Simon Segars, the CEO of Arm, announced the acquisition at a town hall of the Cambridge staff, he wanted to make sure that Arm felt as enthusiastic about this new direction as he did. He set out the whole rationale for why Arm had accepted SoftBank's offer, including that they would now have billions of dollars to invest in new technologies, such as AI and the Internet of Things. This made sense for SoftBank, and it also made sense for Arm. But he did more than make the rational case: he also communicated that this new direction was something in which he, personally, believed. He did that by talking about how he had joined Arm as a young electrical engineering graduate, 15 years earlier. He had been employee No. 16 and he'd spent almost his entire career at the company. He spoke about how proud he was of what Arm had built over the past 25 years and how he wouldn't be supporting the deal if he didn't think it was the best thing to do – for employees, but also for customers and partners.

Segars' communication of this new direction for Arm was a perfect example of **Making it Personal**. As a result, many of the Cambridge-based engineers who had come to that town hall a bit sceptical about what this new Tokyo-based investment fund parent meant for their future left reassured that they were safe, and – critically – motivated by the opportunities the future now held for them. Arm was, and remains, a client and so I asked some of these engineers what Segars' message had meant for them. One of them told me:

> It made me feel that enough of the old Arm would remain, which was important, but that we now had the financial muscle and support to do all the new things we wanted to do. The fact that Simon – like he said, Employee No. 16 – was in this with us, that he was leading us on this journey, that made a big difference.

And as another long-standing employee put it:

> He was clearly committed to this. He told us that in no uncertain terms. And that meant that I was prepared to commit to it, too.

Making it Personal will often require you to talk about your own story and experience – as Segars did here – to give your fellow employees faith in the future. They want to see that you're in this with them, even if they also recognize that your positional power means your role in the change is different from theirs.

Element 2 of Clarity: Explain why it's necessary and how it fits

Next, leaders need to create a credible narrative for the change. A narrative is a story that links the past and the present and, in that context, helps us understand what the future might look like. When kicking off a strategic change, leaders need to talk about why this new strategy is needed – and why now. That's critical if people are to understand what's driving the strategy – a context that can help them decide how to deliver it – and if they are to get a sense of urgency as to why this is now a priority for the business. But leaders also need to talk about how this new strategy relates to previous and current strategies. When leaders explain a new strategy in the context of the past, it enables managers to understand how this new strategy links with what has gone before. This is important because, other than in a brand-new business, a new strategy will typically be announced against a backdrop of existing work. By understanding how the new strategy fits with what's gone before, managers can work out which of their existing initiatives they will be able to keep – i.e. the ones that fit with, and may help deliver, the new strategy – and which parts they can stop. Knowing the parts of their existing work that can be stopped is critical if bandwidth is to be freed up, with which to give the new strategy the time and focus it needs.

What the Ideal Case got right

The CEO of the Ideal Case did exactly this. As one of the change team from that case recalled:

> [The CEO] talked about the history of the business, about where we'd come from, how fast we'd grown and how, with all the increasing regulation and the fact customers were getting more demanding, growth wouldn't continue if we didn't change how the business operated and what we focused on. It wasn't that the growth was over, but it wasn't going to be as easy as it had been up to now. So, we needed to get a bit smarter and more considered about *how* to grow. This meant we had to pay more attention to certain bits of the P&L – like cost per new customer acquired – and less to others, like new revenue at any cost. From that, I understood we'd needed to change – sure. But I also understood the kinds of projects we'd need to work on to make that change. I knew that some of the work I'd been planning wouldn't now go ahead and some of what we were already working on would need to stop.

Similarly, in the Early Momentum Case, senior leaders talked about why the change was necessary and explained how it fitted with what they had done before. Again, this meant managers had a sense of what existing work could be stopped.

What the other cases got wrong

It is here we begin to see some differences emerging between the cases. As the Head of Change in the Under The Radar Case put it:

> So, the CEO was clear about why we needed to do this now, but he didn't really talk about how this was different from what we'd done before. I didn't know what bits of the old strategy were no longer relevant, what I could ditch, so I came away thinking, 'What's *really* changing? Am I just *adding* this new stuff onto everything we're already doing?' Because it seemed like *all* the old stuff was still important, and now we had to do this new strategy *as well as* everything else?

Ironically, this failure to spell out the implications of the new strategy for the existing work – although intended to make the change feel *less* daunting – meant managers felt this was a bigger, and more confusing, ask than it actually was.

Science Spotlight: Strategy as Choice

As we saw in the Under The Radar and Road Runner Cases, a lack of explanation from leaders as to how the new strategy fitted with the existing strategy meant managers found it hard to make choices about which of their existing work to keep and which to stop. The strategy literature may help explain why this leadership failure causes managers such problems.

Harvard Business School Professor Michael Porter famously noted: 'Strategy is not just what you decide to do; it's what you decide *not* to do.'[3] The strategy thinker Roger Martin has also argued that strategy requires leaders to make clear and specific choices about what to focus on. Writing with A.G. Lafley, he argues that strategy 'requires making explicit choices – to do some things and not others'. They go on: 'Yes, clear, tough choices force your hand and confine you to a path. But they also free you to focus on what matters.'[4] Without making clear and specific choices to do some things and not others, any new strategy stands much less chance of succeeding because it is not getting the focus it needs. And the organization, and the people within it, become confused and overwhelmed by the plethora of so-called 'strategic' priorities.

But the way strategy books are written often suggests that the new strategy or change is being introduced onto a greenfield site – one where no current strategy exists. In reality, teams will already be working on implementing existing strategies when any new strategy comes along and so these new strategies just get layered on top of what's already there. Old strategies aren't stopped and there's no clear or shared understanding in the business of how old and new strategies fit together.

The impact at a micro-level is that managers try to do everything, meaning the new strategy is short-changed on time and attention. At a macro-level, the reality is that many of these strategies, all of them deemed equally important, will likely *not* fit together; indeed, some may be in direct conflict with each other. The result of this? First, it reduces the likely impact of the new strategy – muted as it is by the inherited strategies with which it is competing. But, second, it also makes it much more likely that managers will need to ask leaders for clarification and guidance about what they ought to prioritize. So, the words 'Strategy is not just what you decide to do; it's what you decide *not* to do' need to be augmented to include 'and what you decide to *stop*'. Only then will the organization be clear about what its strategic priorities now are – and have the bandwidth needed to give this new strategy the best chance of succeeding.

Things were even worse in the Road Runner Case, where the CEO failed to explain why this change was needed now, let alone how it fitted with the existing strategy or work. As one of the managers tasked with delivering the new strategy told me:

There wasn't really any explanation of why we needed to do this, or why now. And certainly nothing that I could pass on to my team. The other issue was how this fitted with what we were already doing, because we were already pretty busy. As the team leader, it was hard for me to decide what my team should be working on and what we should be stopping.

And so here we see the first signs of managers not knowing how to make choices on their own, because of an initial lack of Clarity (in this case, Clarity about what remained of old strategies and how they fitted with this new strategy). These failures, even at this very early stage, by two out of four of our CEOs, would become reasons for even greater failures in their businesses later down the track.

	Ideal	EM	UTR	RR
Element 2: Explain why it's necessary and how it fits				
Leaders need to create a credible narrative for the change. This means:				
a) they need to talk about why this new strategy is needed – and why now; and	☑	☑	☑	☒
b) they also need to talk about how this new strategy relates to previous and current strategies so that it's clear what can be kept (the bits that fit with the new strategy) and what might need to be stopped (the bits that don't).	☑	☑	☒	☒

Practice Spotlight: Explaining Why it's Necessary and How it Fits

A good example of how to do at least the first part of Element 2 – explaining why the new strategy is needed and why now – was how Anthony Jenkins, the relatively new CEO of Barclays Bank, introduced his new RISES strategy in 2013. Six months earlier, Jenkins had become CEO, replacing Bob Diamond. He wanted to change the culture at Barclays to respond to the criticisms of market-fixing and regulation-dodging, introducing a new culture of Respect, Integrity, Service, Excellence and Stewardship ('RISES') throughout the bank.

The new culture was the product of extensive interviews with bank employees – they essentially chose these five new cultural values. Jenkins launched the new culture and clearly explained where the RISES idea had come from, why it was needed and why now. He talked about why this was important to him personally (he'd joined Barclays as a graduate 30 years earlier) and he even sought to position this 'new' culture as a link with the bank's Quaker past. So far, so good – he'd made it personal (Element 1 of Clarity) and explained why it was needed and why now (the first part of Element 2).

What Jenkins wasn't able to do, however, was to explain how this new culture fitted with the current strategy. The bank made the majority of its profit from its Investment Banking division and this remained a key part of Barclays' strategy going forward. While the new culture was warmly welcomed by the Retail and Card divisions, at sessions where Jenkins or the Culture Team explained the new strategy to groups of investment bankers, it was met with silence in the room and open derision outside it. The issue the investment bankers had was not that they didn't *like* this new culture: rather, their questions were, how did it fit with the existing strategy (and culture) of that part of the bank? While there may well have been plausible answers to these questions, the i-bankers didn't feel that Jenkins had a sufficiently clear explanation in the sessions he ran with them. For many, this was a test of the new CEO's credibility.

I was working with Barclays at the time, leading one of their leadership development programmes. As one banker remarked to me the day after one of Jenkins' 'culture sessions', 'I just don't think he understands this part of the bank. I'm not saying that RISES couldn't work here, but it's absolutely not how we do things right now. So, if he wants this, then other things – and pretty fundamental things like how we work and how we get paid – will have to change. So what does he want us to stop? And by the way, stopping even some of what we're doing was *not* the message we got. What we heard was, "Keep doing what you're doing because it's profitable, but do this as well." And that won't work.'

Jenkins' failure to explain how the new culture would impact the existing strategy – even though he had delivered virtually all the other Elements of Clarity – shows why this part is so important.

Perhaps a better example of how to deliver on *each* part of Element 2 of Clarity was Brian Moynihan, Chairman and CEO of Bank of America, when he decided that the bank needed a new strategy. Like Barclays, Bank of America was a banking conglomerate comprising retail, private, commercial and investment banking divisions. Moynihan's new strategy, introduced in 2017, was to grow by focusing on what he termed 'responsible growth'. Moynihan explained why the new strategy was needed and why now – because, in the post-GFC world, both risk and cost needed to be managed much more tightly than before. But what he *also* did was explain first what this new strategy meant for the old strategy and, second, for each part of the bank – the Elements of Clarity that Jenkins hadn't been able to provide.

First, Moynihan contrasted the new strategy with what had gone before. Bank of America would no longer grow by acquisition.[5] Nor would it grow at any cost. The focus would be on profitable growth, even if that meant lower rates of growth in the top-line. Second, Moynihan and his senior team explained what this new strategy implied for the various parts of the bank. The new focus on margin meant that Bank of America would be exiting its lower-margins businesses. And because in some of its business units, the largest proportion of costs was people, that meant salaries and bonuses would be lower at BofA than at other firms. This was not a 'Do exactly as you've done before, but do this as well' message.

Dubbed by some a retrenchment strategy, it saw significant cost-cutting over the next four years, especially in the non-US and investment banking operations. Many senior i-bankers would leave the firm, including Christian Meissner, then head of Investment Banking. Leaving after seven years in the role, he had reportedly clashed with senior management over what he saw as the bank's diminished risk appetite for M&A business.[6] But although such departures grabbed the headlines, they were merely a consequence of Moynihan's Clarity. By explaining what the new strategy of 'responsible growth' meant for every part of the bank, and specifically how it fitted with what had gone before, employees could understand what it meant for them personally and decide whether this was a 'bus' they wanted to be on.

Shareholders have certainly appreciated the Clarity: with pre-tax profit margin up from 26.9 per cent for FY 2016 to 31.3 per cent in FY 2018,[7] BofA stock has more than doubled over the same period,[8] comfortably outpacing the sector. And the employees who remain with the bank are also enjoying the clarity of knowing what it's now focused on – as one senior banker commented to me recently, 'When you know what the CEO wants, it makes everything easier. You can then just get on with delivering it.'

Element 3 of Clarity: Specify the outcomes and behaviours you want

Having explained why the change is needed and why now; *and* how it fits with what's gone before, it would be tempting now to get down to some activities. But that's the old approach. What leaders need to do now is dial down that urge for action and instead spend more time thinking and talking about what this new strategy will produce.

The first critical part of doing this well is to talk about outcomes (rather than activities) and to specify targets for the outcomes you want the new strategy to deliver. This is essential if managers are to be able to make good decisions about which activities to work on. Without an outcome to target, they're deciding blind.

It also helps if these target outcomes are big improvements compared with current performance. This is what signals to the business that what you're looking for really is a step-change; and, if it is, then don't mess around. Spell it out. Because, having chosen your outcome metric, you should use it to signal the extent of the change you're looking for.

Now a step-change (by definition) is not something that can be delivered in the short term: it takes time. To help people understand this, leaders should also structure the new target outcomes over different time frames. Specifically, there should be a long-dated, multi-year target for the big performance improvement that's being asked for; and then shorter-term milestones to help track progress. Note that the *target* is not the milestones themselves – these are just signposts along the way. The *target* is the big, hairy, multi-year objective. And the combination of these different metrics (both targets and milestones) across different time frames means long-term change is set up to succeed.

Finally, to help people translate these outcomes into action, leaders should also communicate the new behaviours they are expecting to see. This means people can start making immediate changes (in their behaviour) even before they're able to change what they're working on (their activities).

What the Ideal Case got right

This was really where the CEO in the Ideal Case started putting clear blue water between himself and the CEOs in the other three cases. As his Head of Change recalled:

> OK, so he's saying 'Here's why we need to do it and why now'. He's saying 'Here's how it fits with the existing strategy'. And he's saying, 'And by the way, I really believe in this.' So, that's all fine. But, what *really* made the difference for me was that he said, 'Here's what I expect to change as a result. Here's the main metric I'm going to be looking at.' And it was an *outcome* metric. We weren't just saying we were going to work on some stuff, or even that we wanted some indicators to change, like we wanted to be 'more customer-friendly' or even have higher customer satisfaction. No, we were saying that we were going to improve the outturn customer retention metric by 30 per cent. That made people sit up and take notice. That said, 'This is serious.'

You'll notice that there are a few things going on here. First, the CEO is explaining the change in terms of the outcomes he's expecting to see. By being clear and prescriptive about the outcome, he then *didn't have to be prescriptive* about which activities would be worked on. He could, instead, leave the choice of which projects to work on to managers further down the organization. After all, managers were closer to the business and better understood the processes and activities that would deliver this outcome. And because managers knew what they had to deliver (because they had a clear outcome to target), they could decide, within this constraint, which activities would best achieve this. (For more examples of this, see the Practice Spotlight 'Making the Outcomes and Behaviours Clear' on page 98.)

Second, this CEO talked about making a *big* improvement on this outcome metric. Because of this, there could be little doubt about the full extent of the change that was being asked for. As another member of the same change team pointed out:

> We all knew we couldn't get to 30 per cent by just tinkering around – that wasn't going to cut it. Thirty per cent would take fundamental root-and-branch reform of how we did things, how we thought about customers, all our processes, our data – the lot.

The extent of the work required also meant that some current activities – deemed priorities up until now – would have to go. As the Head of Change recalled:

> I remember very early on, we cleared the decks. Because it was obvious to us that delivering the 30 per cent improvement was going to take a lot of our time. For some people, it would be the only thing they would be working on. So, we needed to stop what we were doing on other things.

This big improvement that was being asked for also meant managers immediately started looking at the fundamental parts of the business – things like the data the business had on its customers, and how this could be accessed and used through its IT systems – to make sure these were up to the task. Changes to underlying structures and systems such as these take time to show a return and so this work needs to be started early. Indeed, one of the important lessons from the Ideal Case is that, if these more fundamental changes are not made early on in the change, the danger is that they will never happen.

There are two reasons for that. First, because it's only in the early stages of the change that enough political will exists in the business to embark on changes this big and expensive. If you leave this more difficult work until later in the change, this political will may have waned – as might the enthusiasm (and budget) for the hard grind of this unglamorous kind of work.

The second reason has to do with how long the results from this kind of fundamental change take to emerge. Unless you start the unglamorous work on data and systems early, the results may not have come through by the time leaders are starting to get impatient. Although there is currently no empirical evidence for what I'm about to say,[9] my experience is that one of the reasons change efforts 'fail' is actually because they are prematurely *stopped* by leaders who run out of patience for what was always going to be a long-term effort. A large initial target delta can help businesses focus on the need for this fundamental work early on in the change – which is exactly what produces the lasting change that leaders want.

The CEO in the Ideal Case also set out how he expected people to behave as a result of this new strategy. As the Head of Change recalled:

> Because this was a big change, he was clear that we'd need to be much more experimental than maybe we'd been in the past, where we'd expected everything to work first time. We were going to have to try, learn and try again. He was really big on that. And we were going to have to share good ideas openly across teams.

The reason why leaders should include some direction on how people should be behaving differently is that, in most cases, fundamental change requires humans to behave differently in order for it to happen. Quite what that behaviour should be will, of course, depend on what the new strategy is. If you're looking for higher growth, you may need managers to be more outward-looking in their focus, to help trigger more innovation.[10] If you're looking for a higher share of wallet across business lines, you may need managers to work more collaboratively across silos.[11] And if – as in these cases – the new strategy is to become more customer-focused and increase customer retention, then you may need managers to be more curious about why customers are leaving; more creative and experimental about what can be done to stop them; and better at sharing ideas so improvements can be scaled more quickly. Either way, behaviours matter just as much as projects at this early stage of the change. If you can be clear about the behaviours you want in the new business, as well as what the change should produce, then managers will be able to work out what to do in response.

What the other cases got wrong

This is where the differences between the Ideal and the other three cases really begin to stand out. Although the three other cases all communicated some new behaviours they wanted to see, not all of them specified the outcomes that the new strategy should produce. As a manager in the Road Runner Case remembered:

> The CEO had said this was important. And he'd said we needed to think outside the box and be more innovative. But he didn't say what should change as a result. We immediately started working on projects we thought would help us be more customer focused, but there were no target outcomes, so we didn't know what we were aiming for. And, as a result, I'm not convinced we chose the best projects.

While target outcomes would later be introduced, these managers had nothing for the first 12 months. Instead, the Road Runner CEO relied on specifying behaviours and advising the team which projects to work on. It's easy for leaders to throw out some advice to managers, such as 'Think outside the box' and 'Be more innovative', but the whole point of specifying new behaviours is to produce specific outcomes. So, how can you know which behaviours to ask for until you've specified the outcome you're targeting? Such behavioural asks are worthless until they are grounded in the outcome they will lead to.

It was a similar story in the Under The Radar Case. In this business, the CEO communicated the new target outcome to the managers working on the change – along with some new behaviours to adopt. But, critically, this new target outcome was not communicated to the rest of the business for fear of 'scaring the horses'. As a result, the change team were left to shoulder the burden of delivering the change alone. As the Head of Change recalled in the conversation that gave this case its name:

> The CEO was clear that he wanted this change, but for a lot of the old guard, it was potentially disruptive. So, he didn't spell it out to them. We

had a target but it wasn't widely shared. It was almost like we were doing it 'under the radar'.

And none of the three 'non-Ideal' cases asked for a *big* improvement in the target outcome, nor did their leaders make it clear that this improvement would need to be delivered over a long time frame. As one of the change team from the Early Momentum Case explained:

> So, we had a clear outcome to target but the target we were given in Year 1 was just for Year 1. And it wasn't that much of an improvement. It was actually in Years 2 and 3 that the targets *really* increased for us. But in Year 1, we thought we could get away with some of the easier, lower-hanging fruit. And we did – I mean, we knocked it out of the park that first year. But by the time they announced the bigger targets in the next few years, we realized that actually we should have spent more time in that first year on the fundamentals. It wasn't until the target got *big* that we realized we'd have to get serious about how fundamental this change was. That happened later for us than it did for other people and although we did an amazing job in Year 1, I think that delay cost us in the long run.

Notice here that the issue is not the level of the Year 1 target *per se*: actually, the Year 1 improvement that was asked for in the Early Momentum Case was at a comparable level to that being asked for in the Ideal Case. No, the issue here was that this single-year target was *a target at all*, when it ought to have been simply a milestone on the way to a big, multi-year target. But in this and the other two 'non-Ideal' cases, there was no *big, multi-year* target given right at the start.

The absence of a big, multi-year target had two consequences. First, it meant that these businesses felt comfortable choosing to work mainly on 'quick wins' in the first year: in contrast with the Ideal Case, hardly any work on data or systems was begun in the first 12 months of the change. Second, it allowed managers to feel that they could continue with all of their existing initiatives – just adding the new strategy onto their existing work – because the change felt manageable. As a result – and in contrast with the Ideal Case which had 'cleared the decks' – none of the three other cases had culled any of the projects they had already been working on when this new strategy was announced.

When I went back to the CEOs of these three cases and asked them why they hadn't specified a large multi-year target right at the start – and had instead chosen to announce annual targets that progressively became more ambitious – they all had perfectly good reasons:

- **for the Under The Radar Case**, it was because he was trying to be savvy about how to get the change (in which he personally believed) through a divided senior leadership team. He wanted to kick off the work without 'scaring the horses' and needed the change to be relatively low-profile if it wasn't to provoke a fight;
- **for the Road Runner Case**, it was because the CEO didn't yet believe that this new strategy really would require a step-change. He was able to hold this view in part because he still hadn't signed up publicly to a target outcome. And by the time he did so, it was more than a year into the change – by which time, momentum had been lost; and
- **for the Early Momentum Case**, it was because she just didn't want her managers to fail so she gave them a relatively unambitious target in Year 1, which she felt they could easily achieve. She then followed this up with more ambitious targets when she felt they had 'got the hang of the change'.

These reasons all sound plausible – and each of them was done with the best of intentions. But my advice to each of these CEOs is clear:

- **for the Under The Radar CEO**: It would have been better to have the fight early, rather than risk the change dying a slow death as a result of it being unsupported by all the senior leaders. While he thought that playing a savvy political game was helping him get some change through, the price for this was paid by the managers working on it – who were denied budget and clout because there was no shared commitment to the extent of the change required – and so their work was harder than it ought to have been;

- **for the Road Runner CEO:** Delaying clarity about the target outcome, and instead spending the first year on activities that might or might not have impacted the change, is just a waste of time and money. Better perhaps to have done nothing at all in that first year, rather than to have wasted the effort and goodwill of some of his best managers in those early days; and
- **for the Early Momentum CEO:** Delaying the increase in performance improvement cost her business. The problem was that, by *only* having a Year 1 target (rather than a large, multi-year target with interim, annual milestones), there was no sense that this was a big change or that it would require a fundamental re-making of the organization. She effectively lost a year while she delivered 'quick wins' rather than invested in more fundamental change.

So, while all of our four cases now have managers busy with change projects (i.e. from the outside looking in, all four of these cases still look similar at this stage), actually very real differences are already emerging between them. It's now *only* the Ideal Case which is properly laying the foundations of a successful change, by delivering fully on this third Element of Clarity – clear target outcomes that are big enough to drive fundamental change, *measured* using a multi-year *target* (the big delta) and *tracked* using short-term *milestones;* as well as specifying the new behaviours needed to make this happen.

	Ideal	EM	UTR	RR
Element 3: Specify the outcome and behaviours you want				
Leaders need to talk about what will change as a result of this new strategy. This means:				
a) they need to communicate the outcomes this new strategy will result in;	☑	☑	☒	☒
b) that these target outcomes are big improvements compared with current performance;	☑	☒	☒	☒
c) that these target outcomes comprise both long-dated, multi-year targets (the big delta) and shorter-term milestones; and	☑	☒	☒	☒
d) leaders need to communicate the new behaviours they are expecting to see from people	☑	☑	☑	☑

Practice Spotlights: Making the Outcomes and Behaviours Clear

Spotlight 1

When Michael Chavez became the new CEO of the executive education provider Duke CE in 2016, he knew he needed to drive sustainable revenue growth, but also profitability. He recognized that, in some teams, there wasn't a culture of taking responsibility for winning new business – even among senior staff.

Chavez set out an ambitious plan, asking for growth in revenue and even higher growth in margin. The new CEO ticked all the boxes when it came to delivering Clarity. He was clear why this change needed to happen and why now; and which parts of the previous strategy could be kept and which ones stopped. He was also clear about the critical outcomes he wanted this new strategy to produce. The target outcomes were revenue growth of 8–10 per cent over the next five years, a significant increase on Duke's previous target growth rates that merely mirrored GDP growth in its core markets. This signified to people that this would require fundamental change. By structuring this big increase as a multi-year target to which he added interim quarterly milestones to help track progress, he also signalled that the business was more serious than ever about accountability.

He was also clear about the ways in which he expected people – and especially senior people – within the organization to behave. These eventually took the form of 'Operating Principles' which he wanted all senior managers to live by. As Chavez put it: 'While my senior team and I made growth targets clear early on, I realized later that I also needed to specify the new behaviours this would take. For example, we needed to be much more commercial in how we approached work. We also needed to be more accountable for the long-term health of our business. So, I wanted us senior folks to begin to talk behaviours. Eventually I asked all senior, client-facing leaders to sign up to some operating principles that would help us get there.'

As Chavez recalls: 'We rolled out the new Operating Principles at a gathering of all our top leaders from around the world. The principles were "We're here to win together; we speak the language of commitment (not complaint); we own the problem, creatively and adaptively; we ask and listen in order to learn from each other; and we support each other".'

People made their own sense of these principles, in part because the target outcomes provided the context to help each of them decide what the principles meant for them individually. As Chavez remembers: 'For this last one, some people translated it as "We fight in the kitchen, not in the street", which I thought was a perfect description of how we needed to come together without hindering open debate among senior people.'

The combination of understanding why the change was needed and what it needed to deliver (expressed as large target outcomes with interim milestones) and the behaviours (the 'Operating Principles') meant that people had a context for the numbers they were tasked with delivering. Chavez talked extensively about these targets and principles in each of Duke's six offices worldwide, both in the regular town halls (held every other month) and in ordinary, impromptu conversations.

Many of Duke's Managing Directors – the key client-facing leaders in the organization – responded accordingly. In some cases, they simply didn't renew their lower-revenue, lower-margin projects and focused instead on the projects that would deliver the outcomes that had been asked for. As one Managing Director said at the time: 'Now we know. Before there were some indicators that we needed to grow and get more profitable, but no one was coming out and saying it. Now Michael [Chavez] has, and so we all know what to do. It's made my life a lot easier – because instead of trying to be all things to all people, I am now choosing, because I know the basis for the choices I need to make.'

Since this new strategy was kicked off, Duke CE has achieved both its annual revenue and operating profit targets and Chavez feels the business is now on a path to sustainability. He admits that this would not have been possible without being clear early on about the outcomes being targeted and the new behaviours that were needed:

> We win new business and deliver for clients when we collaborate and hold each other accountable. To do that, we need clear, simple, shared goals and a shared sense of what's expected from all of us.

Spotlight 2

In 2015, one of the world's leading technology companies was seeing increased chatter among its sales teams about how frustrating their work was becoming. Now, to get a job on one of these sales teams you needed to be very smart and very driven. Having worked with many of them I can vouch for that. Motivation is not usually a problem, so something was definitely wrong.

Digging a bit deeper, this company discovered that a major source of frustration for the salespeople was having to report on a myriad of very micro targets each week. These included how many meetings they'd had with clients and how many fields they'd completed in the company's CRM and lead management systems. Managers felt that these tedious, low-value-add activities were sucking up their time. They also felt a bit insulted that leaders wanted to micromanage them to this extent.

Well actually, leaders didn't. What leaders really cared about was that the sales teams made their numbers and that they increased the overall share of wallet with their largest accounts. When they looked at how input data (things like seeing clients regularly and making sure CRM entries were up to date) correlated with outcomes (in this case, sales numbers), there was a clear, positive relationship. Seeing your clients regularly and making sure your CRM was up to date were two of the strongest predictors of whether you'd make your sales numbers.

But these were correlations rather than causes, based on looking at indicators rather than understanding the links between indicators and outcomes. What the sales teams wanted was to be held accountable for delivering the *outcomes*, and to be left to decide on the activities that would achieve this. So the senior sales leaders responded by clearly stating that it was outcomes that mattered, not activities. They reiterated the key outcomes they wanted to see, talked also about the behaviours they believed would lead to sales success and said they were leaving the activities to the sales teams. 'I don't care about how many meetings you have. I *do* care about revenue and share of wallet' was the clear message from one of the most senior sales leaders in the business.

With this clarity, this business saw an increase in motivation and engagement (measured in their annual employee survey) and ultimately, an increase in exactly the two outcome metrics the sales teams needed to deliver on. Turns out smart, motivated people will do their best to deliver what you want – but it does help if you are very clear about what that is.

Spotlight 3

And if, with hindsight, you realize that you may have been too prescriptive about activities and not prescriptive enough about outcomes, then go back and re-do the clarity. A few years ago, I worked with a client whose instinct had been to prescribe activities rather than outcomes.[12] Their change programme was losing traction even though managers in the change-team were extremely busy on a number of projects.

I worked with leaders to help them re-state what they wanted as outcome-level targets. For example, 'Conduct exit interviews with all departing customers' (an activity) became 'Reduce the customer attrition rate' (an outcome). And a target to 'improve cross-selling rates through more outbound calls per month' (an activity) became, simply, 'improve profit per customer' (an outcome). We spent a significant amount of time sweating these outcomes: were they the right ones, had we used the right words, was there any conflict with existing priorities? In fact, several of the leadership team clearly thought we were spending *too much time* getting these outcomes right: they would often ask me something along the lines of 'When are we going to get on with the real work?' For them, the 'real work' was choosing activities.

But because these leaders went back and clarified the outcomes they wanted, it was managers who could now do the work of choosing activities. And because managers now had clear outcomes to target, within weeks they were able to identify better, smarter and cheaper ways to deliver them. Instead of nine projects, they settled on just two, which also helped drive alignment across activities and greater accountability for them. When I asked them why they had chosen these particular two projects to work on, the managers looked at me as if it was a trick question: 'Well, we knew what the outcomes had to be. And we know how the business works, so it's not that hard.'

By setting clear outcomes for managers, rather than choosing activities for them, leaders enabled managers to make better choices about how those outcomes should be delivered. And that's the division of labour in a functioning organization: leaders choosing outcomes and managers choosing activities.

Element 4 of Clarity: Emphasize this change is fundamental, not cosmetic

Having specified the outcomes this change will produce, and having set some big, long-dated targets, leaders now need to talk about how fundamental the change is. This means they need to make clear that, while there may be some 'quick wins' to help build motivation and reassure people that progress is happening,[13] most of the early work will be decidedly unglamorous and will relate to the data, measurement and systems of the business. Leaders also need to take every opportunity to show they believe this work is important and that they care about it and the people doing it.

This fourth and final Element of Clarity is of course predicated on the first three Elements being in place. How can you fully appreciate the fundamental nature of the change, or how long it will take, unless you've already specified that the target outcome and the improvement expected on this metric is a big, multi-year one? How can you know which 'quick wins' are worthy of your time, and which might be counterproductive, unless you have a clear outcome in mind? And how can you know which parts of your data and systems need to improve unless you know the outcome you're targeting and therefore the data you need to capture?

What the Ideal Case got right

As a result, it was only the Ideal Case that could deliver Element 4 of Clarity – because it was only the Ideal Case that had fully delivered on the first three Elements. As the Head of Change at the Ideal Case explained:

> Because we had to deliver a 30 per cent improvement, we knew this was a fundamental change. And so, in those early days, before we could even attempt to move on to perhaps more interesting projects, we worked on quite boring initiatives. But we had to focus on those first if we were to deliver the step-change we needed.

And as one of the team working on the change put it:

> We didn't really have this concept 'Quick Wins'. So much of the early work was about improving the quality of the customer data and really cleaning that up, and believe me, that wasn't quick. It was slow and hard and pretty dull. I mean – really, *zero* glam! And maybe that cost us some early advantage. But we knew we needed to get it done if we were going to make the 30 per cent.

And actually, the amount of time and effort spent on these 'boring', 'zero glam' projects (for example, data validation, customer ID clean-up, metric definition and baselining) rather than on the more glamorous, high-visibility 'quick wins' being done in, notably, the Early Momentum Case, *did* cost the Ideal Case some early advantage. It's what explains one of the odd things we noticed in the Progress Charts in Chapter 2 (page 39) – that the Early Momentum Case outpaced the Ideal Case in the early days. This was precisely because the returns on 'quick wins' are greater in the short term than the returns on data or systems improvements. But the *long-term* results are very different – as we will see in the later stages of the change.

It's important to be clear about the sequence that the Ideal Case used in these first three months:

- First, it decided on its outcome metric AND agreed to target a big improvement in it over multiple years;
- This signalled that fundamental, 'boring', 'zero glam' work was required and that they couldn't get away with just a bit of low-hanging fruit-harvesting – the typical kind of 'quick wins' chosen in the early stages of many change programmes;
- By knowing what the outcome metric was, they could also decide on which data they needed to capture in order to assess and, more importantly, *understand* progress;
- But this early 'zero glam' work takes time and effort, so, at least in the early days of the change, it can feel like the change isn't working;
- But if you do the work, and you keep the faith, this 'zero glam' work lays the foundations for fundamental change – and therefore the possibility of delivering the big, long-term improvement in the outcome being targeted.

And what was it that helped the managers to 'keep the faith' in this 'zero glam' work before it produced improvements in the outcome metric? It was their CEO showing he believed this work was important and that he cared about it and the people doing it. Here, we can see a CEO use an interesting combination of skills and behaviours to help managers. Essentially, the CEO was using his charisma for *mundane purposes*. As the Head of Change in the Ideal Case recalled:

> [The CEO] kept evangelizing not only about the importance of this change, but also about the importance of this 'boring' early work. Things like having clean data and accurate metrics. He kept arguing that, without this kind of work, more fundamental change would be impossible later on. He was always calling out the people who were working on it – people several levels below me who were doing the grind. He'd single them out and say what a good job they were doing and how important their work was to the new strategy.

Now it's worth saying that, although they were mainly doing 'zero glam' work at this stage, the Ideal Case chose to add into the mix a few of what we might recognize as 'quick wins'. These produced quick results and showed that progress was possible – and this can be important as a source of motivation for people. But the 'quick wins' in the Ideal Case were carefully chosen. They all exemplified the change that had been asked for – in this case, they illustrated why customer retention mattered and what could be done about it. They offered managers the opportunity to learn what worked in their business. And, although they delivered quick results at the small scale at which they were initially tried, they could then be scaled into producing much larger results over the longer term. In this respect, the Ideal Case's 'quick wins' looked more like pilots or prototypes than traditional 'quick wins'. And so, even though the time and effort spent on them detracted from the full time and effort that could have gone on the fundamental work at this stage, the upside – the power of seeing progress and of learning what worked – meant that this was worth it. For more on how to choose **good** 'quick wins', see the Practice Spotlight overleaf.

Practice Spotlight: Emphasizing the change is fundamental, not cosmetic – Choosing Good 'Quick Wins'

If you decide you need at least some 'quick wins' to help build momentum for the change, then by all means choose some. But choose 'good' ones. Good 'quick wins' are totemic rather than toxic. They communicate what's important about the change and help people understand what it will require.

In 2016, Linklaters, the Magic Circle law firm, decided that in order to execute on its strategy, it need to be more collaborative across practices and offices. It decided it needed to grow a culture of regular feedback-giving to boost collaborative behaviour. Led by the firm's Managing Partner, Gideon Moore, the most senior partners started talking about how important this behaviour was and role-modelling it whenever they could. They also devoted budget to training 400 partners globally on the skills of giving and receiving feedback: over the space of 10 months, I ran 23 sessions for Linklaters' partners worldwide to train them in how to give and receive feedback more effectively. They also chose a 'good' quick win to help prompt partners to remember to give feedback to their teams and to each other. They introduced 'Feedback Fridays' where, every Friday, people were asked to look for opportunities to give and receive feedback.

What made 'Feedback Fridays' a 'good' quick win, rather than merely a cosmetic gimmick? First, it wasn't just randomly chosen – it was chosen because it was a way to deliver a key part of the new strategy for greater collaboration. Second, it was backed up by leader messaging, role-modelling and significant investment in partner training. The messaging was that people should be giving feedback *every* day, but until this new habit was built, the device of 'Feedback Fridays' would prompt people to do so. As such, we can think of Feedback Fridays as a 'quick win' that actually built capability within the firm because by getting into the habit of regularly giving and receiving feedback, partners strengthened their feedback muscles and learned how to use them.

Had 'Feedback Fridays' been done with a different motivation or without the support (and resourcing) of all the other Elements of Clarity, this 'quick win' would have been purely cosmetic. But because this was just one small part of a more fundamental change, it is a good example of how to use a visible, totemic event to push forward the change you've asked for. And while the new culture of regular feedback is still a work in progress, the firm has made considerable strides. The well-chosen 'quick win' of 'Feedback Fridays' played its part.

To help you choose your own **good** 'quick wins', here's my suggested checklist for making sure these are totemic rather than toxic:

1) **Do they exemplify and represent the change you're asking for?** For example, the new behaviours or the new focus for the business? Feedback Fridays at Linklaters exemplified the new collaborative behaviour the strategy required.

2) **Do they help build capability within the organization?** For example, because they ask people to practise a new behaviour or try out new ways of working. Feedback Fridays did this – by asking everyone in the firm to practise this new skill on a particular day each week. As a result, people were more likely to do it and therefore more likely to improve through practise.

3) **Are they a small part of a larger and more fundamental project? And are those linkages clear?** Feedback Fridays are again an example of this, because ultimately, every day could become a feedback day once the habit of giving and receiving feedback had been established. Feedback Fridays were the trigger, or cue, that helped this new habit become established.

4) **Can you learn from them?** In other words, will the information you glean from trying out this small quick activity help you understand how and why larger change might happen (or not) within the firm? Feedback Fridays didn't work everywhere within Linklaters, but the information about how and why they worked in some practices and not others helped the change teams to focus their next interventions more effectively. By trying something small and learning from it, they built the case for a larger piece of work on how to embed the change within the firm.

5) **Do they pass the gimmick test?** This requires you to think carefully about how you message and label the 'quick win' and to properly explain how it fits with, and progresses, the new strategy. Feedback Fridays could have been a gimmick, but for how they were messaged: this was just a small first step and one that was supported by leader role-modelling and a significant development effort.

If your potential 'quick wins' pass these five tests, then they are potentially helpful for – and even totemic of – the change you've asked for. If they can't, then they are probably just a bit too cosmetic – and, as a result, potentially toxic for the change.

One final caveat to how to choose 'good' 'quick wins' in practice. Even if you have agreed a target outcome or some critical new behaviours to help guide your choice of 'quick wins', it's also important that people believe that these activities are part of a more fundamental, long-term change. If on the other hand, people believe that this is a short-term change effort, then they will be pulled into relatively cosmetic 'quick wins'.

An example of this was Bob Diamond's announcement in 2011 of Barclays' '13 by 13' strategy – i.e. that the bank would deliver 13 per cent return on equity by 2013. Now, Diamond may well have wanted people to look for ways to fundamentally change the bank and behave differently, but the imposition of such a short-term target meant that no one took that seriously. Knowing they needed to deliver results within only two years meant ideas that needed investment or time to produce additional ROE were immediately discounted. Instead, people looked only for easy-to-do activities that would produce a short-term filip to returns. Speaking to Barclays bankers at the time, they recognized that this meant they were short-changing returns in 2014 and beyond, by failing to invest time and capital in more fundamental improvements. But given a target that was less than two years away, they had no incentive to do anything else. So leaders need to be careful to communicate *all* the Elements of Clarity (why the change matters and why now; what it will produce in terms of outcomes and behaviours; and that it will take time and require fundamental change) if employees are to respond in the way they want them to and, specifically, if the 'quick wins' they choose are to be more than just cosmetic.

What the other cases got wrong

The other three cases had compromised one or more of the first three Elements of Clarity and so it was hard for them to deliver on this fourth and final Element, even if they'd wanted to. As a result, all three failed to do much 'zero glam' work at this early stage, choosing to focus instead on more traditional 'quick wins'. As the Head of Change in the Early Momentum Case put it:

> We wanted to make progress on the Year 1 target as fast as possible and that meant doing the easiest, fastest initiatives we could.

Notice again that it is the idea of a Year 1 *target* – rather than a Year 1 *milestone* towards a large, multi-year target – that is largely driving this choice. Star managers want to deliver the targets they're given, so focus them on a target that's big and long-term. It was a similar story in the other two cases. The Head of Change in the Road Runner Case – which did not at this stage even have an outcome to target – recalled:

> It was all about activities. We immediately got projects kicked off and they made a difference pretty quickly. But a lot of what we worked on, we did just because it was work we could do. We did nothing that required better data or better systems. And I realize that some of what we worked on in those early days was just lipstick on the pig. But at least we were getting something done.

As we'll see, it was the absence of this fourth Element of Clarity – emphasizing that the change is fundamental, not cosmetic – that set the scene for subsequent failure in these three cases, just as the Ideal Case was now set up to succeed.

	Ideal	EM	UTR	RR
Element 4: Emphasize the change is fundamental, not cosmetic				
Leaders need to talk about how fundamental the change is. This means they need to make clear that:				
a) while there may be some 'quick wins', most of the early work will be decidely unglamorous and will relate to data, measurement and systems; and	☑	☒	☒	☒
b) this work is important and they care about it and the people who are doing it.	☑	☒	☒	☒

Science Spotlight: Why 'Quick Wins' Can Be Toxic to Fundamental Change

The popular folklore of how to lead change has given 'quick wins' an almost mythical status in a change effort, particularly in its early stages. Choose some 'quick wins', the advice goes, get them done as quickly as possible and this will communicate urgency and momentum for your change.[14]

The problem with this is less with the advice *per se* and more with how it has been interpreted. 'Quick wins' were never meant to be the *only* thing that a business was doing in these early stages. They were always meant to be done in conjunction with other, more 'zero glam' work – work that held out the promise of being able to make much more fundamental change within the business. As I sometimes say to my class at MIT, 'quick wins' are like chocolate – you can have some as a treat, or if you're in need of a quick sugar-rush, but sadly, it can't be the only thing you eat. If it is, you'll run out of nourishment. And it's the same when it comes to your change effort: if it's solely focused on 'quick wins', the immediate sugar-rush they give the change might be gratifying and give it some energy, but the fundamental improvement won't happen if this is all you do.

The fact that this has become lost in translation – again, perhaps because of the Activity Delusion with a bit of Magic Delusion thrown in – shows how far we've strayed from what the empirical research tells us will and won't work. It also shows the power of basic psychology: humans want to believe that change will be easier and faster than they, rationally, know it's likely to be, and so 'quick wins' are our ideal drug of choice when it comes to helping us delude ourselves about how hard and slow the change might actually be.[15]

One of the most interesting pieces of research that throws light on *why* 'quick wins' can hurt an organization that needs fundamental change was done by my MIT colleague, Professor Nelson Repenning.[16] Imagine a business decides it needs to produce more output. At a certain point (we'll call it t_0), it starts devoting more time to production (by working harder) and less time to learning and improving (what we might term working out how to work smarter). This change in the distribution of effort is shown in the 'Effort over time' diagram overleaf:

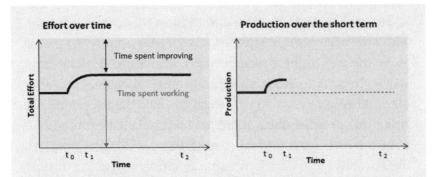

Sure enough, this effort pays off and production increases. As shown in the 'Production over the short term' diagram above, production has increased at t_1. In the short term this is a good result. The problem, however, is that this short-term increase in production comes at a long-term cost: the extra time and effort spent on *working* has crowded out the time and effort that could have been spent on *improving*. This means although the short-term results look good, the long-term results will look very different.

The first problem this creates is that the business now has less capability than it did at the start (t_0), thanks to having less time to work on improving (see the 'Capability over time' diagram opposite). This reduction in capability is already happening at t_1, but the business doesn't notice. At this point, the business is only paying attention to the much more visible increase in production. The result is a more fragile organization, less able to adapt to fundamental change.

The second problem – because of this reduction in capability – is that the business now produces less at t_2 than it did at t_0, even with the same effort – see the 'Production over the longer term' diagram. That's the impact of the capability reduction in practice: the business is now less productive as a result of trying to raise production, because it did so by crowding out the time it could spend on working out how to be more productive.

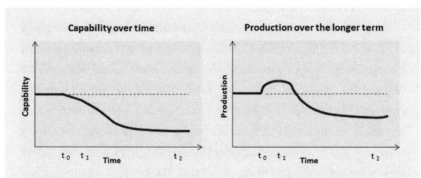

In the context of organizational change, this is exactly the impact that badly-chosen 'quick wins' can have. Suppose a dynamic new change manager – let's call him Dave – responds to the request for change by scoping some 'quick wins', i.e. projects that can be done easily and that will produce quick results. These still take time and effort, but they require much less time and effort than 'zero glam' work on data and systems. Critically, the results from such 'quick wins' are produced without the need to iterate, which means that learning loops aren't required. And that means time spent 'working' (the lower area in the 'Effort over time' diagram on page 112) increases, while time spent 'learning' (the upper area in the 'Effort over time' diagram) is crowded out. That triggers exactly the same reduction in capability we see in normal organizational settings and a long-term cut in the business's ability to generate value from a given level of effort.

Perhaps even more pernicious is the fact that no one *sees* the impact of this – at least not at the time. People are still lauding the great results that are being achieved so easily by Dave and his 'quick wins' and wondering why anyone ever said this change was going to be hard. In fact, why isn't everyone as amazing as Dave?

Well, actually, Dave isn't amazing: he just made short-term gains (from his purely cosmetic 'quick wins') at the cost of long-term capability (the time and effort that should have gone into what managers in the Ideal Case termed the 'zero glam' work). But no one realizes this at the time.

It may be that Dave leaves his current role on a wave of glory around t_1 – i.e. before the downturn in his results sets in. Perhaps he even gets a promotion on the back of his 'amazing' results. Maybe he becomes the new Head of Change for the global business. Let's hope not because what he left behind him was a depleted system that is now less able to deliver even ordinary results, let alone fundamental change. This will become visible as time goes on, but, by the time that happens, someone called Amanda is in charge of the change. She's inherited Dave's 'amazing' results (i.e. a fundamentally depleted system) and been unable to sustain the progress he made. Leaders are concerned. All too often, the conclusion they come to is that 'Amanda's just not up to it' and 'I wish we could get Dave back – he knew how to deliver'. When, in fact, even if Dave *was* still working on these projects, the impact of his exclusive focus on these early 'quick wins' would have been revealed. Because the early success wasn't due to Dave at all, but rather because the projects he chose were ones that could be done quickly, easily and with no fundamental change to the system being necessary.

From this, we can say that 'quick wins' are bad for business if they have two features. First, if they can be done without any learning loops or if they do not add to our understanding of how and why the business works as it does. And second, if they are the main or only activities at this crucial early stage of the change. If both these conditions are true, then 'quick win' projects – so tempting for your organization – may well turn out to be toxic.

Choosing the wrong 'quick wins' not only helps create these Capability Traps that deplete what the organization can do for a given level of effort; they also help foster many of the Leadership Delusions we encountered in Chapter 1. They especially feed the Activity Delusion because they foster the belief that change is all about getting some activity going rather than thinking hard about the narrative of the change and what it will produce. 'Quick wins' also feed the Magic Delusion, because they enable leaders to continue to believe that none of the boring, mundane work matters, that this change won't be that hard or take that long, and therefore their magical powers will be sufficient to see it through.

It's worth noting that the corollary is also true: that just as 'quick wins' can produce cosmetic improvements while depleting fundamental capability, equally non-'quick wins' (or 'zero glam' work) can mute early performance improvements while building fundamental capability. We see this when we compare the early progress made in the Ideal Case with that of the Early Momentum Case. This is why, as Nelson likes to remind students at MIT, 'Things will usually get worse before they get better.'

Now it may be that your business doesn't want to see things get a *lot* worse before they get better. Sometimes leaders don't quite believe that worsening performance will only be a short-term thing. And sometimes the optics around performance reduction are just too hard to manage. So, you may want to do what the Ideal Case did, which is to add some traditional 'quick wins' into your fundamental 'zero glam' work. It's true that this means that not all of your time and resources are being invested in the fundamental work – so arguably you are still diluting the speed and power of this work. But having a mix of 'quick wins' *and* fundamental work (or what one of my clients now terms 'high glam' and 'zero glam' work) may make the early days of the change a bit more palatable – politically for those above you and motivationally for those working on the change. As long as you have enough 'zero glam' work happening right at the start, to lay the foundations of the fundamental change you need to see, then choosing to add a few 'quick wins' into the mix shouldn't do you much harm. Especially if the 'quick wins' you choose pass the five tests we talked about in the 'Choosing **good** "quick wins"' Practice Spotlight earlier in this section (page 106).

As we've gone through this chapter we've summarized how each of the four cases delivered each Element of Clarity. As we'll see in the next chapter, this will have a significant impact on the next stage of the change: Alignment. But for now, and so that we can see them all in one place, take a look at Diagram 4.1 overleaf to see how each of the cases compared, at the end of the first three months of their change.

Diagram 4.1: Summary of how the Cases delivered Clarity

	Ideal	EM	UTR	RR
Element 1: Make it personal				
Leaders need to talk about why they believe this new strategy is the right thing to do, and that it's something to which they are personally committed.	☑	☑	☑	☑
Element 2: Explain why it's necessary and how it fits				
Leaders need to create a credible narrative for the change. This means:				
a) they need to talk about why this new strategy is needed – and why now; and	☑	☑	☑	⊠
b) they also need to talk about how this new strategy relates to previous and current strategies so that it's clear what can be kept (the bits that fit with the new strategy) and what might need to be stopped (the bits that don't).	☑	☑	⊠	⊠
Element 3: Specify the outcomes and behaviours you want				
Leaders need to talk about what will change as a result of this new strategy. This means:				
a) they need to communicate the outcomes this new strategy will result in;	☑	☑	⊠	⊠
b) that these target outcomes are big improvements compared with current performance;	☑	⊠	⊠	⊠
c) that these target outcomes comprise both long-dated, multi-year targets (the big delta) and shorter-term milestones; and	☑	⊠	⊠	⊠
d) leaders need to communicate the new behaviours they are expecting to see from people.	☑	☑	☑	☑
Element 4: Emphasize this change is fundamental, not cosmetic				
Leaders need to talk about how fundamental the change is. This means they need to be clear that:				
a) while there may be some 'quick wins', most of the early work will be decidedly unglamorous and will relate to data, measurement and systems; and	☑	⊠	⊠	⊠
b) this work is important and they care about it and the people who are doing it.	☑	⊠	⊠	⊠

Leadership lessons from Ask #1

It is important, at this stage, to reflect on the type of work that Clarity requires from leaders. There are two early lessons leaders can take from this.

The first one relates to the type of leadership that needs to be used here. When we look carefully at these four Elements of Clarity, we can see why both transformational *and* transactional leadership are needed from leaders – even in this early change initiation phase. Yes, leaders need to be charismatic. They need to be compelling in how they sell the change, making sure people understand why it's needed and why now, and how it fits with what's gone before. Think evangelist!

But they also need to use, and honour, the elements of the more mundane, transactional leadership. In other words, they need to temper the evangelism with a bit of boring reality. They need to spell out what they want and how long it will take. To help people see the extent of the change that this entails, and to help them make their own choices about what to do to deliver it, leaders need to ground the new strategy in a clear, unambiguous target outcome – which they've had the business take the time to clearly define and baseline. And they need to embrace their inner nerd and evangelize also about the importance of data and processes and all the 'zero glam' work that needs to be done.

Of course, leaders won't be the ones doing this 'zero glam' work: managers will be doing that. But leaders need to care about this work and honour it at every opportunity by talking about how important it is and by giving it – and the people who do it – their time and attention. A classic mix of transformational *and* transactional leadership endeavours.

The second lesson we can take from this early stage of the change is one that we will see play out over its duration. Namely that, perhaps ironically, it is precisely by being clear and pretty prescriptive at this early stage – about *why* the change is needed and *what* it should deliver – that leaders lay the groundwork for managers' autonomy about *how* they will deliver it.

The way I have come to think about this critical distinction between WHAT needs to change and HOW that change should be delivered is by using what I call the 'Green and Blue' Diagram – albeit that, in this book, it's in greyscale! Having used it with thousands of leaders and managers over the past few years, I have found it resonates. It speaks to the work that both leaders and managers need to do.

Diagram 4.2: The 'green' and 'blue' zones of organizational work

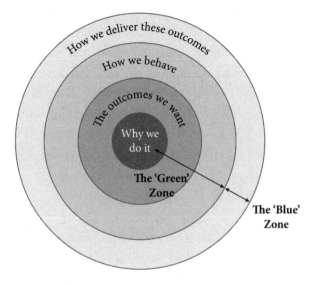

Adapted from Johnson, 2016, *Harvard Business Review*, 'How Leaders Can Focus on the Big Picture'
Reprinted in *HBR's Guide to Thinking Strategically*, 2017, Harvard Business School Press

Let's start with the 'green zone'. This is the zone which leaders need to occupy. Which means they first need to explain the 'why' – whether it's why your organization exists, or why this new strategy and why now; or why we're doing these particular initiatives. From the macro-level to the micro, people need to understand why they're working on what they're working on. That's how they start to see how their 'bit' contributes to the whole – and that matters. Not just so that all the 'bits' join up to create a whole, but also so that people are motivated by seeing real meaning in their work.[17]

Having explained the why (or the purpose) of the organization and its strategy, leaders then need to be clear about what their company, or the new strategy, or these projects will deliver – and by when. In my experience, this is often the missing link in many organizations these days. However, it's clear from my research that 'why' on its own is not enough. If it was, then all four cases would have succeeded. So in addition to 'why', leaders *also* need to say in clear, specific terms what outcomes they want to see. Ideally, these outcomes would not only be expressed in terms of outcomes for customers or employees, but also in financial terms. This helps the causal links between business interventions and customer behaviour, and, ultimately, the P&L be more clearly understood throughout the organization.

Leaders also need to give clear direction about how they want people to behave – whether that's with customers or with each other. What behaviours do they think will help deliver this new strategy and re-make the firm? What old behaviours, including ones that may have served us well in the past, do we now need to drop? This behavioural direction helps people know how to show up – especially important during times of change – and can help sustain them in the months before the outcomes of their new efforts start coming through.

This 'green zone' work – covering Purpose, Outcomes and Behaviours – is where leaders need to **step up** because it is in this 'green zone' that leaders are best able to act as points of leverage in the system. That's because it's leaders who have the broadest understanding of context across the firm and so are in the best position to explain that context to others. It's also leaders who have the greatest visibility in the system and so are in the best position to have what they're doing noticed by others. And it's leaders who have the greatest positional power with which to intervene and make the structural changes that may be necessary at this time. If the system is to be remade, then leaders need to own and occupy the 'green zone': this, now, is the true realm and work of leadership.

This is in contrast with the 'blue zone'. The 'blue zone' – or the Activities zone – is where decisions are made about how the change (and the outcomes that have been asked for) will be delivered – i.e.

what activities to work on. This 'blue zone' is not the domain of leaders – at least not any more. It may once have been, but they are now too senior (and, frankly, too expensive) to be occupying the 'blue zone'. Rather, this 'blue zone' is now the domain of managers. Which means leaders need to get out of that zone so that managers can occupy it fully. Because it's their turn now. They are the ones who deserve to shine in this role, just as leaders once did. So, leaders, do them (and yourselves) a favour and get out of their way.

When I present this 'blue/green zone' idea to senior leaders, they often accept it intellectually. They understand that they are now too expensive and too senior to be spending their time doing 'blue zone' work – and none of them want to take a pay cut or a demotion, which is what being in the 'blue zone' again would require. Nevertheless, they are usually still a bit uneasy.

This uneasiness appears to come about for three reasons. The first is that these leaders really *liked* their time in the 'blue zone'. And they were really *good* at it. In fact, being really good at 'blue zone' work was usually the reason they were promoted to be leaders in the first place. They slightly hanker after that time and for the immediate and visible value they felt they could add in that zone. So here's what I say to them: you need to get over it. It's hard to get over because those were good times for you, and, to be candid, there are far more opportunities in the 'blue zone' to add quick, visible value and that is self-validating. Put simply, there were a lot more dopamine hits available to you in the 'blue zone' – and that's really nice (and highly addictive).

The 'green zone' is different: the dopamine hits on this kind of work are fewer and they are longer-dated. Sure, you might get great feedback on a town hall session, or appreciation from people for how clear you've been about what they should target, but you need to prepare yourself for the fact that self-validation is harder to come by the more senior you are.

OK, so say they buy that. They want to be leaders and so they're going to bite the bullet on this. But now comes the second reason – and it sounds really plausible. Leaders often say to me, 'But my managers come to me and say they need help. What am I going to do, just turn them away?' And of course you don't just turn them away. But if they are coming to you with what we can term 'blue zone' problems ('What should we work on?' or 'What should we be prioritizing'?) then you help managers best by not giving them 'blue zone' answers. That is *their* job now, not yours. And you don't help them do that job by taking their place and doing it for them.

Instead, the work of leadership in this situation is to make it a 'green zone' conversation. Say someone comes to you and wants some direction about whether to continue with a particular project or not – i.e. they're asking you a 'blue zone' question. Your job now is to ask them about, and talk them through, 'green zone' context – i.e. why we're doing this, what it will achieve and how we are behaving – so that they can make their *own* choices about how to deliver the purpose, outcomes and behaviours you want. And then, with that 'green zone' context set, you need to ask *them* the question they've asked you: do *they* think they should continue with this particular project? Because it's *their* job – not yours – to decide on the answer to that question.

If they're still struggling to come to a view, keep pushing them with questions like:

- What is your instinct here? Why is that?
- Why do you think we're running into issues at the moment?
- What do you think an immediate way forward might be? How long would you like to run with that before we chat again?[18]

These kinds of questions push the manager to do more of the 'blue zone' thinking for themselves. They also boost the accountability they are likely to take for the answer they come to – because it's their answer, not yours. You should not be the one giving managers the answers to such questions, but you absolutely *should* be the one helping them think about their answers, and taking the time to listen to and coach their thinking. In other words, you need to give the 'blue zone' work back.[19] That's how you teach the next generation how to think through these kinds of issues and develop high-quality answers of their own – thereby *building* capability rather than reducing it. In fact, it's only when, having set 'green zone' context, leaders leave the 'blue zone' to managers, that they build capability in those managers. If leaders stay in the 'blue zone', or too readily go back into it when managers ask them for help, then instead of building manager *capacity*, they will invariably build manager *dependency*.

Whereas it's in the 'green zone' that leaders make the best use of their time and experience. Here, you most effectively leverage your position in the firm. In fact, we can think of 'green zone' work as a *high leverage* use of leader time, whereas if leaders use their time on 'blue zone' work, that's very much a low-leverage activity – that costs them, their managers and the organization. It costs leaders the opportunity to practise 'green zone' effectiveness – and this definitely takes practice, as does any other kind of work. It costs managers the opportunity to develop: after all, it's their turn now to learn and to shine and leaders take that away from them every time they tell them what to do. And it costs the organization because it compromises the most efficient use of resources and the most effective building of capability.

OK, say a leader accepts that being a good leader is about teaching and bringing on the next generation. There is still a third, and perhaps more fundamental, reason for their uneasiness with staying in the 'green zone'. And it is this: they don't (yet) believe that this 'green zone' work is really work – and they certainly don't believe it could ever be a full-time job.

All I can say to leaders, when they get around to admitting this, is – trust me, the 'green zone' is definitely a full-time job. At least for C-suite leaders. And, for those leaders one or two levels below the C-suite, the 'green zone' needs to be much more of your job than you currently imagine. Because there is a lot to do in this zone and the only people who can do that work are leaders. The reality – borne out in hundreds of conversations with leaders, and especially with newly-promoted ones – is that the more 'green zone' work you do, the more you will see the need for 'green zone' work in your organization, because the more you will come to see how much of it is currently missing. Until and unless you step up into this zone, you won't see the extent of the need for it. You may have to take this on trust initially but, when you do, the power of – and the need for – this 'green zone' work will be clear to see. You need to step up into this 'green zone' so that you devote enough of your time and effort to doing it properly, rather than being tempted back into the 'blue zone' – with its instant validation. Because if you are, that 'blue zone' work will end up crowding out the critical 'green zone' work you really need to do and you will never give it the time, skill and attention it needs.

The 'work' of Clarity

Back in Chapter 3, when I first introduced the concept of Clarity, I argued that the reason leaders need to **step up** for this stage is that there is a *lot* to do here. Having spent this chapter going through the detail of what Clarity entails, I hope you now see what I meant. Giving the organization the Clarity it needs, to kick the change off in the best possible way, is involved. It requires leaders to think perhaps more than they may normally do at this stage – and to act less. It requires them to work at developing, and then communicating, a clear narrative of the change. And to honour the nerdier aspects of it – by having clarity about the metrics and understanding the less glamorous parts of the business that may need to change.

It's worth making two additional points about the 'work' of Clarity. First, I sometimes hear leaders complain that their strategy is hard to communicate and they ask me to work with them so they're able to communicate it more clearly. They talk about this as being a communications problem. In my experience, though, it is rarely a *communications* problem. It's usually a *clarity* problem. And that's because unless and until the strategic choices you've made are clear (to you in the first instance), it's hard to communicate them to others, regardless of how articulate you are as a leader. And therefore the work that needs to be done here is not wordsmithing how the new strategy will be explained – though that work is important – but rather the work of thinking and clarifying the strategic choices you've made so that they're easy for you (and anybody else) to communicate.

The second point to bear in mind relates to what leaders are up against here, in their efforts to leave the 'blue zone'. Because it's not just *people* who love the 'blue zone': organizations love it too. After all, this zone contains the activities that most people define as 'work'; and the art and science of *doing* things – what Berger and Luckmann called 'recipe knowledge' – is highly privileged within most organizations precisely because it's this kind of knowledge that appears to be critical to 'adding value'.[20]

But that's just how things appear. What actually adds value to organizations – and, in my days as an equity analyst, I had quarterly proof of this, in every results presentation – is when people *understand how and why things happen in their businesses as they do. That* is what makes outcomes more predictable and less risky over time. And you can only develop such an understanding by having clear long-term outcomes, monitored by short-term milestones, to which you can link the various activities you have worked on over the period.

Of course leaders will need to judge whether or not they have actually delivered Clarity – because, as I said in Chapter 3, all organizations are different because all organizations are human. To help both leaders and managers assess what this means for them in practice, this chapter ends with some tips and watch-outs for both groups.

Where the four cases stand at the end of the first three months

After the first three months, the four cases had made quite different levels of progress. You can see in Diagram 4.3 below that the Early Momentum Case was already 10 per cent of the way towards its target – what would equate to 100 per cent on the y-axis; whereas the Ideal Case had barely moved the dial. What explains this stellar progress by the Early Momentum Case?

Well, justified by having only a short-term (Year 1) target – that created a lower expectation within the business about how fundamental the change needed to be – they had focused much of their early work not on data or systems but on more traditional 'quick wins'. The result was huge early progress, precisely because the return on this kind of work is typically very short-dated – otherwise they wouldn't be 'quick wins'.

Diagram 4.3: Progress at the end of the first three months

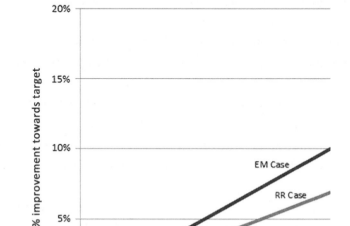

Focusing too much on 'quick wins' at this stage, and too little on the work needed for more fundamental change, would impact the Early Momentum Case in two main ways. First, it meant they squandered the early days of the change – with all the enthusiasm and political will that that time offered – on things that were easy rather than hard. Better to have done the hard things now and saved the easy ones for when people were starting to flag.

Second, the easy, early progress that came from these 'quick wins' may well have fuelled this business's belief that actually 'zero glam' work might not even be necessary. But, as we will see, by Year 2 the fallacy of this argument would become clear: with all the low-hanging fruit already harvested by then, no further improvement could be made without doing some of the 'boring' work. Only this kind of work could lay the foundations for real, fundamental change. As the Head of Change in the Early Momentum Case put it:

> I think we should have done that work sooner. The data, the de-duping. We left that too late, I think. We wanted to get more scores on the doors first, but I think that cost us in the long run. And by the time we did get round to it, we had much less appetite for that kind of work than if we'd done it at the start.

The Ideal Case, on the other hand, was targeting a significant improvement in its outcome metric over the long term. This meant they understood the fundamental nature of the change required and so most of their early work focused on the more fundamental issues of how the business ran (data quality, processes, metrics and the like). They recognized that if they didn't spend time and effort on these fundamental things at this early stage, they wouldn't be able to deliver the delta they'd been asked for in the time frame they'd been given. But, by their very nature, the short-term return on these boring 'zero glam' projects produced virtually no short-term improvement in the outcome metric, so their three-month progress chart looks disappointing – at least relative to that of the Early Momentum Case.

Meanwhile, the Under The Radar Case was the worst performer at this stage. That CEO's concern about 'scaring the horses' had meant he'd underplayed the extent of the change needed in the business. As he later admitted:

> With hindsight, I wish we'd done more in those early days. I wish I'd have spelt it out – that we need to go from x to y and that's going to mean a lot has to change. But I was still a relatively new CEO and there were a lot of people here who did not want to change. So I made the call that we wouldn't shake things up too much in those early days. It's clear to me now that that cost us big time later on.

But what about the Road Runner Case? It was doing well at this stage – almost as well, in fact, as the Early Momentum Case. Why was that, when it had failed to achieve most of the Elements of Clarity in the first three months? The reason was partly that, like the Early Momentum Case, it was doing virtually no work on data or systems, instead focusing all its effort on 'quick wins' – albeit with significantly fewer resources. But the other reason was that this business had been able to get off to an immediate start because it had spent no time analyzing or baselining metrics – something that all the other three cases had done. This freed up time to dive straight into activities which gave it a small but immediate head start on the other cases. As a result, at the end of the first three months, this business looks like it is doing well.

But this short-term gain would lead to long-term pain. Because, without the context of a target outcome, let alone a large, multi-year one, this case couldn't make assured choices about which activities to work on. And without any early work on data or metrics (which even the Under The Radar Case was beginning at this point), the Road Runner Case wasn't able to understand how and why some of its activities were working, while others weren't.

What was true of all of these 'non-Ideal' cases, whatever progress they had made by the end of the first three months, was that the managers working on the change were doing their best: they were working hard and they were personally committed to the change. There was no lack of effort or willpower or resilience on their part. But in the absence of the kind of Clarity that the Ideal Case had, it was hard for them to know what to work on, and almost impossible to make the case for looking beyond traditional, easy 'quick wins' to work on the more fundamental systems-related issues that their businesses faced. Without having all four Elements of Clarity in place, it was hard, also, for the 'non-Ideal' cases to know how best to Align their businesses around the change they'd asked for. That's what we'll turn our attention to in the next chapter.

Tips and Watch-outs to Help You Get Clarity

Tips and Watch-outs for Leaders

- **Don't succumb to the Four Leadership Delusions**. By all means, be your charismatic self – talk about the new strategy with enthusiasm and show your personal commitment to it. But start thinking now about the structural changes you'll need to make – including to target outcomes and data – and get these started as soon as possible;
- **Keep selling the narrative of the change – why do we need it and why now; what will it deliver and how does it fit with what's gone before?** This narrative is critical so that people understand what they're doing and why. You'll need to repeat it long after you've grown tired of it. Never underestimate how many times you will have to say it. From this narrative, people should be able to work out what the strategy requires, what they should keep from the past and what they should ditch;
- **Sweat the detail on the outcomes and then leave the details about activities to others**. You're now paid too much to be in 'blue zone' detail – if you want to do 'activities', then you need to give some of your salary back. But in order for managers to be able to choose the best activities to work on, they need you to be clear about what these activities should produce. What's the outcome being targeted? Deciding on that, and explaining that, is most definitely your job;
- **Choose a big target to be achieved over a number of years**. Tempting though it is to dip your toe in the water and take things relatively easy in these early stages, it's best to go with a relatively big delta if this is really to be a strategic change. This will focus everybody (including you) on the full extent of the change the organization needs, as well as force choices about the level of budgets and resourcing needed to deliver this size of delta;
- **Think hard about behaviours**. Identify the behaviours you need to see more of if this new strategy is to be delivered. Equally, think about what you'd like to see less of. Then give clear directions about these behaviours and role-model them – even when you think no one's looking;
- **Show you care about the 'zero glam' work**. Give your time and attention to the mundane; seek out opportunities to talk about, resource and celebrate the 'zero glam' projects on which real change will be built. And never miss an opportunity to honour those working on them. This is how you really signal that this change is different and about more than just some 'quick wins'.

Tips and Watch-outs for Managers

Don't settle for anything less than all four Elements of Clarity in the first three months of the change:

- **Making it personal**. Actually, most leaders will go some way towards doing this: they know they need to show belief in, and personal commitment to, the new strategy. But what about the other three Elements of Clarity?
- **Explaining why it's necessary and how it fits**. Where's the narrative that explains how this new strategy fits with what's already being worked on, and why we need it now? Does it help you know what to keep and what to ditch? You may have to help craft this narrative if bits of it are missing, but it's essential if people are to be clear about what to do;
- **Specifying outcomes and behaviours**. You may have to coach your leaders until you get this, but keep pushing for the target to be expressed in terms of outcomes, not activities. And ask for a big delta in the target over, say, a three-year period, which is then broken up into regular milestones. This may seem like you're making your own life harder here, but if you're serious about being part of a long-term, strategic change, then the sooner everybody understands that this will take real work and not just tinkering, the better. An ambitious multi-year target helps send that message. It will also help you justify a larger budget for the change. Finally, if your boss wants to determine the activities you work on, tell her that that's your job, not hers. Offer to come back to her with your project shortlist that you can talk through together – but make it clear that this will be FYI for her;
- **Emphasizing that this change is fundamental, not cosmetic**. This means no *cosmetic* 'quick wins'. Instead, sufficient 'zero glam' early work to lay the foundations of fundamental change. If the organization is to be prepared for the long-haul effort that fundamental change requires, then the potential toxicity of traditional 'quick wins' needs to be dealt with early. You need to be asking your leaders to get out there to message how important these 'zero glam' projects are. And as a manager, you want to get your fair share of this 'boring' work so that you're close enough to the guts of the data and the processes to understand what will drive fundamental change. And if you have a CEO who's giving you credit and visibility for taking on such work and who's celebrating it at every opportunity, it will be no hardship – so ask them to do just that. You may also have to placate parts of your organization with some early wins, but your boss needs to know that this can send a truly toxic message if left unmanaged – namely, that this change is easy and it won't take too long. So, make them *good* 'quick wins' – i.e. visible, totemic projects that illustrate the change (and perhaps some of the behaviours) you're asking for, but which you can learn from and scale.

CHAPTER FIVE

Ask #2: Alignment

Get all your signals right

For the first three months of the change, leaders will have been working on achieving Clarity. But during this time they also need to start work on aligning the organization around the change that's been asked for. This is the second way in which leaders need to **step up and do more** than they perhaps ordinarily would at this stage of a new strategy or change. This Alignment work also takes much longer than just three months. In fact, the Alignment effort will take the best part of a year to get right and, along with Clarity, it will lay the foundations for the success of the change – and for manager autonomy.

As we saw in Chapter 3, the new approach to leading change I set out in this book specifies **four Elements necessary for Alignment**. These are, in essence, the signals that managers are looking for, to help them make sense of the change and to understand how important it is.

Element 1: Alignment by Conversations

Leaders need to talk about the change at every opportunity, whether formally or informally, with large groups or one-on-one. This keeps it front-of-mind for managers and reinforces its importance – an effort that leaders started during the Clarity phase, by *Making it Personal* and *Explaining why it's necessary and how it fits*. Alignment by Conversations is particularly important in the first few months of the change and so should be done in parallel with the Clarity effort.

I have called this Alignment 'by Conversations' to try to reflect the fact that Alignment should be happening in ordinary conversations, rather than merely by communication 'events', such as formal announcements, press-releases or set-piece gatherings like town halls. These should all be taking place, of course, but such communications 'events' are usually more about gaining that initial Clarity. What we're talking about here is leaders using the ordinary, everyday conversations they are having with managers to align the organization around the change they've asked for. For example, it needs to be what leaders mention if you bump into them in the corridor or what they ask about, even if you're presenting on another topic. It also needs to be the context into which they put every other topic they talk about at this time – again, so that managers can understand how this change fits in with everything else that's going on. (A good example of how to do this is given in the Practice Spotlight opposite.)

What the Ideal Case got right

This was exactly what the CEO of the Ideal Case was doing, as one of the change-managers recalled:

> This [new strategy] was what he was talking about. This was what he was asking you about. And it would be in every meeting. Even when he'd just bump into you. You'd meet him in the lift and it would be 'How's the new strategy going? Are there any issues?'

And, at this stage, the leaders in the Early Momentum Case were doing the same. Now, of course, both of these businesses had already specified target outcomes that the new strategy should deliver and this provided a context for all the conversations about progress.

Practice Spotlight: Alignment by Conversations – Talking About the New Strategy at Every Opportunity

Back in 2004, Pankaj Razdan, the then CEO of Pru-ICICI, the largest private mutual fund company in India, was spearheading a new strategy within his business. He wanted the business to start focusing more on long-term customer value, rather than accepting the churn rate that was deemed normal for the rest of the Indian mutual fund market.

'We needed to keep customers for longer and have them buy more from us. That was the secret to reducing marketing and servicing costs, because we spent less acquiring each customer and we spent less servicing them for every Rupee they invested with us. The economics was simple.'

To help embed this new strategy within the business, Razdan organized lunches with staff members at least four days a week. The point of these lunchtime meetings was to talk about the new strategy, explain why it mattered and what it would deliver. It was a classic example of a leader aligning people around a new strategy by having conversations with them.

As Razdan recalls: 'I used to ensure that every lunch meeting, I'd be there with four or five of my senior managers from right across the business – maybe one from customer service, two from sales and one from operations. We'd all sit down together and we'd discuss the new strategy, why it mattered and what it meant for each of them. Each of them brought different perspectives, and hearing each other's take on it meant they could start acting in a much more joined-up fashion. I think this made a difference – I mean, it helped me understand what more needed to be done to make this happen, but it also showed people that, both formally and informally, this is important and this needs to become part of everything we do.'

Notice that these conversations were not only a way of aligning each individual with the new strategy, but also of driving alignment across different teams and functions so that the business overall understood what it needed to do.

Razdan supplemented these personal staff meetings with sufficient resources and revised KPIs, which as we will see later in this chapter, are the other critical ways in which leaders can drive Alignment. Nevertheless, these daily lunchtime meetings were an early way to reinforce the message that this change was important and needed to become part of everybody's job. The new strategy went on to be a huge success for the business, which saw a significant reduction in its rate of customer churn and an increase in net margin as a result.

What the other cases got wrong

The leaders in the other two cases – the Under The Radar and Road Runner Cases – were also working hard to try to align their organizations by talking about the change in ordinary conversations. Indeed, leaders in both these cases spent roughly the same amount of time now, in the first six months of the new strategy, talking about it and trying to keep it front of mind, as did the senior leaders in the Ideal and Early Momentum Cases. But these efforts had much less impact. This was largely because these leaders had failed to deliver on the Clarity 'ask' right at the start of the change.

For example, because managers in the Under The Radar and Road Runner Cases hadn't got the message that this was a big change that needed fundamental work – and how could they, given that the change had been downplayed (in the Under The Radar Case) and there was as yet no target outcome to point to (in the Road Runner Case) – when the senior leaders in these cases now talked about the new strategy in ordinary conversations, this message just blended into the noise of all the other work they were doing. As the Head of Change for the Under The Radar Case recalled:

> Sure, they talked about it. But there was no shared understanding that this would take a step-change or what work we could drop in order to focus on this new strategy. So when they talked about it, my reaction was, 'Sure, but it's just another thing we have to do.'

And so, even at this early stage, we are starting to see how dependent the subsequent dimensions – in this case, Alignment – are on the critical first dimension, Clarity.

With leaders from all four cases delivering on the need for Alignment by Conversations – albeit that their efforts were yielding very different results, largely depending on whether they had achieved sufficient Clarity – this is where we stand on this first Alignment Element:

	Ideal	EM	UTR	RR
Element 1: Alignment by Conversations Leaders need to take every opportunity to reinforce the importance of the new strategy – formally and informally, in groups and in one-on-ones	☑	☑	☑	☑

And, by the way, for those leaders who question whether they really need to be talking about the new strategy *at every opportunity* for the first 12 months, the answer is do not underestimate how many times someone needs to hear something before they understand what it means and that it's here to stay. To help persuade you of that, and to help you calibrate the difference between how successfully you think you communicate and how successfully your *listeners* think you communicate, see the Science Spotlight on 'Overcoming the Curse of Knowledge' overleaf.

Science Spotlight: Overcoming the Curse of Knowledge

I'm fascinated by what people choose to do their PhDs on. A particularly interesting one came out of the University of Stanford in the early 1990s. Completed by Dr Elizabeth Newton (as she became), it sought to articulate and calibrate something called the 'Curse of Knowledge'.

The Curse of Knowledge – a phrase first used in a 1989 study[1] – is the idea that, once you know something, it's impossible to remember what it was like to *not* know it. The very fact of knowing something, changes how you behave relative to that knowledge. It's an example of a cognitive bias – in this case, hindsight bias, i.e. that with the benefit of the knowledge you've acquired, you now have a different view about how likely or easy that knowledge is to understand. In particular, the Curse of Knowledge makes it hard for you to empathize with people who don't yet know the thing that you know. And that makes it harder to explain what you know to the people who don't yet know it. This is the essence of what makes the communication of new ideas (such as new strategies or change) hard.

Here's how Elizabeth Newton demonstrated this phenomenon.[2] She recruited 80 volunteers and put them into pairs. Sitting opposite each other, one member of the pair was designated the 'Tapper' and the other the 'Listener'. The Tapper was asked to choose three songs from a list of 25 and then tap out each song on their knees. The Listener had to guess the song being tapped out, writing down their answer after each of the three tapping sessions.

But before the tapping started, Newton asked the Tappers to estimate the chances of their Listeners guessing the song correctly. With the song already running round inside their heads, the Tappers assumed that this would be an easy song to guess and so they invariably overestimated the chances of the Listeners guessing correctly. Once the tapping had begun, however, the Listeners struggled to make sense of what was being tapped out. I know this from my own experience: whenever I run the 'Tappers and Listeners' exercise in a class, it's the same story. 'What on earth are you tapping? How am I supposed to make sense of *that*?' is what's etched onto the Listeners' faces as they try to translate the tapping into something meaningful.

This is an example of the Curse of Knowledge in action. When you know the song, when it's already playing in your own head, it's easy to think that someone else will be able to pick it up too. Whereas, in reality, this is – as Newton herself described it – 'a near impossible task'.[3]

And so it is in organizations. When you've spent months working on and agreeing a new strategy, when you've been through all the arguments for and against and looked at all the evidence, it is easy to think that the new strategy you're now announcing is obvious, or will be easily understood by the people who are now hearing about it for the first time. But they weren't with you in the data-rooms, or in the meetings where you thrashed it all out. They weren't there when you distilled down the new strategy to a few pithy catchphrases that make sense to you, but may well seem too abstract to those hearing them without the background knowledge that you have. You take this knowledge for granted – even though you have not shared it. And your attempts to communicate are cursed as a result.

So what can you do about this? Well, it helps to understand what you're up against. Tappers expected their Listeners to guess the song on average 50 per cent of the time – in other words, to get one song out of two correct. Some of the Tappers went as high as guessing their Listeners would get it right 95 per cent of the time. Whereas what actually happened was that Listeners guessed correctly only three times out of the 120 tries – in other words, only 2.5 per cent of the time, or one song out of 40.

That 'calibration gap' – between what Tappers expected and what Listeners actually understood – gives us a sense of how much more effort leaders need to be putting in to communicating new strategies or change efforts, relative to what they think might be OK. This is why leaders need to be talking about the change at every opportunity because, for much longer than you think, there will be people in the organization who still haven't heard what you're trying to tell them and still haven't understood what they need to do differently as a result. The tune might have been playing loud and clear in your head for a while now, but it still isn't yet playing in theirs. And you, as a leader, still have work to do until it is.

But talking is not enough. As well as senior leader conversations, the change should also be supported by senior leader actions and behaviours.

Element 2: Alignment by Actions

The second way leaders can help align their organization around the change they've asked for is by how they choose to act. This is about making choices that reinforce the change. Specifically, leaders need to role-model it; they need to make time for it; they need to give managers whatever decision-rights they need to make the change happen and they need to put the change on the agenda of their senior team meetings. Collectively, I call this 'Alignment by Actions' to cover each of the ways in which leaders need to enact the change.

By role-modelling it

The first way leaders can enact the new strategy is by role-modelling the change-behaviours they've asked for. For example, if leaders have asked for the business to become more collaborative in how it works, then they need to show how to do that by themselves collaborating more, especially with peers. Equally, if leaders have said that this will take time, then they need to honour that by showing patience, however much they'd like to see immediate results.

Now, of course, knowing what to role-model depends on leaders having made it clear what new behaviours they expect as part of the new strategy. But whatever behaviours you've asked for, you're the first person who ought to be demonstrating them.

By making time for it

The second way leaders can take action to align the business around the change they've asked for is by giving their own time to it and making sure they always make time to discuss it. Giving your time to the new strategy is an important way to signal how important it is, as illustrated in the Practice Spotlight below, 'Role-modelling and Giving Time to the Change They've Asked For'.

Practice Spotlight: Alignment by Actions – Role-modelling and Giving Time to the Change

Let's return to the example of Pankaj Razdan, who was leading the change to make his mutual fund business more customer-focused as a way to drive long-term margin improvement. As we saw in the Alignment by Conversations section earlier, Razdan had regular conversations with staff (organized as staff lunches in the CEO's office, held at least four days a week) to drive alignment around the new strategy. The purpose of these lunchtime meetings was to talk about the new strategy, explain why it mattered and what it would do. It was a classic example of a leader aligning people around a new strategy by having conversations with them about it.

But these conversations were important not just because of what was talked about, but also because of the signal they sent to the organization. By deciding to devote time to the change, Razdan signalled that this change mattered. As he put it: 'It was a big time-commitment for me, of course it was. But you have to invest if you want to see the rewards and here, the currency of investing in the change was my own time.' As he added: 'It wasn't just the conversations themselves that we had in the room, though those were a great way of me re-explaining what was expected. It was also the *fact* that these conversations were happening, four days a week. That sent a really big signal to the organization. Pretty quickly after we started those lunches, I was hearing feedback that, if this thing is important enough for the CEO to have lunchtime meetings about it four days a week, then it must be pretty important. Which is exactly what we wanted people to believe.'

The other way Razdan used Actions to signal that this change was important was by role-modelling it. He had asked the organization to become more customer-focused and so he himself decided to spend more time with customers. He scheduled regular meetings with groups of customers at which he could find out their concerns: 'The point of this wasn't just to educate myself about what customers were thinking and feeling about doing business with us, although that was interesting for me. It was also to signal to the folks who worked in my business that customers mattered. Because if I could spend my time listening to them, then so should everyone else in the business. And equally, if I hadn't decided that customers were important enough for me to spend my time with, what did that say about this new customer-focused strategy? I needed to put my diary where my mouth was.'

Here, the bottom line is that if you're not making time for the change, then don't be surprised if managers interpret this as signalling that this change isn't important to you.

The time leaders make available for the change matters to managers especially in this early stage of the change because, at this point, they will likely still need to regularly meet with leaders to get feedback on the progress they're making; they may also need leaders to help them work through issues that are arising or roadblocks that are getting in their way. At this early stage – before the more structural changes have been made that would solve these issues – this is perfectly legitimate. And to help managers get *quick* resolution on any issues they're having, leaders need to be available for meetings at relatively short notice. (A good example of this is described in the Practice Spotlight 'The Power of the Diary', below.)

Practice Spotlight: Alignment by Actions – 'The Power of the Diary'

In 2018, I did a series of 'Leading Change' sessions for a global universal bank. The firm had recently pruned its less profitable operations and successfully cut operating costs. I knew a lot of senior bankers at other, comparable firms who envied the position these guys had got themselves into. But the change wasn't done. This bank needed to double down on cost-cutting and efficiency and the 250 Managing Directors with whom I was working would be the ones to drive that change. I presented the four Elements of Alignment and asked them what more they could do to align their business units around this cost-cutting effort.

We started talking about how they were using their own actions to drive alignment. The MDs I worked with in these sessions had given their managers the decision-rights they needed, the new strategy was also regularly discussed at senior team meetings and they believed they were already role-modelling it (for example, they'd cut back their own expenses and their own headcount). But when I asked whether they were properly making time for it, many of them realized that this might be an area they needed to give attention to.

I asked them what was stopping them devoting more time to the new strategy – and to the managers who were working on it and who might still need their help or guidance. The main issue was that they didn't feel they had extra time to devote to the change. I argued that, if they dedicated time to help managers as soon as issues arose, they might find this saved them time overall. They bought that idea and agreed to set aside some time every week that would be devoted to the change.

So how could they structure this time most effectively? After all, they didn't want to get sucked into too much detail or give managers the impression that they were micromanaging them. We talked about the type of help that managers most frequently needed from them, what kinds of issues were coming up and how frequently. From this, we developed an understanding of the cadence of leader involvement that would be most effective for managers. The MDs realized that they needed to block off at least one chunk of time (circa two hours) each week. This time would be ring-fenced and kept for managers to come to them with queries or issues, as and when these arose.

I asked these MDs to email me to tell me what happened as a result of this seemingly simple change to how they used their time. Three themes emerged from this feedback. First, the fact that this time was now in the diary, and managers knew that it was there if they needed it, was interpreted as an important signal that this change mattered. Second, managers appreciated that this made talking about the change much more routine: one MD told me that her managers now felt they were being 'less of a pain' when they came to her with issues, because by routinely making time available to discuss them she had now signalled that issues were expected. This meant issues were raised more freely and were discussed more openly.

Third, by blocking off time each week, managers were able to see leaders for guidance as soon as something arose, meaning fewer issues were left festering. This meant issues were dealt with much more quickly, and, critically, *given back to managers for resolution*. This increased productivity and maintained the proper 'green/blue zone' demarcation of work.

To increase the speed of resolution, and make their use of time even more effective, many of the MDs chose to split their 'chunk' of time between two separate slots during the week. This was especially helpful for MDs managing global teams, across different time zones – a call with the West Coast and another with Asia-Pac could now be accommodated within the same week without needing to schedule additional time. All this was possible because leaders chose to set aside this time in the first place, using 'the power of their diary' to drive change.

By giving managers the decision-rights they need

The third way leaders can take action to align the business around the change may seem an obvious one, but it's critical. It is by giving managers the decision-rights they need to make the change happen. An example of transactional rather than transformational leadership behaviour, it's important because without the power to decide on which initiatives to pursue, or how to spend the budget they've been given, managers will get a lot less done and will be coming to leaders for a lot more input and help.

By putting it on the agenda of senior team meetings

The fourth way leaders can take action to align the business around the change is by making sure it is discussed every time the senior team meets. Again, this is a transactional rather than a transformational leadership endeavour – and, again, it is very important because of the signal it sends. Put simply, if something isn't important enough for you to discuss when you and the other senior leaders of the business meet, why should it be important enough for your managers to make and keep as their priority?

Now, of course, being able to put the new strategy on the agenda of the Senior Leadership Team depends on the extent of the Clarity that you achieved in the first three months. In particular, it helps if you were clear about the target outcomes because these will provide the right frame for a board-level discussion about the change. Focusing the conversation on outcomes helps ensure that senior people don't get sucked into the minutiae of individual projects – these would constitute 'blue zone' conversations. So without clear target outcomes, it's hard for leaders to put the new strategy on their agenda *and* keep within the 'green zone'.

It is important not only to put the new strategy on the agenda (literally), but also to place it sufficiently *high up* the agenda that it will always get the air-time it deserves. The importance of doing this is illustrated in the Practice Spotlight 'The Power of the Agenda', below.

Practice Spotlight: Alignment by Actions – 'The Power of the Agenda'

One company I worked with a number of years ago is a good example of what it takes to get the 'Power of the Agenda' right. They were a global insurance company, with operations in the US, Europe and Asia-Pacific. In each of these operations, they wanted the business to become more focused on cost efficiencies. How this was delivered was up to each of the regional operations, but options on the table included outsourcing, off-shoring and headcount reductions. This was an important new part of the firm's overall strategy and the Senior Leadership Teams of each region were asked to report to Group HQ on their progress each quarter.

This organization did lots of things right. They communicated that this new strategy was important and they set clear outcome-based targets. They took every opportunity to talk about the new strategy and set aside time to discuss it. They also put it on the agenda for their Senior Leadership Team meetings, held each month.

But this is where details matter too. Their existing SLT agenda had the following items on it, in this order: Sales, Broker Issues, Customer Issues, New Products, Regulation & Compliance, Any Other Business (AOB). They added in a new item on the Cost-Cutting strategy just before AOB. As a result, although there were some meetings when it was discussed, there were some when the meeting ran long, they ran out of time and so this important new strategy wasn't talked about.

The effect was demoralising for those who were working on the change. Asking for a debrief on what the SLT had said about their progress, managers were sometimes told 'Sorry, we ran out of time, we didn't get to it'. The signal this sent was that actually, this new strategy wasn't that important – and certainly not as important as the things they *did* have time to talk about.

The lesson from this example? Don't just put the new strategy on your SLT agenda, but make sure you place it close enough to the top of the agenda so that it is always given the time it deserves. Managers are looking at all the signals you're giving at this stage in the change – and what you discuss as a senior leadership team is a critical one you can't afford to miss.

What the Ideal Case got right

The leaders in the Ideal Case had specified the behaviours they wanted to see right at the start of the change – as, indeed, had the leaders in all four of our cases. Leaders now role-modelled these same behaviours. As a manager in the Ideal Case recalled:

The CEO had said that we needed to be much more experimental. Actually, I wasn't sure he really wanted this at the start, but, honestly, he role-modelled it. Every time we suggested a new idea, he'd push us to think beyond what we'd done before and to try things out. Whenever we met with him, he'd always push us to be thinking differently. And he was keen to experiment with the new ideas we were having. I don't think I would have embraced that whole experimental mindset if he hadn't been such a good role-model for it.

Similarly, leaders in all four cases made time for the change, making themselves available to discuss the progress managers were making and to deal with any queries or issues that were coming up. As one of the Early Momentum managers recalled:

> Whenever we needed to see [the CEO], to check in or maybe get help with brokering something with another part of the business, she always had time. I guess because she *made* the time. That showed this was a priority for her. Her diary was always open for us.

It's also true that leaders in all four cases gave managers the authority they needed to make decisions without having to check-in. As one of the change team in the Early Momentum case told me:

> The CEO told us really early on that we'd be the team working on this and we'd have whatever power we needed to make this happen. She followed that up with sign-off and other decision-rights on budgets, resources and projects – and so we had all the power we could ask for.

So far, so good, then. Whatever shortcomings we might find in leaders aligning the business around the change, it wasn't because they failed to role-model it, or make time for it or give managers the authority they needed – it must be something else.

What the other cases got wrong

It was in respect of the fourth way to deliver Alignment by Actions – namely, by putting it on the agenda of their senior team meetings – that we see some differences between the cases. In fact, only two of the four (the Ideal Case and the Early Momentum Case) got this right, and it made a big difference to the managers involved. As one of the change team from the Ideal Case put it:

> Because it was on the agenda for every SLT meeting, we knew it was guaranteed to get air-time with the senior guys. And that meant a couple of things. First, it reinforced that all the effort we were putting in was worth it, because it was being noticed at the highest level. And second, it was further proof that this was very much on the agenda. Literally.

But the other two businesses – the Under The Radar and Road Runner Cases – weren't able to put this on their senior team's agendas. Why was this?

You'll remember that, in the Under The Radar Case, the CEO hadn't communicated to all of his senior team the extent of the change required. He had actively chosen this route (hence the 'Under The Radar' term) because he knew that some of his team wouldn't agree with the change and, as a relatively new CEO, he didn't want to rock the boat too much. Now, that is not an illegitimate choice *per se*. As a leader you may sometimes feel that you need to make a similar one, if you judge that the political context won't let you do more. But understand that this will come with consequences, both for the change you want and for the managers working on it. As one of the change team in the Under The Radar Case told me:

> How could this be on the agenda when half of the senior team didn't even know the extent of the change that he'd asked us to deliver? I didn't mind doing it under the radar, but it definitely made things harder. Especially when it came to getting issues fixed and justifying a decent budget.

The senior team in the Road Runner Case weren't regularly discussing the change at their meetings either. Remember, in this case the CEO hadn't yet agreed a target outcome. This meant that 'progress discussions' were largely bilateral affairs (between the CEO and his Head of Change) about how well individual projects were going and so, rightly, didn't warrant being on the senior team's agenda. As the Head of Change remembered:

> [The CEO] always made time if I needed to speak to him about progress – that wasn't the issue. The issue was that this still wasn't being talked about across the whole senior team. So, if there were issues, he would help me sort them out, but this was never something that everybody talked about or helped with.

For both these cases, the failure right at the start to specify and socialize the outcomes they wanted the change to deliver – whether for fear of rocking the boat, or because a clear target outcome hadn't yet been agreed – meant it was then hard to openly discuss progress at an enterprise level with all the members of the Senior Leadership Team. As the table below shows, these two cases did everything else right, but by failing to put the change on their SLT agendas, they left managers relying too much on their personal, bilateral relationships with individual leaders in order to move things forward. In turn, these individual leaders were left being the solution in too many 'blue zone' conversations with managers.

	Ideal	EM	UTR	RR
Element 2: Alignment by Actions				
Leaders need to make choices that reinforce the change that's been asked for:				
a) by role-modelling it;	☑	☑	☑	☑
b) by making time for it;	☑	☑	☑	☑
c) by giving managers the decision-rights they need; and	☑	☑	☑	☑
d) by putting the change on the agenda of senior team meetings.	☑	☑	☒	☒

But leaders can't be omnipresent for all their managers all of the time. So what happens when leaders aren't there to personally align the organization, by either conversations or actions? What signals are managers paying attention to then?

It turns out there are two additional signals that managers are paying attention to – and, helpfully, these don't require leaders to personally be around to speak about or role-model or give time to the change. These other two Elements of Alignment are more structural than personal – and, in leadership terms, more transactional than transformational. But if leaders get them right, it's these next two Elements of Alignment that can increasingly do more of the signalling for them.

Element 3: Alignment by Resourcing

This is the first 'structural' way leaders can align the organization around the change and signal to managers that this change is important. Here, the bottom line is that leaders need to put their money where their mouth is. But actually, money is not enough. 'Resourcing' here means not only sufficient budget, but also the right people. While budget is important, on its own, it's not enough. Equally, the right people are important, but on their own, they're not enough. Both parts of the resourcing equation need to be in place.

And when we say the 'right' people for the change, it isn't enough that they are smart and hard-working. What's important here is that they are experienced (they've done something similar before), they are well-connected (they have a good network within the firm to help get things done and to help recruit others to the team) and they are sufficiently senior (they have status and power to make things happen and, often, are recognized as 'stars' within the firm). This signals to everyone in the firm that this new strategy is the real deal – otherwise, why put such people on it?

Having got the 'right' people on the change, you also need to make sure they are spending most of their time on it – at least in the early days of the change. If they are working on the change as only a small part of a larger role, this probably won't be enough to gain traction.

What the Ideal Case got right

Helped by having clear target outcomes in place, both the Ideal and Early Momentum Cases allocated sufficient budget to the change. As one of the change team in the Ideal Case put it:

> He talked about how it was important, and he put budget behind it too.

Both managers and leaders anchored their budget conversations in the outcomes being targeted. As another manager in the Ideal Case recalled:

> The budget conversation was absolutely had in the context of the outcomes we were targeting. If we were going to deliver a 30 per cent improvement, then we needed real money – that was our argument. And equally, senior leaders could feel better about a larger budget being allocated because they knew they would hold us accountable for the outcome. My sense was that having the target outcome made it possible to justify the budget.

Our first two cases – the Ideal and the Early Momentum – also made sure that the change had the right people allocated to the new strategy and that they were dedicated to this effort. This was another important signal for people. As one of change team in the Ideal Case remembered:

> [The CEO and CFO's] willingness to throw good resources, and enough resources, at this new strategy spoke volumes. And it wasn't just budget, it was people. Really good people, whom everyone at that level knew were on the fast track. This was now what those people were working on. That said 'this is important'.

But while both the Ideal and Early Momentum Cases had sufficient budget, and the right people, allocated to the change, what these two cases were *spending* their budget and time on (at least in this first year) was quite different. Because of a big, hairy, multi-year target in the Ideal Case (the 30 per cent improvement mentioned above), as we saw in the last chapter, this team was already working on fundamental 'zero glam' projects to improve data and systems. In contrast, while the Early Momentum Case had specified the outcomes to be delivered, they had set only annual targets – and a Year 1 target that was relatively unambitious. As a result, this case was focusing almost exclusively on activities that would deliver short-term and relatively cosmetic improvements at this stage. *This* was where their equally generous budget was being spent. Indeed, as we'll see at the end of this chapter, by the end of Year 1, the Early Momentum Case had made stellar progress, whereas the Ideal Case was languishing behind. Arguably, the glut of budget available in the Early Momentum Case – which meant even more 'quick win' activities could be started – only augmented the sense that this was going to be easy and wouldn't need fundamental, long-term change.

So the lesson from the comparison of these two cases at this still-early stage? Just sorting out the budget and allocating the right people isn't enough. You also need to make sure they're being deployed on the right things. And it is Clarity – in particular, clarity about outcomes and the need for fundamental, long-term change – that ensures that resources are being well spent in these early days.

What the other cases got wrong

It was a different story for managers in the Under The Radar Case. This business had allocated the right people to the change, and for most of them, it was also now their full-time role. The issue for this case was budget. And the reason it was hard for managers to argue for budget, and for leaders to give it? Largely because the extent of the change required hadn't been explained right at the start. As one of the managers told me:

> Where we really paid the price for it being 'under the radar' was when it came to budget. All of this was supposed to be no big deal, all done a bit quietly. If the CEO suddenly announced a large budget for this effort, how could he have squared that with the message that this wasn't a big change? So it was really all on me and the team to try to make this work, but without the proper means to do it.

Meanwhile, in the Road Runner Case, while they also now had the 'right' people working on the change (experienced, hard-working and well-connected), it was not for most of them their full-time role. They also lacked budget. This was largely because they still had no clear target outcome – something the Head of Change found frustrating:

> We were caught in a vicious circle. We hadn't agreed an outcome to deliver, so it was hard for us to make the case for resources. And because we didn't have resources – and by that, I mean not just budget but also dedicated people working on this – we were incredibly stretched, and progress started to fall back. That made it even harder to say 'Give us more money and people' – for what, a failing effort?

This, then, is where the pressure on managers starts. As in the Road Runner Case, having *some* Clarity (about what activities to work on and how to behave) but not enough to actually help (no clear target outcome, no large, multi-year delta, nothing about the need to make fundamental change) coupled now with a lack of budget and too few dedicated resources, meant the pressure on this team was huge. In fact, the lack of budget is arguably more damaging when good people are put on the effort, because they try all the harder to deliver, despite not having the means to do so. Leaders are setting them up to fail – and to work extremely hard in the process.

The personal cost of being on several projects at a time, especially for star managers who want to do well, is high. This is something my friends Heidi Gardner and Mark Mortensen researched recently and their findings are discussed in the Science Spotlight below. But the impact is also felt at an organizational level: having key people overcommitted to several projects at the same time detracts from the quality of the work they are able to do on any one of them, meaning that less is achieved from a given level of effort. This may be one of the most important consequences of the failure to specify and socialize clear target outcomes right at the start. Because only by doing so can managers choose the right activities to work on which, in turn, gives them confidence to work on fewer activities. And working on fewer activities does two things. It helps you make better second-order decisions about what your stars should be giving their time to and how much budget this effort needs. And second, it helps drive accountability in the firm, because the smaller number of activities increases the focus and attention that each one receives from leaders.

Science Spotlight: The 'Overcommitted Organization'

Heidi Gardner of Harvard Law School and Mark Mortensen, a professor at INSEAD, recently published their research into what they have called the 'overcommitted organization'.[4] What they mean by this is an organization that has too many things on. While this can mean conflicting priorities for the business, what it means for the people working on these myriad priorities is arguably more serious.

Gardner and Mortensen surveyed more than 500 mid-level managers in global companies across a wide range of industries. They wanted to understand the impact of sharing people across multiple teams all working on different projects. Their findings showed that teams lost traction as their members dipped in and out of the work. This impacted the speed with which results could be delivered, as well as the cohesion of the team.

But in addition to these organizational and interpersonal impacts, there was also a psychological impact for the individual team members. Many felt that they weren't doing a good enough job – a worry in particular for a firm's high achievers. This increased their levels of frustration and stress. It also reduced their motivation, since it was less clear how and why their contribution was translating into team or project-level outcomes.

Team leaders also suffered. They now had a bigger job to do to co-ordinate the members of their team whom they shared with others, and to manage the deliverables schedule against a much less certain resourcing situation. This required them to engage in much more political work within the firm, as they negotiated access to key team members at particular times. Team leaders reported feeling their roles (and their own performance) were now riskier than before, because they felt less in control of the outcomes which their much more fluid team would produce.

The benefits of sharing personnel across teams can of course enrich learning across the organization, as well as the individual's own work experience. But the downsides – and the risks – of not having dedicated resources for a high-profile change are considerable. So if it matters enough for you to call it a priority, it ought also to be a priority for the people working on it.

The result for these businesses was that only two of them – the Ideal and Early Momentum Cases – fully used resourcing to drive Alignment:

	Ideal	EM	UTR	RR
Element 3: Alignment by Resources				
Leaders need to allocate sufficient budget and the right people to deliver the change:				
a) sufficient budget;	☑	☑	☒	☒
b) the right people (i.e. experienced, connected, sufficiently senior); and	☑	☑	☑	☑
c) for whom the new strategy/change is now their main role (i.e. dedicated resources)	☑	☑	☑	☒

These relatively early failures to use resources to support the change would take a heavy toll on managers, leaders and the change itself. But even putting your money – and your best people – where your mouth is isn't quite enough to set managers up to run the change themselves. There is a final, and really important, signal leaders need to use to make this happen – and it is another 'structural' way to show managers that you're serious about this new strategy, even when you're are not personally there.

Element 4: Alignment by Metrics

The fourth and final way leaders can align their business behind the change is to use data, metrics and KPIs to help support it. Specifically, leaders need to introduce revised, outcome-based KPIs for both themselves and their managers to reward the new strategy. They also need to focus on data and metrics to help the business understand, and refine, the projects that are now being worked on.

KPIs refers to the 'Key Performance Indicators' by which managers' and leaders' performance is assessed and rewarded as part of the regular performance review process in a firm. But there are lots of different terms used for such things.[5] Data and metrics in this context means the information leaders and managers use to assess how well their initiatives are progressing and why.

The words 'data' and 'metrics' are often used almost interchangeably in businesses, but they are different things. The main difference is in their purpose. The reason you collect data is to *understand* what's going on in your business or change programme – how do certain actions or inputs result in outcomes over time? And because you are collecting data to understand what's going on, you don't ever have a 'target' data-point in mind, at least not in the traditional sense. You might well have some hunches about where you think the data will come out, but nothing more than that. In fact, the idea of 'target data' is really an oxymoron: you are interested in the data whether it comes in above or below your hunch because of what it can tell you about what's going on and why.

The reason you produce 'metrics', on the other hand, is to measure and reward what's going on. As a result, you will, quite rightly, have some target metrics in mind, to help you to judge whether performance is good or not. (For more about what this looks like in practice, see the Practice Spotlight opposite – 'The Difference Between "Data" and "Metrics". ')

Why does it matter that leaders are paying attention to data and metrics at this stage? Obviously, leaders aren't the ones poring over this intel, but they need to be asking about it and honouring its importance because this signals to people that learning how and why projects are working matters almost as much, at this early stage, as what these projects are delivering. Getting the balance right between performance and learning will, it turns out, be a critical differentiator for successful, sustainable change in Years 2 and 3.

And why does it matter that new, outcome-based KPIs are introduced early on? Because until you do, people are left wondering how important this new strategy really is, or how long it might be around for. How can it really be a priority for the firm if it's not important enough to affect how people are paid and recognized? As one academic paper put it: 'Reward systems direct attention to [the] activities that reinforce strategic objectives'.[6] So don't give people any excuse for doubt: signal clearly that this matters by making these changes to KPIs as early as possible in the change. And, before these changes take effect, talk regularly about the changes that you'll be making to the KPIs and when these will come on-stream.

The new KPIs need to be based on outcomes (rather than activities) so that managers and leaders focus on doing what delivers value. If all leaders do is prescribe some activities, then they will be the ones responsible for deciding what managers work on, whereas we need to make managers responsible for the choices about activities – they are, after all, usually closer to the operations and often to the customers.

And these new KPIs need to be for both leaders *and* managers so that everyone has skin in the game. What's the point of managers being accountable for an outcome if the leaders, who asked for it, aren't? Of course, they will be doing different roles to deliver the target outcomes, but leaders and managers are in this together and their KPIs need to reflect that.

Leaders and managers sharing KPIs helps drive alignment *vertically down* through the organization. But in order to drive alignment *horizontally across* the organization, we need *all* leaders to share these KPIs, whatever part of the business they are running. For example, every member of the C-suite should have a KPI related to the change so that it is no longer the responsibility of just one department or function, but is shared across the organization to get everyone feeling responsible for it and so more likely to help where they need to.[7]

It's also worth noting that metrics and KPIs matter to good managers not because they need to be *paid* for performance – nothing that crass. KPIs and metrics matter to good managers mainly because of the *signals* they send. As Professor Dan Ariely has put it: 'Human beings adjust behaviour based on the metrics they are held against. Anything you measure will impel a person to optimize his score on that metric. What you measure is what you get. Period.'[8] And the reason for that is not that you are *paying* for this metric, but rather because you are measuring it and holding someone accountable for it. Good managers want to do a good job – and part of that is delivering on the metrics you set them. They also want to be able to demonstrate – to themselves as well as to others within the firm – that they are delivering. So if metrics drive performance, it pays to choose your metrics carefully.

Practice Spotlight: Alignment by Metrics – The Difference Between 'Data' and 'Metrics'

Too many businesses, in my view, have way too many metrics and actually not enough data. I know that sounds weird in this age of 'big data' that we're always hearing about. But in my experience, businesses don't have enough data to help them understand how and why things are happening within their business, and from which they can then generate insights about what to do instead.

And equally, they often have way too many metrics that they are trying to deliver – which then means they have even less time and inclination to capture data and generate insights.

Returning to the example of the large global technology company we mentioned in the Clarity chapter (page 100), this business had a whole raft of metrics on which it measured its sales teams. Even after leaders had clarified that it was outcomes that mattered rather than activities, there were still a lot of activity-based measures in place. The result was that some of the sales teams were still trying to deliver specific activities – increasing the number of client meetings being the best example – even when this was actually counter-productive to the outcome.

Here's what was happening. The number of client meetings (an input metric) was sometimes positively correlated with higher sales (the outcome metric), but only if certain things went on before, during and after those meetings. And this organization realized it didn't have enough data about these things, such as how well people were preparing for meetings, and how they were showing up in the meeting itself. Because the causative factor here wasn't the meeting *per se*, but rather the quality of the conversation between the client and the salesperson. And while this business had lots of *metrics* to *measure* inputs and outcomes, it started to realise that maybe it didn't have enough *data* to *understand* the dynamics of these meetings and how and why they produced good outcomes.

So they looked at which teams were producing the best outcomes and drilled down to understand what these teams were doing differently in their client meetings. The answers were interesting. The salespeople in these successful meetings were better prepared than their peers, they also listened more and talked less, and the conversation was more about what the client needed and less about what the salesperson could offer.

But the real lesson here is not just about what this business discovered about its successful sales teams, but also *how* it discovered these insights. These sales leaders put the work in to properly understand *how* and *why* some activities produced better outcomes than others. They committed time and effort to working out what was going on. By collecting and analyzing the necessary data, this business started to understand what was going on in its sales teams and therefore which activities (and skill-sets) should be prioritised.

It's worth noting that most of the data this business collected to help them understand the difference between good meetings and bad meetings weren't numbers either. Most of the data used here were qualitative data, such as verbatim quotes from client meetings and feedback sessions. They also started filming some of their internal client meetings, so that people could watch themselves back and see where they could improve. As one sales manager told me: 'It sounds creepy to film yourself, but it was so helpful. It was only when I watched myself back that I realised all the things I wasn't conscious of doing – whether it was my body language or my tone of voice. Watching it back, I also realised that, although I'd thought I'd done a lot of listening, actually I'd done a fair amount of talking!'

In my experience of working with these teams, they are a committed bunch – they are interested in their work and always keen to do better. But being this committed to data and what it can tell you about how to improve is rare. The result, though, was a huge increase in client satisfaction for those teams who were now collecting this kind of data and using it to coach their teams on how to improve; and in employee satisfaction and learning as people got better – because they now had the right data to help them know what to get better at.

What the Ideal Case got right

The Ideal Case – along with the Early Momentum and Under The Radar Cases – was collecting and using data and metrics to understand and refine the projects being worked on. This had several benefits, including that managers were starting to fully use the autonomy they had. As the Head of Change in the Ideal Case told me:

> The new data and metrics we were collecting meant that we could start understanding the links between what we were doing and the outcomes that was producing. If I do this, then this happens. That helped us make better choices about what work to do. So it was us deciding what particular activity to prioritize and leaders accepting that – because we now understood how and why things happened as they did. I think it also made us all feel like the effort was less risky. Less random.

The Ideal Case – along with the Early Momentum Case – also introduced new, outcome-based KPIs for both leaders and managers. This had a big impact on those working on the change (as it has had for other businesses I've worked with – see the Practice Spotlight 'A Test of Seriousness', page 162). As the Head of Change in the Ideal Case explained:

> We'd been working on this [change] for around six months but when the new KPIs came in, that was a big deal. Especially since they applied to leaders as well as to us. That said to me, 'This is serious and we're all in it together'. I also felt vindicated in all the things I'd been asking the team to do up until now. I mean, we'd known the outcome we were working towards, but before the KPIs, all I'd had to call on was quoting the CEO, or reminding them that the senior team were looking at the numbers. But now, I had KPIs to point to. KPIs for me, for the team, and for leaders. Outcomes written into all of our KPIs. After that, *that* was what drove us on. I'm not saying we didn't need the CEO talking about it any more, or the senior guys paying attention to the numbers, but I'd definitely say we needed them less.

In this statement we see the kernel of the autonomy that will grow in the later years in the Ideal Case, as their dependence on the CEO's continued involvement reduces. By giving managers a macro-level target (based on the outcomes, rather than activities), leaders left it up to them to decide what to do (rightly, a 'blue zone' activity). As a consequence, the conversations between leaders and managers focused on how and why the change was progressing – rather than merely reporting on what was being delivered. And by pushing for the right data to be captured and analyzed, leaders helped ensure that these 'how' and 'why' conversations were always high quality and therefore always worth their time.

The fact that these new outcome-based KPIs were for *all* senior leaders in the business also had a huge impact. The burden on individual managers was reduced because the target outcome was now shared by the whole organization. As the Head of Change in the Ideal Case remembered:

> So, whereas right at the start I would need to spend time persuading other departments to get on board with what we were doing, that changed when all the leaders had the new KPIs. That meant they were all paying attention to these outcomes – it wasn't just me and my team now – and that meant they were a lot more focused on helping when we needed it. I definitely didn't need to do as much brokering with other teams to get the help we needed.

Now, of course the structural changes made to KPIs and metrics required personal effort by senior leaders to get it done. And sometimes that came at a cost. The CEO of the Ideal Case recalled a particularly difficult conversation with one of the most critical members of his SLT. This senior leader didn't *disagree* with the new strategy, but he didn't want his bonus to depend on it. The CEO held the line:

> It was a difficult few weeks. This guy didn't want to see his KPIs changed. He didn't want to share in the pain of this new strategy. He said to me, 'If we all have to have this and you force it through, then I will leave this

organization.' I said, 'I respect you, I value what you've done for us, but this is a fundamental change for our business and if you don't really agree with it, then thank you for your work, but ...'

The senior leader in question left the business shortly afterwards. Jim Collins would call this a 'bus' conversation[9] – as in, leaders need to make sure that they have the right people on the bus, people who agree with the destination and are prepared to invest in the journey. But as this CEO remembered, in the real world, these conversations are hard and personal – even if the message they send to the wider organization is powerful. As the Head of Change recalled:

> This guy had been there for a long, long time. He was trusted. A safe pair of hands. Always made his numbers. But the way the CEO explained it, he wasn't up for this new strategy. And so he went. That was a powerful message for all of us. It came just as we were coming up to the first anniversary of the change, and it really galvanized us in the team. This was another signal that said, this is important and there's no going back.

Once again, we see how both personal and structural Elements support each other here, with the CEO still having to step up and deliver a difficult message, but being able to base this on the initial Clarity of what the new strategy would deliver.

Practice Spotlight: Alignment by Metrics – 'A Test of Seriousness'

Back in the Clarity chapter, I talked about how Michael Chavez, the CEO of Duke Corporate Education, introduced an ambitious new plan to deliver growth in revenue and even higher growth in margin. Chavez's initial clarity about the outcomes, right at the start of the change, was already enough to produce reactions from some of Duke's Managing Directors – as they exited low-revenue, low-margin client work and chose to focus instead on projects that would help them meet the new goals. But much greater traction was to come when these new outcomes were written into these MDs' individual job descriptions and KPIs. It was at this point that *everybody* started paying attention to the new ask – not just those who had been minded to do the right thing when it was first announced.

Here's what Duke CE did. First, they translated the overall target outcomes into individual-level targets for each Managing Director. Then they shared these with the individual MDs, so that each MD had the opportunity to give feedback on how appropriate the expectations were. The result was rewritten job descriptions and KPIs for each MD in the firm, stating the minimum revenue each one needed to deliver – this varied by geography and client portfolio. And because they had started measuring the right data at the start of the change, they knew that an MD's ability to sustain profitable revenue depended on having the right mix of revenue from new and existing clients. So they included a metric that required that their revenue comprise a certain amount of new work won each year, along with revenue from retaining or growing existing clients.

The impact of introducing these new KPIs was two-fold. First, the business was now properly acknowledging the efforts being made by its best client managers. Prior to these KPIs, these managers would of course be lauded, but in a relatively informal way – by Chavez calling them out at town halls or by their local offices celebrating their efforts. Notice that these are all great things to do, but they remain informal, personal interventions. Back in the formal part of the organization (KPIs, targets and performance management) there was no such recognition – at least not until the KPIs were changed. Only once role expectations were rewritten and new KPIs introduced was it possible for managers to gain formal recognition (whether that entailed money or not). Now the recognition that had previously only been through informal and personal means (all of those good ideas, mind, which leaders continued to do) was being reinforced by the formal and structural means as well. Now all the signals were pointing in the same direction.

The second impact that these revised KPIs had was on those who hadn't so far changed. They had heard Chavez talk about the new outcomes being targeted, they'd also heard him praise those who were starting to make the right decisions (about how they used their time and which clients to focus on). But, before their KPIs were changed, they seemed to view this change as optional for them.

We can see the impact these revised KPIs had on two different MDs. The first had already changed her focus in response to the new strategy and was delighted to now have her KPIs changed to reflect this: 'It's great that this new strategy is now written into my job description and my KPIs. This proves Michael, his team, and the whole business is serious. It's not just something that he talks about, it's how our performance gets assessed – and that totally works for me.'

The second MD had, up to this point, been reluctant to change her behaviour, despite the new strategy being clear about what was now expected. She had not wanted to take the decisions to let long-standing clients go, even though many of them were low-revenue and some of them were even loss-making. While the means of assessment was simply informal (i.e. the absence of praise) and personal (i.e. not being celebrated by the boss or her colleagues), she could tolerate the impact and therefore still decide *not* to change. However, when the means of assessment became formal and structural, the costs of not changing (i.e. failing an annual appraisal or not receiving a bonus or promotion) became too high for her. She now had to decide whether to change – i.e. start actively managing her book of business by letting some of her old projects end and replacing them with higher-revenue, high-profit ones – or leave the organization. She decided that the cost to her was still too high and so she chose to leave the organization – joining a not-for-profit educational organization that she said suited her better. By having both Clarity and Alignment by KPIs, she could make a choice that was right for her and right for the rest of the organization, given its new direction.

As Michael Chavez put it: 'Changing the KPIs, and *changing them early*, was absolutely critical to us delivering the change. Once we were clear about the strategy, I said to people, this is serious, this isn't optional. I could have continued to talk about this at every town hall and in every meeting I was in, but I learned fast that clear talk, while necessary, isn't sufficient to change behaviour. It was really only when we changed the KPIs for people that they got what we were trying to do. If we'd delayed the change in KPIs, as some said we should, we would have delayed the results that we're now seeing. Why would anyone do that?'

What the other cases got wrong

Now actually, *all* of the four cases went to the trouble of revising the KPIs for the managers working on the change. They all invested a comparable level of time and effort (by HR and team members) to make these changes. But, largely because of the lack of Clarity right at the start, these efforts didn't have the same impact as in the Ideal Case.

In the Road Runner Case, the new KPIs for managers were based on activities (for example, 'Get these four projects up and running') rather than outcomes. It could hardly be otherwise, given this case failed to agree clear outcomes as part of the Clarity stage. That deficiency now meant they had nothing to translate into outcome-based targets, whether for managers or leaders. As the Head of Change remembered the type of KPIs she and her team were given:

We had new KPIs, but they weren't outcomes. They were activities. Sure, they were specific – get such-and-such project up and running by a certain date – but they were tactical, micro.

Because of the 'tactical, micro' nature of their new KPIs, managers ended up checking in much more with senior leaders to report on progress – or, as the Head of Change put it, to 'get our homework marked'. The result for the CEO and other senior leaders was that they became the homework-markers, checking too much and too often, policing the effort rather than leading it. They didn't want to be micro-managers, but nevertheless that's what they became; that was the dynamic which their failure to achieve Clarity had set up between them and their managers. They were spending far too much time in the 'blue zone' largely because they hadn't been clear or prescriptive enough about the 'green zone'.

They made this worse than it needed to be, though: they also failed to introduce any new KPIs for leaders at all. This meant that the horizontal alignment that we saw in the Ideal Case – across different departments in the organization – didn't happen here. This worsened the impact of one of the Road Runner Case's other failings – namely, a lack of dedicated resources, as the Head of Change recalled:

> Most of my team weren't full-time on this. They'd be off doing something else for so-and-so, who had different objectives and different KPIs. That hurt my KPIs, but it didn't hurt his. I guess if we'd have had dedicated resources on this, that would have helped. But we probably could have survived that if only we'd all had shared KPIs. What we couldn't survive was having neither of those things.

It was a similar story in the Under The Radar Case – albeit for different reasons. Here, if you remember, the CEO had agreed a target outcome with the team working on the change, but he hadn't publicized this outcome to the rest of the organization. Not even all his senior team were aware of it. This led to arguably the worst of all possible worlds for these managers – they were given new, outcome-based KPIs (a higher standard than the activity-based KPIs given to the Road

Runner team), but their leaders were not. The impact on managers was felt immediately:

> The new KPIs were just for me and the team. If anything, that made things worse for us, because now we had more pressure personally, but that pressure still wasn't spread across other departments. We felt very much on our own.

The final failing in the Road Runner Case was that, in contrast with the other three cases, it didn't start producing data and metrics in these early days and so wasn't able to start understanding the linkages between activities and outcomes – i.e. 'how' and 'why' certain things worked better than others. This was largely because leaders weren't talking about outcomes – so why bother understanding the specific actions that produced them? What mattered to them was that the feedback from customers on the activities was positive, rather than the value this delivered for the business. As it would turn out, the lack of data to help them understand what was going on in their projects would come to dog this business in Years 2 and 3 – causing them to be busy but ineffective.

And so here's where we stand across the four cases: only two fully delivered on Alignment by Metrics, the other two had some signals missing:

	Ideal	EM	UTR	RR
Element 4: Alignment by Metrics				
Leaders need to introduce revised metrics and KPIs to measure and reward the new strategy:				
a) data and metrics to help understand the projects being worked on;	☑	☑	☑	☒
b) revised, outcome-based KPIs for managers; and	☑	☑	☑	☒
c) revised, outcome-based KPIs for leaders	☑	☑	☒	☒

And let me reiterate: all the evidence from these cases suggests that it was the fact of *having* the KPIs and metrics, and being judged against them, that seemed to matter more to these managers than being paid for them. These people cared about succeeding and being seen to succeed – so leaders needed to give them the right targets to strive for. That intrinsic motivation was the basis of what kept them going. If they also got paid a bonus for their efforts? Well, then that was just what the name suggested it was – a bonus. (For more on the science behind this, see the Science Spotlight below.)

Science Spotlight: The Impact of Metrics and Rewards

The impact that metrics have on organizations is almost taken for granted: every organization has myriad dashboards, KPIs and scorecards. But not all of these will drive value. Some will be badly conceived and, as a result, produce perverse outcomes. Care needs to be taken when designing KPIs and rewards if they are to produce the impact you want.

We can see the potentially perverse impact of incentives by investigating when rewarding individuals for doing something actually makes them *less* likely to do it. For example, a recent study of 15,000 US schoolchildren suggested that being rewarded for attendance made them less likely to attend school.[10] Similarly, in one well-known study,[11] a school wanted to reduce the incidence of parents being late to pick up their children. They introduced small fines for late pick-ups. Bizarrely, this actually increased the incidence of parents turning up late.

These findings seem counter-intuitive to conventional wisdom that you ought to reward the behaviours you want to see more of. So, what's going on in these studies? The best interpretation is that people view rewards (and any other measures that seek to shape the choices we make) as signals about what they ought to do. For example, by rewarding schoolchildren for perfect attendance, the new rewards inadvertently signalled to them that perfect attendance was no longer the social norm or expected by the school. And by signalling to parents that they could now make amends for being late by paying a small fine, more parents came to believe that being late was an acceptable choice. The introduction of the fine had replaced a powerful social motivation to be on time ('my kids will be upset, other parents will think I'm a bad parent') with an economic mechanism that enabled them to assuage their guilt or concern ('OK, now I can buy off my guilt at being late by paying a small fine'). Had the fine been of a larger amount, or indeed of a social nature (such as being named and shamed to other parents), perhaps fewer would have made this choice.

The lesson then is, as it would be for any intervention in a social setting, that you need to design and implement the right reward in the right way for the people whom you are trying to influence. Just thinking that money for X will make X happen suggests a relatively unsophisticated understanding of human beings. That is because, at least for people earning enough to cover the basics, money serves a symbolic as well as a literal purpose. Therefore, you first need to pay people enough so that they aren't worrying about money and so they can feel good about working for you.[12] Only then can you use money and other rewards for more symbolic purposes, such as rewarding certain outcomes or behaviours.

Research suggests that rewarding people for outcome-based targets and leaving them free to decide how to achieve those outcomes is particularly effective, not only in delivering the target outcomes but also in increasing employee satisfaction and retention.[13] In a study of 34 outlets of a major US retailer, 15 of which implemented a new incentive plan to support their new customer-focused service strategy, while the other 19 did not, researchers found significantly different outcomes between the two groups of stores. The new incentives paid bonuses based on the target outcomes (higher customer satisfaction and higher profit) being achieved. The results of the 77-month study – a good example of longitudinal change research for once – showed that the stores with the new outcome-based incentives not only achieved better outcomes but also had higher rates of employee satisfaction and lower incidents of store manager monitoring. In fact, in the stores with the new outcome-based incentives, supervisory monitoring was reduced over the six-year period, largely because employees could now make the decisions about what would best deliver these outcomes on their own. This, in turn, improved not only the outcomes being targeted but also their own levels of job satisfaction.

As importantly, then, it seems that *not* changing rewards or recognition to reflect the new strategy signals to people that, whatever leaders say, this new strategy isn't important and may not be around for long. In Steven Kerr's famous 1975 article, 'On the Folly of Rewarding A, While Hoping for B',[14] he shows that where there is misalignment between what the organization wants and what it rewards, employees (and especially the most conscientious employees) suffer. They then have to navigate mixed signals about what's important and what's required of them. Kerr makes the point that, in such an organization, leaders need to rely on employees being 'good citizens' – after all, there is nothing to reward them for their extra effort yet leaders still ask them for it. A more recent study[15] suggests that aligning incentives with what is asked of people has a more positive impact on less conscientious people (in this case, undergrads at a US university earning course credits): the most conscientious students studied hard anyway, whereas the less hard-working studied harder *because of* the new incentives.

From all of the research on measures – including studies on incentives, rewards and recognition – we can say two things. First, if your only means of rewarding and recognizing people's efforts involves money then you need to augment that with social sources of recognition for managers and their teams – things like public appreciation, praise, promotion, writing up successes as case studies that others should follow. Every one of these is a source of validation for people who've done a good job, so use them all. And second, if rewards (even social ones) are the only source of alignment you are using, then you need to augment this with the other three ways to drive Alignment – Conversations, Actions and Resourcing. Otherwise, the signal provided by metrics alone might be too weak and therefore open to misinterpretation by managers who lack the additional context that leader conversations, actions and resourcing can give them.

The sequencing of these four sources of Alignment

The sequencing of Clarity first and then Alignment is pretty obvious when you see it played out over time. You need to be clear about what the change will deliver (as well as why it's needed and how it fits) so that you know what you need to align around. What is perhaps less obvious is the internal sequencing of the four Elements of Alignment we've been focusing on in this chapter. In other words, some happened before others.

The two personal sources of Alignment – by leader Conversations and by leader Actions – can happen immediately. As a leader, you are the most immediate source of meaning for managers, so they will be looking at what you're saying and what you're doing to help them work out what this new strategy means for them. So as soon as the new strategy is announced, leaders can and should change what they're choosing to talk about and the actions they're taking to support the change.

Changing the two *structural* sources of Alignment – by Resourcing and by Metrics – isn't usually as immediate. Part of this is for practical reasons. Budgets will have been set for the year based on the old strategy. While there ought to be some flexibility for mid-year re-allocation within the firm, achieving all the budget that is necessary for the change may not be possible within the first 12 months of the change – you may have to wait.

The managers in these cases understood this – they accepted that it might not be until the beginning of Year 2 and the next budget cycle that they got all the funding they needed. But there needed to be commitments from leaders that the funding was on its way. For example, in the Ideal Case, this was done by a relatively small mid-year allocation from a previous priority to this one, but it was material because of what it signified:

> It wasn't a huge amount of extra money for us at that stage, but it was what it represented. It said this is now more important than what we were doing before.

Equally, allocating the best people to the change might not be immediately possible either – typically, good people aren't sitting around waiting for a new strategy to be announced. So reallocating them and ensuring they are dedicated to the change may take time. But leaders need to be talking about getting the best people to work on this new priority to signal that the right resources will be given to it.

It's the same story when it comes to changing KPIs and metrics. New KPIs in particular need to be defined, agreed, baselined and then measured before being fully introduced. New data may need to be validated and new systems built (or at least new routines established) to collect it. None of this can happen quickly and, again, managers in these cases recognized this – not least because they were often the ones doing the work of baselining and collecting the data and metrics, and so could see that this would take time.

What is it that leaders need to be doing during this time, while we wait for the change in KPIs to come through? They need to be talking about the new KPIs that are coming, talking about why they matter for both leaders and managers and talking about how important high-quality data is for the change. As the Head of Change in the Ideal Case recalled:

> It took longer to get the KPIs fully sorted. That wasn't really done until nearly the end of that first year. But it was OK because in the meantime, the leaders were talking about it regularly, so we knew the KPIs would be changing, and actually, we were behaving and making choices as if the new KPIs were already in place long before they were.

These are examples then of where leaders can use the *personal* Elements of Alignment – Conversation and Actions – to keep momentum going until the *structural* changes to Resourcing and Metrics are in place. But while Alignment by Conversations and Actions helps fill the credibility gap in the early days of the change, the structural changes that drive and support alignment *do need to be made*. And, ideally, before the first 12 months are up.

It's these two structural Elements of Alignment – Resourcing and Metrics – that will come to be seen by managers as the litmus tests of whether the change is here to stay; and it's these two structural Elements of Alignment that set up the possibility that the change, and the managers working on it, can become less dependent on leaders to see it through.

Equally, when these two structural Elements of Alignment are missing, leaders will be needed much more as the change progresses. They will still need to devote time and effort (by Conversations and Actions) to signalling that the change is important because the structural signals (Resourcing and Metrics) aren't there to share the burden. Managers too will have to commit more time and effort – again in personal endeavours such as brokering, negotiating and doing favours for other departments – just to make progress on the change, because they can't rely on the structural changes made in Year 1 to help them out. As the managers in our two cases that failed to change the structures to support the change put it:

> Even at this stage, I was starting to see that this change never just happened on its own. It always required effort – whether more input from the CEO, or another conversation to broker a way forward with another department. It never became business as usual for us. (The Under The Radar Case)

> The thing I remember most as the first year ended was just how much time this was taking. Going backwards and forwards, checking in with the CEO, then back to the team, having to have a million conversations to get something kicked off and to keep it moving. It was hard work. (The Road Runner Case)

It was harder than it needed to be because the structural Elements of Alignment hadn't been sorted by the end of this first year and, driving this, harder than it needed to be because Clarity hadn't been achieved in the first three months.

For each of the four Elements of Alignment, we've been scoring the cases as we've gone through this chapter. So that we can see them all in one place, take a look at Diagram 5.1 opposite. As we shall see in the next two chapters, these Alignment scores will have a significant impact on these businesses' ability to sustain progress in the second year of the change. They will also in part determine how successfully managers use the autonomy they've been given.

Diagram 5.1: Summary of how the Cases delivered Alignment

	Ideal	EM	UTR	RR
Source 1: Alignment by Conversations				
Leaders need to take every opportunity to reinforce the importance of the new strategy – formally and informally, in groups and in one-on-ones.	☑	☑	☑	☑
Source 2: Alignment by Actions				
Leaders need to make choices that reinforce the change being asked for:				
a) by role-modelling it;	☑	☑	☑	☑
b) by making time for it;	☑	☑	☑	☑
c) by giving managers the decision-rights they need;	☑	☑	☑	☑
d) by putting the change on the agenda of senior team meetings.	☑	☑	☒	☒
Source 3: Alignment by Resources				
Leaders need to allocate sufficient budget and the right people to deliver the change:				
a) sufficient budget;	☑	☑	☒	☒
b) the right people (i.e. experienced, connected, sufficiently senior);	☑	☑	☑	☑
c) for whom the new strategy/change is now their main role (i.e. dedicated resources).	☑	☑	☑	☒
Source 4: Alignment by Metrics				
Leaders need to introduce revised metrics and KPIs to measure and reward the new strategy:				
a) data and metrics to help understand the projects being worked on;	☑	☑	☑	☒
b) revised, outcome-based KPIs for managers;	☑	☑	☑	☒
c) revised, outcome-based KPIs for leaders.	☑	☑	☒	☒

175

Leadership lessons from Ask #2

The first lesson for leaders again relates to the type of leadership you need to use here. As you will recognize, some of the ways in which you create Alignment rely heavily on transformational leadership – for example, the need to continue to evangelize for the new strategy and to talk about it at every opportunity; and the need to role-model it with authenticity and enthusiasm. But the other ways to create Alignment require what would best be described as transactional leadership. Things like making sure the change has sufficient budget and the right people on it, working out what the revised KPIs should be and how these link to outcomes, being interested in the data and metrics that help you understand why the change is working and the micro but totemic changes to your own diary and to your senior team's agenda. Each of the things on this list would qualify as transactional leadership behaviours or actions and yet, despite this, we now know they are all extremely important for managers who are interpreting the signals leaders are sending at this stage of the change.

So, the same thing that was true for achieving Clarity is also true for achieving Alignment: you need *both* types of leadership – albeit in different ways – to deliver what managers need from leaders at this stage. And while it may be tempting to use the two personal, agentic sources (by Conversations and Actions) more than the two structural sources (Resourcing and Metrics) – because it may feel easier and faster for you to do and there's nothing structural to change – as Diagram 5.2 opposite shows, you only gear the system properly if you make sure you have *all four* of these signals in place and pointing in the same direction.

Diagram 5.2: Leaders' Signals – Do They Fit Together to Drive the System Forward?

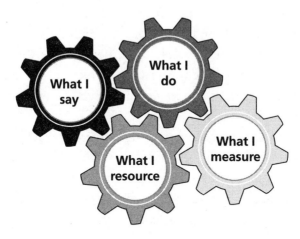

The second lesson for leaders about Alignment is: don't send mixed signals. Mixed signals happen when leaders don't manage their signals to all point in the same direction. For example, when leaders are talking about one thing and role-modelling another, or saying something's important but not resourcing it, or continuing to reward something completely different.

But notice that mixed signals can also happen passively or inadvertently – in other words, when leaders change some of the four Elements of Alignment, but not all. The most likely missing Elements will be the structural ones – Resourcing and Metrics – because they are the hardest and most time-consuming ones to change. But bear in mind how managers will interpret a lack of action here – because they will be looking at what you're *not* finding the time to fix, as well as what you *are* doing. As my friend and colleague Professor John van Maanen put it: 'Consider also the fullness of the empty sign'.[16] Leader inactivity or inaction might inadvertently signal to managers that this change isn't really important to you.

When leaders send out mixed signals, they sow the seeds of confusion. We know that this misalignment within the organization hurts effectiveness *and* efficiency – meaning things work less well *and* they take longer. Economists would say that the organization has increased its internal transaction costs, because there is now more interpretation and checking time required before every decision. But what about the impact at a more practical level? How do these mixed signals play out for employees?

The fact is mixed signals can have very different effects on your best managers compared with the impact they have on your worst – and however good your business is, you'll know who both of those groups are. Your best managers hate mixed signals. They want to come to work and perform. And mixed signals compromise their ability to do that. Should they be doing the thing that was asked for, or the thing that's being role-modelled? Should they continue to do what's been asked for even though it hasn't been resourced and still isn't being measured?

As a result, mixed signals increase manager anxiety because they make their daily choices harder. And we'll see in the later chapters of this book that mixed signals also corrode managers' autonomy for the same reason: eager to make the best choice, managers flail and often don't make any choice at all, because it's now hard for them to know what the *best* choice is.

While your best managers hate mixed signals, often mixed signals are exactly what your less conscientious managers are waiting for. Mixed signals give them a 'get out of jail' card. How could they possibly be expected to perform, when it wasn't clear what leaders wanted them to do? Saying one thing and doing another, or saying one thing and measuring something else – this is what gives a poor-performing, low accountability manager a plausible excuse for not delivering.

The anxiety of these managers *doesn't* increase because of these mixed signals; in fact, it may well *reduce*, because they know that mixed signals will give them a plausible excuse for under-performance without being held to account. It also enables them to continue as they were doing before – working on their pet projects and perhaps not engaging at all with the new strategy – because the visibility of and accountability for what they are doing is much less in a 'mixed signal' environment.

So why on earth would leaders do this? Why would they set up their best managers to either fail (they make bad choices about what to do), or at best succeed but with much more effort (they end up making good choices but it takes time and anxiety)? And why would they enable their worst managers to feel less accountable for poor performance?

In my experience, no leader sets out to cause these effects. Most intuitively get that 'walking the talk', 'putting your money where your mouth is' and 'measuring what you want to manage' are all management proverbs that work in practice. Most leaders send out mixed messages either accidentally – because they're not really noticing all the ways in which they signal to people – or because, perhaps still beholden to the Magic and Drama Delusions, they put too much emphasis on what they can do personally to drive Alignment – by what they say and what they do – and not enough on how they need to tweak the structure – by changing what they resource and what they measure.

The third and final lesson we can take from this early leadership work on Alignment is one that will only really be seen in the later stages of the change, but here's a headline of the story to come. If you don't do the structural work of Alignment now – and if, instead, you rely only on the personal work of Conversations and Actions – then you will be stuck doing this personal work for the rest of the change. It is only by doing the *structural* work of Alignment (changing budgets, securing dedicated resourcing, capturing good data and introducing new KPIs for leaders and managers) that you will be able to be less personally involved – because these structural changes are doing more and more of the Alignment work for you. Long after you have stopped talking about the change at every opportunity, and when you are perhaps even role-modelling it less, it's these structural Elements that will still be signalling to managers that this change matters. So, the reason to step up and do more on these structural Elements now is not only to ensure that all four Elements of Alignment are working for you – all the cogs in the system working in the same direction as in Diagram 5.2 on page 177 – but also to lay the foundations of managers not needing you.

So, the question for leaders at this stage is: Have you made sure that you now have all four sources of Alignment working for you, all four cogs in the system in place and driving in the same direction? And the question for managers is: Which of these cogs isn't working as hard as it could – even if it's not actively working against the change? Working that out, and then giving leaders feedback on the effectiveness of each of these four Elements of Alignment, is a critical part of a manager's job at this stage in the change.

The 'work' of Alignment

As this chapter has shown, leaders need to pay attention to all four of the ways in which they're driving Alignment during this first year of the change. Even if you kick the change off by relying more on the personal sources – by what you say and the actions you take, because you can alter those things faster and more easily – you need to quickly follow this up by work on the structural sources – resourcing and measurement. And because these will take longer to change, you need to get this structural work started early, in order to have these two Elements in place by the end of Year 1.

If you don't achieve that, one of two things will happen: either managers will start downgrading the change, in terms of what they are personally prioritizing for themselves and their teams; or it will remain important but only because you are having to personally be involved. In other words, if you short-change the two structural sources of Alignment at this stage, you will have to spend more time and effort on the other two, personal sources – because that's all you have left. And that continued time commitment is unlikely to go away until those structural supports are in place.

As we know, Alignment is the second area where leaders need to step up and do more than they might typically do at this stage of the change. Having spent this chapter setting out the detail of what Alignment requires from leaders, I hope you can see where this extra work is required. Because for most leaders, advising them to talk about the change at every opportunity and role-model it regularly isn't new advice. What *is* new, at least for some leaders, is the advice to start thinking at the very earliest stages of the change, about the more structural Elements of how they signal to their organizations. These Elements are sometimes taken for granted by leaders, some of whom may feel that making changes to these areas will make less of an impact than them personally signalling, by what they say and how they act. Of course, the reason for that continued belief is our old friends, the Magic and Agency Delusions that we met in Chapter 1. Once we embrace a different version of leadership, where the work of leadership relates not just to the personal magic a leader can bring, but also to the more mundane work that the leader is seen to support, then leaders are more likely to see the value in using both structural *and* personal means to signal what's important.

To help leaders and managers remember what Alignment requires in practice, I am including some tips and watch-outs at the end of this chapter.

Where the four cases stand at the end of Year 1

The first 12 months of the change had seen the leaders of our four cases take very different approaches to initiating it. This led to very different choices being made about:

- the targets to be set;
- the projects to be worked on;
- the data to be captured and analyzed.

These early choices meant the four cases made noticeably different rates of progress (towards the 100 per cent level on the y-axis of the graph below) during this first year.

Diagram 5.3: Progress at the end of Year I

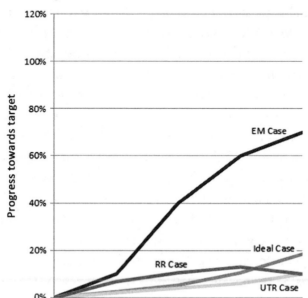

As you can see, the Early Momentum Case opened up a huge gap on the other cases during this first year. They had doubled-down on the 'quick wins' which dominated their work in the first three months and these paid off for them – at least up to this point. If you were the Ideal Case, still battling away with a lot of 'zero glam' work, it might have been tempting to look over at the Early Momentum Case and wonder whether all this 'zero glam' work was such a good idea, given your relative lack of progress.

But this is about to change. In fact, you can already see in Diagram 5.3 the Ideal Case starting to move upwards towards its target – a movement it would sustain for the next two years. You can also see that the Early Momentum Case's progress is starting to slow.

During Year 2, we will see it plateau and then reverse. Year 2 will also see the Early Momentum Case introduce a much bigger target for that year – remember, they hadn't had a big, multi-year target at the start, but instead had focused on annual targets that became increasingly ambitious. As a result, it would only be in the second year that the Early Momentum Case realized it would need to devote time and effort to some fundamental 'zero glam' projects, such as data and systems, if it was to achieve this new, ambitious target. But, by that time, some of the political and financial will of the early days had dissipated. As a result, as the Early Momentum's Head of Change commented:

> It felt like we almost had to start again in Year 2. And that was hard. We had less political will by this stage and so it was probably harder than it should have been.

This case did, however, have all the Elements of Alignment in place to help them as they went into Year 2. Having sufficient resources for the change, in particular, would ease the pressure they would soon be under.

This wasn't true for the Under The Radar Case who now had to deliver outcomes but without the budget they needed, and where there still wasn't shared agreement at a senior level about the extent of the change required. Nor was it a happy picture in the Road Runner Case. The impact of their initial 'quick win' activities was starting to tail off even by the end of the first year. Going into the second, they lacked not only budget and dedicated resource, but also clear outcomes. These wouldn't be agreed until into the second year – at which point, like the Early Momentum Case, they would re-evaluate their early work. Again, they would realize that cosmetic 'quick wins' wouldn't cut it and more 'zero glam' work was needed. But starting this a year after the Ideal Case, without the budget or people to do the job properly, these managers would soon find themselves overworked and frustrated.

You'll notice that there is no lack of resilience or effort on the part of either leaders or managers in any of the four cases as we come to the end of Year 1: everyone is working hard and believing that they will succeed. But the die has already been cast for some of these cases. Whether by failing to achieve Clarity right at the start of the change, or by failing to deliver the structural Elements of Alignment later in this first year, three out of four of these cases are about to have a harder second year than they needed to have.

Tips and Watch-outs to Help You Get Alignment

Tips and Watch-outs for Leaders

- **Use your personal charisma to keep the change front-of-mind for people** – this means talking about the new strategy at every opportunity and role-modelling the new actions and behaviours you've asked for. Remember, people are looking at you all the time in the early days of the change, so pay attention to what you're doing even when you think no one's noticing;

- **'Action' means more than just 'role-modelling'.** While role-modelling is important, it's not enough. You also need to make changes to how you use your time so that you always have time for people who need to talk to you about progress or issues. And to make sure it's on every SLT agenda. Put it close to the top of the agenda, too, so that it always gets discussed;

- **But personal effort – alignment by Conversations and by Actions – is not enough.** You also need to use your power to put in place the two structural sources of Alignment – Resourcing and Metrics. You can make these changes faster and more easily than others because you have more power, so use it. The result of doing this now is that you'll need to deploy your time and power much less in the later stages of the change, because more will be happening automatically and without your involvement;

- **Resourcing isn't just about money.** Although securing the budget needed for the essential early work – especially the 'zero glam' work – is important, who's working on this change effort matters too. Make sure you're giving it your best people – those who aren't just smart and hard-working, but also well connected, can make things happen and are widely seen as the future stars of the organization. That signals this matters;

- **But great people aren't enough on their own.** If you allocate your best people to this without dedicating them to the effort or giving them sufficient resources, you risk creating anxiety and wasted effort for them. Make sure you support them with sufficient budget so that they are set up to succeed;

- **Devote time and effort to the data – and show you care about it.** Keep honouring the 'zero glam' work and the exploratory projects that help you understand why some initiatives produce results and others don't, by asking about the data as well as the outcomes that emerge from this work. That shows you care about learning from the change, as well as simply delivering it;

- **Change the KPIs and change them early.** Make sure also that the new KPIs are based on the macro-level outcomes (what the change should produce), not on micro-level activities. Managers ought to be choosing these for themselves. The new KPIs should be for all leaders as well as managers, so that everyone has skin in the game.

Tips and Watch-outs for Managers

Don't settle for anything less than all four Elements of Alignment in the first 12 months of the change:

- **By Conversations:** most leaders know they need to talk about the change in these early days. Make sure they do and show your appreciation for this effort;
- **By Actions:** you may find your leaders role-modelling the new behaviours and that's great. Show your appreciation for this when it happens, but make sure that they're also freeing up time in their diaries so you have time with them when you need it. If this isn't happening, keep pushing for it and ask what you can do to help make this time available. Make sure also that the new strategy and the progress you're making is on the SLT agenda and close to the top. Help make this easier by making sure it's a 'green zone' conversation and by getting feedback on the first few presentations you make and seeing what lands best with them;
- **By Resourcing: the right people.** Well, *you're* on the change effort, so that's good, but who else do you need on your team? Where are they and what can senior leaders do to help make these people available to you? This is a major way leaders signal that this change matters – and that it's more important than other, existing initiatives. So ask them for their help here or call out that this could be a mixed signal;
- **By Resourcing: changes to budget.** So this might not be immediate either, but what signals have leaders sent that this new strategy will be a priority in the next budgeting round? And what reallocations can be made in the meantime? Again, one of the most totemic ways to use the budget as a signal is to take money away from one area and give it to the new strategy, so look for these 'hypothecation' opportunities and explicitly ask leaders to take them;
- **By Metrics: changes to KPIs.** Assuming you've agreed a target outcome in the first three months, make sure that this is the basis of the new KPIs for you and your team – and also for senior leaders. Don't accept micro-level, activity-based KPIs; these are choices you should make for yourself. And if you haven't already got a target outcome, use the KPI conversation to insist on getting one. Better late than never;
- **By Metrics: changes to data.** Make sure also that you are capturing and analyzing all the data you need to help you understand how and why things are working (or why not). This will help you refine initiatives over time without the need for leader input. Make sure also that the metrics that track progress are sufficiently visible within the firm to help motivate people.

CHAPTER SIX

Ask #3: Focus

Give it the time it needs

When it comes to delivering strategic change, time is pretty important because, by its very nature, strategic change is not a short-term endeavour. It takes time to make the changes and even longer for them to bed down. To help this happen, leaders and managers need to use their time (from the begining of Year 2 onwards) in specific ways. The first thing they ought to be devoting time to is Focus – and that's what this chapter is about. The second thing they ought to be using their time for is to show Consistency and I'll cover that in Chapter 7.

Crucially, whereas the first two stages of successful change – Clarity and Alignment – required leaders to **step up** and do more than they might typically do, the next two stages – Focus and Consistency – require leaders to **step back** and do less.

By the second year of many strategic change efforts, typically one of two things is happening. Either the change is starting to unravel, as progress flags; or else leaders act to prevent this, by becoming involved in more of the work than in Year 1. The additional work for leaders in this scenario is typically 'blue zone' work – helping managers decide which projects to work on, rolling their sleeves up and helping push initiatives forward, and generally reinvigorating a change that is running out of steam.

My argument is that this kind of work ought not to be necessary. If leaders have stepped up sufficiently during Year 1 – and delivered all the Elements of Clarity and Alignment – then they should be able to step back and do less now – including spending less time overall on the change and certainly spending less of that time making decisions about it.

This period of the change (particularly in the early months of Year 2) can sometimes feel a little bit like a no-man's land, because while leaders are now trying to step back, managers may not yet have completely stepped up. They may not yet be fully occupying the 'blue zone' that leaders need them to. It's important to remember that managers stepping up is conditional on leaders stepping back, so this is really where leaders need to lead – by first doing their part of the bargain that will then enable managers to do theirs.

That said, stepping *back* is not stepping *out*. You are not leaving managers without any support: rather, you are leaving them to do what they do best. Harvard Professor Teresa Amabile made the distinction between 'checking in' with people and 'checking up' on them[1] – and that's a good way to think about it. Stepping back is not a passive endeavour, it still takes work. But this work should have two characteristics. First, it should be 'green zone' work – the kind that coaches and pushes managers to fully occupy their 'blue zones'. And second, this 'stepping back' work should require no new decisions – because these should all have been taken in Year 1.

Indeed, the trick now for leaders is to *not* make new decisions, but instead to give managers the time and space they need in order to focus on the change. As a leader, you best help managers at this stage by not tinkering with it, not interfering with it and not changing your mind about it. That's the essence of this stepping back 'work'. And it will require just as much effort, discipline and self-awareness as you needed for the stepping up stages, if not more. It will also require you to let go of any last attachments you have to the 'Hollywood' version of leadership and the Four Delusions that it fosters. The work of stepping back is – initially, at least – hard work precisely because you may not see it as 'work' at all.

In my experience, while most leaders have no problem with doing more, many have much more difficulty with this concept of doing less. That feels unbecoming of them as leaders. They worry especially about how to navigate the sometimes fine distinction between stepping back and stepping out – i.e. completely disengaging. That's *not* what managers need from leaders at this stage nor, arguably, at any stage. But what's the difference in practice? I will explain that over the next two chapters.

And the message for managers as you read these next two chapters? You have two critical opportunities now, as the change enters its second year. First, just as you were helping leaders deliver Clarity and Alignment – and calling out when you needed *more* input from them – your job now is to be on the lookout for leaders *not* stepping back, so you can call them out when you need *less* input from them. That will take just as much noticing and just as much effort – not least because this may not be 'normal' behaviour for either you or them. Second, and more importantly, this is now your opportunity to fully occupy the 'blue zone' of delivering the change. Setting you up to do this was, essentially, what Year 1 was about. From Year 2 onwards, the floor is yours, so make sure you have it to yourself.

In return for this new effort, the prize for both leaders and managers is to have the change they are working on be delivered and sustained – thereby avoiding the fate of so many other change efforts in Years 2 and 3, namely that the change peters out, before being replaced by yet another initiative that asks for a similar level of effort and belief. Not for nothing is this middle period sometimes referred to as the 'death valley'[2] of a strategic change.

The two elements required for Focus

When I use the term 'Focus', what I mean is the ongoing process by which leaders, managers and the whole organization remain focused on the new strategy. This is what enables managers to keep delivering it and for the results of the change effort to get better and better over time. Without sufficient Focus – for example, if you don't give it the time it needs, or if you crowd it out with too many other 'priorities' – then the change can become just another initiative and will likely become diluted as a result. Focus stops this from happening. Put simply, if you're sufficiently focused on the change, it will get time, resources and attention from the organization – and won't get diluted over time.

The connection between Focus and time manifests in two ways. First, the *individual managers* working on the change need time to stand back, think and reflect on how their work is going. We refer to this as the need for **slack** – and leaders have to help create and protect this for managers. Second, the *change itself* needs time – time for this fundamentally new way of doing things to take effect. This requires leaders to show **patience**. Let's take each of these Elements in turn.

Element 1 of Focus: Give them some 'slack'

'Slack' has a bad reputation. Think about how we use the word. We talk about 'slacking' when we don't think we're working hard enough. We call people 'slackers' when we don't think they're sufficiently committed or contributing enough. These words are pejorative. They certainly seem a long way from something to which we should aspire. But when it comes to delivering successful long-term change – or, indeed, *anything new* within an organization – managers need to have slack in their day. And leaders need to help them *create* slack – by ensuring they don't have too much on – and then they need to help them *protect* it, by actively encouraging managers to refine or even cull projects, rather than adding to the number of activities they're working on.

Slack has been defined as 'a cushion of excess resources' that help the organization adapt to internal or external pressures.[3] This 'cushion of excess resources' definition has led many organizations to view 'slack' as simply 'waste'. This conflation is largely because the earliest conceptions of slack borrowed from the neoclassical economics view that slack only occurred when the firm was not in perfect equilibrium. Slack therefore ought to be minimized to make the firm more efficient.

Now that's fine if efficiency is the goal – because in the short term, the most efficient business will indeed be the most profitable. But what if it's more about effectiveness than efficiency? And what if *long-term* profit – that often requires learning and new ways of doing things – rather than merely short-term results, is the goal? Because, in an organizational setting, slack is essential if teams are to iterate, learn and improve over time – which is what's required in order to generate long-term value let alone deliver a strategic change. (See Science Spotlight page 192: 'Why Organizations Need Some Slack'.)

To understand slack at the individual level, I find that the best way is to define it by its absence. If, as a leader or manager, you feel you are completely up against it just to fulfil your core responsibilities or to meet your basic KPIs, then you don't have any slack. If, on the other hand, you find you regularly have a bit of time to stand back and reflect on how things are going with your team, to learn from mistakes, to think about how your role fits into the firm's overall strategy, and to make fundamental fixes to problems when they arise, rather than just alleviating the symptoms, then you probably have a bit of slack in your working life. Exactly how much slack you need will depend on your role, but having none at all is bad news if you want to *learn from* your actions, rather than just perform them.

In the specific context of organizational change, it turns out that having slack is particularly important, for three reasons. First, because change doesn't always go as planned. Slack gives managers the capacity they need to adjust to setbacks and come up with a Plan B. That won't happen if they are overwhelmed with work under Plan A.

Second, slack enables managers to learn from their initial activities (e.g. the first iteration of a project) and then work out what has worked and why. If managers don't have time to do the analysis of what's working and why, they won't improve the outcomes from their activities (by choosing different points or modes of intervention) over time. Not only does that make managers' jobs much less interesting, it also reduces the effectiveness of what they're doing, reducing the chances that the change will succeed. Slack – i.e. having the time to stand back, reflect, think and learn – is what enables all of that to happen. Without slack, there is no learning; and without learning, there can be no improvement.

The third and final reason why slack is important – and particularly so during change – is that organizations aren't always as joined-up as they should be and because leaders don't always do what they ought to. (And, as we'll see in this and the next chapter, that's especially true in the later stages of a strategic change.) Because of this, managers need to have sufficient time and head-space so they can be on the lookout for things not working as they should.

Harvard Professor Max Bazerman has studied and written about what he calls 'the art of being a good noticer'.[4] This requires us to be paying attention to what is happening around us, seeing things and making connections that others might miss, and knowing when to speak up and challenge with sufficient time to make a difference to the direction of travel. But when we're too busy, we have less chance of noticing the things we need to notice. Having some slack in their working week is what gives managers this time and capacity to notice what leaders are doing at this stage of the change – and, in particular, whether they are truly stepping back. Slack also gives managers time and capacity to look up and see possible connections (or inconsistencies) with other parts of the organization. Time to go for coffee with colleagues in other areas of the business is particularly vital at this stage – to help you assess how your emerging achievements are fitting (or not) with theirs, and how all your activities roll up to deliver the overall outcome being targeted.

Science Spotlight: Why Organizations Need Some Slack

The relationship between having slack (as we have defined it, i.e. having some slack time to stand back, reflect, think and learn) and being more innovative is well established. The academic literature – starting in the 1960s onwards – has shown that when people have slack, they take on riskier and more complex projects, the very ones that can often lead to fundamental breakthroughs in their market or in the way they do business.[5] As one well-known paper put it: 'learning occurs most readily when what is known as "slack" occurs: [learning] can emerge only when there is space for experimentation, foolishness and randonée'.[6]

You might be wondering what exactly the ROI on 'randonée' is these days, but a recent study suggests it might be higher than you think. The authors investigated how the number of new technology ideas being offered on Kickstarter, the world's leading crowdfunding platform, varied with college holidays. They found a 45 per cent increase in the number of new ideas generated after students had been on holiday for a week.[7] Having some slack time gives us the opportunity to be more creative and also to act on the ideas we have.

Having slack time also helps us make connections that we might not otherwise make. The benefit of humans regularly 'coming up for air' to let their minds wander is well-established. It's what Manoush Zomorodi calls 'mind wandering'[8] – the idea that, when you're not thinking about anything in particular, your mind can wander and, in so doing, make connections or come up with ideas that you'd never have done if you were actually 'thinking' about it. And that's exactly what having some slack time gives you the opportunity to do.

This can be particularly important when different teams are working on different projects or work streams within a large change programme, often across different silos within their organization. If all your time is taken up with getting the work done within your own work stream or silo, and you have no time to make connections with and between parallel work streams, vital opportunities for, and threats to, progress can be missed. There is evidence to suggest that ensuring the right people have slack time at the *same* time – what we call 'overlapping slack' – is important if co-ordination and connections across teams, especially where they are working on complex problems, is required.[9]

The *shape* of your slack time is also important. For thinking about complex problems or the connections between projects, it's likely that larger chunks of time are more useful than just 10 spare minutes every hour. (In fact, having 10 spare minutes is really *only* helpful as a way to recover from one activity and prepare for the next. This isn't enough to really constitute slack as we mean it.) This is why some Google teams have moved away from their well-known '20 per cent rule' – where employees' slack time was spread out evenly during the working week – to fewer but longer blocks of time that can be spent on more complex problems. And why many organizations invest in giving their employees sabbaticals – extended, paid leave when they can refresh their thinking.[10] (For good examples of this, see the Practice Spotlight: 'Making Sure Employees Have the Opportunity to Stand Back, Reflect, Think and Learn', page 196)

It's also why many people switch off Outlook when they need to concentrate for a chunk of time without being distracted by email notifications.[11] This also reduces the switching costs of managers moving from one type of work to another, an issue when the slack you have is broken up into short, albeit regular, chunks of time that aren't adequate to get proper, thinking work done.[12] Given it takes around 25 minutes for people doing cerebral work to refocus on their task after an interruption, this is a huge issue for productivity.[13]

This is of course a much greater problem where organizations have multiple, different projects happening at the same time – what my friend Dr Heidi Gardner at Harvard calls the 'overcommitted' organization. In her work with Mark Mortensen at INSEAD, she has shown that when individuals have to switch between teams, there is a high cost to both the individual (greater stress and a lower sense of value being delivered) and the outcome being targeted.[14]

It's worth calling out the residual worry that some leaders may have about employees having slack time – namely, that this will give them the wrong message about how productive they need to be and, as a result, they'll work less hard and productivity will fall. Leaders often base this contention on a belief that people are at their best when they're 'up against it' and so a bit of pressure in the system – high demands and low slack – is what produces the best outcomes.

Some of the empirical research, at least at first glance, appears to bear this out. Several studies show a curvilinear (or U-shaped) relationship between slack time and output[15] – in other words, increasing slack from zero helps output up to a point, but beyond that 'Goldilocks' level, too much slack hurts output. What's noticeable about these studies, however, is that they all asked managers to work on a particular set of tasks. As might have been expected, having more time to do a particular set of tasks did result in people taking longer to do them – although, notably, the *quality* achieved in the activities was not measured, so they could have also been doing them to a higher standard. But where employees were asked not to work on a list of tasks but rather to deliver *a specific outcome* – as I have argued is essential in a strategic change effort – and where the employees were able to choose the tasks that would produce the outcome, then having some slack time increased the creativity of the ideas proposed and the complexity of the projects that were attempted. (In our terminology, fewer cosmetic, low-leverage, capability-killing 'quick wins' and more initiatives that actually make a fundamental difference to the business's long-term performance.)

So it seems the worry about too much slack leading to lower productivity might be mitigated by leaders structuring their asks as outcomes rather than tasks. And, in this context, slack has been shown to improve the quality of the work attempted and the overall delivery of the target.

But it's also worth dealing directly with the claim that people are at their best when they're 'up against it'. I frequently hear leaders claim this about themselves, wearing it almost as a badge of honour. They then translate this belief they have about themselves into the expectation they have for other people.

Except that this belief is just plain wrong. Because virtually all the evidence – from the latest neuroscience to a range of organizational studies – suggests our brains aren't at their best when we're stressed. In fact, our physical response to stress – whereby our bodies produce cortisol and adrenaline – prompts changes in our brain function. Put simply, the activity in the parts of our brain that deal with danger increases, while the activity in the parts that process information and govern our ability to be rational, to communicate effectively, to collaborate and to be creative, is suppressed. This response is designed to boost our chances of surviving physical danger, and makes sense when the threat is of that nature.[16] But when the source of stress is instead an impossible deadline or too many conflicting priorities, then a response that makes us less rational, less articulate, less creative and less likely to collaborate – all things that knowledge work requires – isn't particularly helpful.

So, if you're one of those leaders who still thinks people need to be flat-out with zero slack in order to be 'working', then you probably need to unlearn what it takes for people – yourself included – to truly be productive.

Now exactly how *much* slack time you need will depend on your role. Roles that require more creative thinking (coming up with new products or new ways of doing things) or integrative thinking (working out how different parts of the strategy or the firm should work together) will need to have more slack. Whereas roles where learning, creativity or connectivity are less important (in other words, roles which could essentially be AI-ed) will need less. My rule of thumb is: if your job can't be done by a robot, then you need some slack.

Practice Spotlight: Making Sure Employees Have the Opportunity to Stand Back, Reflect, Think and Learn

Arm, the technology company, offers employees regular sabbaticals to help them gain perspective and develop new ideas. Every four years, Arm-ers can take a four-week period of paid leave. This is in addition to their 30 days' paid annual holiday. As one senior manager at Arm said to me recently as he was about to return to work after his sabbatical:

It's a time when I can stand back and just think. I mean, I catch up with people, I spend time with family, I can take a proper holiday, but in amongst all that 'non-work' activity is some proper 'work' thinking. And it seems to happen without me thinking about it. So I feel that I'm coming back to work with more ideas, and better ideas, than I've had in a while.

And as Kirsty Gill, Arm's Chief People Officer, says of this investment in 'slack' time:

We don't do it to be nice – although we are nice. We do it because we're in the business of having cutting-edge ideas. To do that, people need to have time to really think and time off on sabbatical helps that happen.

Bulgari is another business that actively encourages employees – especially its designers – to refresh their creativity by spending time out of the business. It is famous for being a jewel-based jewellery house, meaning they design their pieces around the precious stones they have bought, rather than houses such as Cartier, which buy stones to populate the designs they have created. All of Bulgari's designs come from its in-house designers, so it's important that they don't get stale. The company believes that encouraging their designers to regularly spend time in other design-led businesses, often within the Milan design ecosystem, exposes them to new and different ideas and helps keep their designs fresh and modern.

Now, to some extent, managers need slack at *all* stages of the change – and, arguably, at all times in their working lives. But in the experience of these four cases – and in all change initiatives I've ever seen – having 'slack' becomes much more of an issue for managers after the first year of the change, because by then, other initiatives and 'priorities' may well have been added into their schedules. And so whatever slack they may have managed to carve out for themselves in Year 1 is now in danger of being crowded out by the amount of activities they have to do by Year 2.

So, what can leaders do to make sure managers have the slack that they, and the change, needs?

What the Ideal Case got right

The leaders in the Ideal Case helped managers *create* slack by making sure they weren't swamped with too many tasks or activities. For the Ideal Case, this didn't take much work by leaders at this stage: their work in Year 1 had laid the foundations. Helped by having sufficient budget and dedicated resources, and by Clarity about the multi-year outcomes being targeted, the managers in this case knew what to focus on. As the Head of Change remembered:

> We'd chosen which projects to work on depending on what fitted best with the outcomes we were targeting. If you are clear about *that*, it's not hard to work out what to do, and then focus on it.

But if the 'time famine'[17] that so many of us experience is to be prevented, then creating slack is not enough: leaders also need to help managers *protect* it by actively encouraging them to work on fewer things. This often requires leaders to say 'no' to managers, when they come to them with ideas for new initiatives. The CEO in the Ideal Case was doing exactly this – as one of his change team remembered:

> Left to our own devices, I think we'd have eaten up the extra time we had now. Our instinct was, 'OK, we've got some spare capacity, what else can we do?' But every time we went to [the CEO] with an idea for some

more initiatives, he'd say two things. One, focus on what you've already got on, unless you've now decided these projects aren't working. But if they're working, then focus on making them better. And two, if they're not working, then stop them and work out what to do instead. But don't do both. This was the mantra. And, honestly, it kept us disciplined in that second year. Without that coaching, I think we'd have piled up the projects and been overwhelmed pretty quickly.

Notice what work the CEO is doing here. He is pushing managers to focus by having 'green zone' conversations with them. This is very different from the old approach of a leader sitting down with managers and 'helping' them decide what activities they should prioritize. Let me say it again: that's not 'helping'. That's doing their 'blue zone' job for them. *Your* job now, as a leader, is to stick to the 'green zone', i.e. to reiterate (if you need to) why the change is needed and what it should deliver and then leave it to managers to decide how to deliver it. And because this CEO was pushing managers to decide and to justify their decisions in the context of what needed to be delivered, managers never felt that he was shutting down their new ideas; rather, they felt they were being coached to stay focused on these outcomes.[18]

Notice that the CEO in the Ideal Case was asking these questions – about what was working and why – to managers who, because of their early 'zero glam' work on data, processes and other fundamentals in Year 1, had a solid understanding of how and why change was happening in their business. As another manager working on the change recalled:

[The CEO] was pushing us to understand what was driving the improvement and then to use that understanding to prioritize the activities we worked on. By the second year, we seemed to have a lot more time. The early work had been done and we had good data by now, so we were looking more closely at what we were working on and we were doing more iterations of each project. Gradually we cut down the number of things we were working on because gradually we developed a much more robust view of what the best things to work on were.

Because of this solid understanding of how and why improvements were happening, the Ideal Case cut the number of projects they worked on. By now, they didn't need as many projects to accomplish the same outcome. This in turn made it easier to understand those projects:

> By focusing on a few things, it's also possible for you to really understand why certain things are working or not, because you haven't got a million things to work out, just a few. So you really *can* understand each project and make it better.

Another benefit of having a smaller number of projects to work on was that these were highly visible. This drove greater accountability for outcomes among the teams. As one of the team members put it:

> So, if you're only doing a few things, then you have no choice but to make those work. You are properly on the hook for those. Whereas if you've got a million things on, you can lose some of the things that don't work, you can hide them in the mass of all the other things you have on.

Accountability was clearly felt in the Ideal Case, but this accountability didn't seem to put pressure on the team. What was it that helped these managers to feel empowered, rather than pressured, by the accountability that comes from working on a smaller number of high-visibility projects?

Well, part of the answer lies in what they were doing with the slack time they had. They were using it to, in their words, 'really understand each project and make it better'. This gave managers a sense of control over the work they were doing, because they understood the linkages between activities and outcomes, and so the work felt less random than in the other cases. Having a sense of control over one's own work has repeatedly been shown to be one of the most effective means of reducing workplace stress at all levels of an organization[19] – and so it proved here.

What the other cases got wrong

The CEO of the Early Momentum Case had supported the change with plentiful resources – both money and people – in Year 1. She'd also worked hard to deliver each of the Elements of Alignment – just as in the Ideal Case. But now, differences between this and the Ideal Case started to emerge. Why was that?

Partly, it was the missing Elements of Clarity right at the start – the absence of a big, multi-year target that would have forced the business to look at more fundamental improvements rather than simply the 'quick wins' on which they'd spent most of their effort so far. But part of it was also something this CEO was doing *now*: she never said 'no' to a new idea. As a result, she didn't help create, or protect, managers' slack. Unfortunately, at the time, her managers saw this as a positive. As one of the team put it:

> Every time we went to [the CEO] and said we could move the numbers a bit more if we did one more initiative, she said yes. There was never a 'no'. And we're all really smart, we like working hard, it feels entrepreneurial, so why wouldn't you want to do lots of new things and do as many of them as you can, right?

Well, actually, there is a cost to never saying 'no'. As was true in this business, it causes Focus to be lost and, as a result, the change becomes diluted. Just when the Ideal Case was culling projects to focus on the most impactful ones, the Early Momentum Case was adding in new projects – the new 'zero glam' work (which they only now recognized needed to be done) being added onto their existing 'quick wins'. The impact was two-fold. First, whatever slack managers had had, thanks to abundant resources, was now eroded. Second, with many more individual initiatives to analyze and manage – and therefore many more dots to join when it came to working out which projects were working and why – the Early Momentum managers didn't have time to learn which ones were most impactful. As a result, the return on their effort was being diluted because they weren't focusing on the projects which could have the greatest impact. The lack of Focus made learning harder, which, in turn, made it harder to know how to improve and what to Focus on.

In this sense, by failing to say 'no', and by failing to coach managers on how best to deploy their efforts, this CEO came closer, in my view, to stepping *out* than stepping *back*. As one of the team remembered:

> We'd been collecting data from the beginning, but by year 2, we had so much on that we didn't always have the time to use it. When the early improvements we'd made suddenly went backwards, we were by then so busy that it was even harder to find the time to work out why.

Of course, it wasn't really that their early improvements were going backwards: those improvements weren't now going wrong or being undone. It was simply that there were no more of them. With no more easy, 'quick wins' to make in Year 2, progress stalled. And so, relative to the previous quarter's results, the numbers looked worse. But the reason lay not in what was or wasn't being done in Year 2; rather, the reason lay in the inattention paid, in the very earliest stages of the change, to the boring, 'zero glam' work.

Another consequence of having too many projects on at the same time was that, in contrast with the Ideal Case, when an individual project failed, it was less visible and so there was less pressure to explain what had gone wrong and to learn from it. Fewer people were asking questions, because fewer people even saw that this individual project – one of around 25 – had failed. And so the teams working on them were much more likely just to move on, turning to something else or starting something new.

The work was even less focused in the Under The Radar and Road Runner Cases. Because their CEOs hadn't publicly specified target outcomes – let alone a big, multi-year one – managers hadn't known how to choose the best priorities to work on during Year 1. Nor had these leaders explained how this new strategy fitted with current strategies, something that could have helped managers decide what of their existing workload to cull.

This early situation was exacerbated by the shortage of budget in both these cases – caused in part, of course, by the absence of a large, clear outcome-based target. The cumulative impact was that these managers were extremely busy. There was no slack for them:

> We had so much on. All the old work we'd been doing before this new strategy, plus all the new work. Plus, not enough budget. It was doable if all the projects were going OK, but if there was an issue, even something pretty minor, we just had to put the fire out. We had no capacity to do more than that. And it was starting to feel like all we were *doing* was putting fires out. It was at this point that the issues with it being under the radar really started to come home to us. (The Under The Radar Case)

> We were so busy. We did our best and I personally focused on the behaviours that had been asked for – because that was something I could do. But it just felt like we were always up against it. There was never a breather. (The Road Runner Case)

Notice a couple of things from these quotes. First, that these are perfect definitions of having no slack. No time to take a breath and reflect on progress, time only to work on the short-term task. No time to fundamentally fix issues, time only to heroically deal with the symptoms.

Second, notice that these star managers were still trying to do their best and so they focused on delivering the parts of the change that they *could* deliver, namely the parts that leaders had been clearest about. And that's an important lesson for leaders: good managers will try their best to deliver the things you clearly ask for. So ask for the things that really matter, or else you'll leave your best managers just trying to make sense of what they should be doing.

As we saw in the Ideal Case, Focus requires a predisposition to tweak existing projects rather than start additional ones. Not only did the

Under The Radar CEO not actively encourage that, he was often the one asking for more projects to be added, as the Head of Change recalled:

> I think the culprit here was actually the CEO … Even when our instinct was to focus a bit more, to improve what we'd started first and only then move on to the next thing, he'd be asking us for something else. Often these ideas seemed to come from him speaking to the important stakeholders in the firm. Perhaps he'd had a meeting with the sales guys and they'd been complaining about something. All of a sudden *that* would become a new project that we'd have to work on.

Notice that the underlying reason why this was happening had occurred a year earlier – when this CEO hadn't fully explained the extent of the change that needed to happen. Exacerbated by not having the change on the regular agenda of the SLT, this CEO had never got buy-in from his leadership team for it. As a result, it cost the sales guys nothing to ask for an additional, and often conflicting, priority to be added to the change team's To-do List – because they had no sense of the trade-offs involved. The CEO *did* have a sense of the trade-offs involved, but because he hadn't established Clarity and Alignment in Year 1, *he* was now the one who had to referee the still-conflicted interests of his SLT. By not stepping up earlier, he now had much more to do – and much less opportunity to step back.

The result for the Under The Radar Case was an increasing lack of integration of their efforts, across their myriad projects. We see from this case how a lack of slack – to foster learning – means managers aren't able to focus on the few projects that matter most. With too much on and not enough time to learn, whatever Clarity or Alignment you achieved in the early days will become compromised. As the Under The Radar's Head of Change put it:

> So, I think we had enough Clarity early on. It might not have been widely shared, but in the team we knew the outcome we had to deliver.

The real problems came later. And it wasn't because our target changed, but because it got crowded out – by the sheer volume of work and the 'fix this' requests that were coming at us.

But it wasn't just managers who were busy in the 'non-Ideal' cases: leaders too were still being pulled into far too many micro conversations about projects and asked far too many times by managers what direction to take. And because they had failed to prioritize – they had simply layered this new strategy onto previous strategies – they too were now suffering under the burden of having too many things to do. It's worth rehearsing again why this was.

- In the **Under The Radar** and **Road Runner Cases**, there was too much on right from the start, because leaders had not explained how this new strategy fitted with existing priorities, and so existing projects were not culled to make way for this new strategy. The absence of clear target outcomes made choosing what to work on even harder, because there was no outcome to link activities to, or to gauge their success against;

- In the **Early Momentum Case**, however, their CEO *had* explained how this new strategy fitted, so those teams *could* have culled projects and started with 'cleared decks' as we had seen in the Ideal Case. The reason this hadn't happened was a failure to give a different kind of Clarity – namely to choose a large, multi-year target and to make clear that this would require a fundamental change and not just some cosmetic 'quick wins'. Choosing to work on lots of 'quick wins' – enabled by abundant resources – meant that by the start of Year 2, the Early Momentum Case already had a myriad of projects on the go. This became worse *during* Year 2 because of the CEO's failure to provide Focus: she never said 'no' to a new idea and wasn't coaching her managers to refine or tweak existing projects, so the cumulative workload grew.

And so, for different reasons, both leaders and managers in all three of the 'non-Ideal' cases found themselves busy with too many activities and therefore not enough bandwidth to be noticing what really mattered. As a result, the senior leaders in these three cases – because of a mix of prior failings, in Clarity or Alignment; coupled with a lack of Focus now – were still having to step up and be involved at precisely the time when they ought to have been able to step back.

In contrast, for the senior leaders in the Ideal Case, they really could start to step back at this stage (Year 2 onwards). They were enabling this by pushing their managers to Focus – ensuring they had slack time and coaching them to refine rather than add to the projects they were working on.

Notice that helping managers create and protect their slack takes discipline from leaders. They can't be asking for 'additional priorities' or loading managers with new work. Nor can they be tinkering with the change, or second-guessing the decisions managers have made about how to organize their work. (See the Practice Spotlight 'How Leaders Can Eat Up Managers' Slack – and What to Do About It' opposite for an example of a leader who did exactly this.) Leaders will also have to decide to say 'no' to attractive new ideas they may come across if these deviate from the objectives of the change. This is the work of 'stepping back' that managers – and the change itself – need from leaders now.

How leaders do this is covered in more detail in the final part of this chapter – in 'The "Work" of Focus' section. But the fact that only one of the cases managed this – see the table below – tells us that this stepping back work is perhaps harder than it sounds.

	Ideal	EM	UTR	RR
Element 1: Leaders need to make sure managers have 'slack'. This means:				
a) they need to help them create slack by making sure managers don't have too much on; and	☑	☒	☒	☒
b) they need to help them protect their slack by actively encouraging managers to refine or cull projects, rather than add to them	☑	☒	☒	☒

But creating slack for managers, and then helping them protect it, is not all that Focus requires. There's a second Element – one that might be even harder for leaders to achieve, especially if they are prone to the Drama or the Activity Delusions.

Practice Spotlight: How Leaders Can Eat Up Managers' Slack – and What to Do About It

Leaders can eat up managers' slack even without meaning to. One of the most common ways they do this is by interfering with the process by which managers prioritize their own work. It's another example of leaders moving in on managers' 'blue zone' territory, causing pressure on every part of the system as a result. Here, leaders essentially decide that they can re-prioritize managers' work, as and when they feel they need to. This messes up the process for the rest of the work – the work that leaders effectively de-prioritize by intervening – and reduces the overall amount of slack available to managers.

I have *lots* of examples of leaders doing this. One of my favourites – and I have anonymized the names here to protect the guilty – is the case of a London-based specialist insurance broker. Originally spun out of one of the Lloyds of London syndicates and backed by the balance-sheet strength of a major insurance company, this small group of experts offered speciality insurance for global shipping firms. This was highly technical work: each risk (for example, a ship going from Singapore to San Francisco at a particular time of year with a particular cargo) would be analyzed and priced by a team of specialist underwriters and brokers working together, using industry data, their cumulative experience of the sector and their knowledge of the market appetite for this type of risk. These terms would be offered to the client and, if they were happy with the premium and the conditions, the deal was done.

When a new piece of work came in – often over the phone, in the first instance – the underwriter would give an initial estimate of how long the quote would take to put together. For the first few months of the operations, the team delivered 95 per cent of all quotes within the time they had estimated.

Helped by their strong relationships within Lloyds, this team quickly built a reputation for pricing risk faster and more competitively than the established companies. They won more and more work. Gradually, the work outstripped the small team's ability to respond. The percentage of quotes being delivered within the estimated time fell to below 80 per cent, and clients were starting to complain about the time they were having to wait.

While the team sought to hire more underwriters – not easy, given the specialist nature of the work – the head of the team (let's call him Derek) had a solution for his clients. A highly respected broker in the sector, he had a number of high-profile clients and he didn't want them waiting longer than the promised deadline for their quotes. So when a request from one of *his* clients came in, he would personally call the underwriter to make sure they were prioritizing his client's quote above whatever else they were working on. Underwriters knew that if Derek called, that client would now become their priority. (In fact, when talking with other underwriters about what they were working on, they would refer to how many 'Derek clients' they had on their books.)

The impact on the work was immediate. An underwriter who may have been halfway through pricing the risk for one client now had to drop this, pick up Derek's work and price that instead. This switching cost ate up time and the disruption of moving from one file to another threatened quality – meaning even more time was needed to check the pricing and terms being offered. As a result, total processing time (for all the quotes being produced) increased. And, within this, some clients – the ones whom Derek had effectively *de*-prioritized when he intervened on behalf of *his* clients – were now waiting much, much longer for a quote than they had been promised. Meantime, the response time for Derek's clients improved, even to the point where he questioned whether additional underwriters were needed after all.

It was only when one of the group's largest clients (who happened *not* to be a 'Derek client') threatened to take their business elsewhere unless response times improved, that Derek agreed to hire another underwriter. This took pressure off the others, response times recovered and client satisfaction improved. But even with the additional resource, which meant his clients were no longer at risk of waiting too long for their quotes, Derek continued to call the underwriters to ask them to prioritize his clients. He'd become used to jumping the queue when the system was broken and he didn't want to stop just because it was now fixed.

The most senior underwriters in the team explained to Derek the impact that his queue-jumping was having, both on clients (greater variability in response times than should be the case, given the balance of work and resource) and on the underwriters (less control over their own work and less slack in which to reflect on and improve their processes). Derek agreed to refrain from asking for special treatment and gave everyone in the group permission to call him out if he lapsed into his old habits. He asked for regular feedback both on how he was doing on this, and on how the new resourcing levels and work design was working. As well as measuring waiting times for all clients, the team split this out between 'Derek' and 'non-Derek' clients, with the aim of normalizing processing times between these two groups. This metric was a good 'canary in the mine' if Derek ever lapsed into his old ways.

And the lesson for leaders from this example? Well, of course you need to fix the underlying problem – whether it's a poor process, or inadequate resourcing. And please also pay attention to problems even when you're not being impacted by them – perhaps because your power has insulated you from their effects, as was the case here. These problems are still causing pain somewhere in the system and you need to use your power to help fix them. But then, even after the problem has been fixed, leaders still need to make sure they are not messing up the new system by abusing their power. Asking for open and honest feedback from other senior leaders is a good way to help you gain some insight on this, as is using indicator metrics to help you see where issues are arising as a result of the unintended consequences of your actions.

Element 2 of Focus: Be patient and focus on the learning

The second thing leaders need to do to enable managers to Focus is to show patience for the change they've asked for. This means they need to focus people's attention on the long-dated, multi-year target, rather than on the shorter-term milestones. They also need to balance the need to deliver with the need to understand and learn about what's being delivered.

Showing patience for long-term progress doesn't mean leaders aren't showing interest in the change, or asking for regular updates on how it's going. But in all these conversations, leaders should be stressing that this will take time and that learning about what is working, and why, is as important as whatever short-term improvements are being made.

Crucially, showing patience isn't a passive endeavour. (For a great example of how to be 'actively patient', see the Practice Spotlight on Hendrick's Gin opposite.) On the contrary, showing interest in the change and asking about progress are critical at this time. There is, remember, an important distinction between stepping *back* – which is what managers need from leaders now – and stepping *out*. So you still need to show interest and give the change your time and attention, but in ways that leave the onus of the work – and the accountability for these long-term outcomes – with managers.

Practice Spotlight: How 'Active Patience' Delivered Long-term Value for Hendrick's

First launched in 1999, and ranked the 'Best Gin in the World' by the *Wall Street Journal* in 2003, Hendrick's is a high-juniper gin made by the Scotland-based distilling family, William Grant & Sons. Sold in an apothecary-style bottle and served with a slice of cucumber rather than lemon, it has a high price point – usually around 50 per cent more expensive than ordinary gin – and, famously, is never discounted in supermarkets. So how did this wonder-product come about?

A major reason for developing a gin – a 'white liquid' – was that most of William Grant's other products were 'brown liquids' such as whiskies that could take up to 30 years to mature in casks. White liquid such as gin could be made and sold without the need for maturation, helping William Grant produce a higher return on capital over time. But this new product still had to be developed and its brand established. And that *would* take time.

It initially took two years (and 21 distillations) for Grant's master distiller David Stewart and chemist Lesley Gracie to decide on the right combination of juniper, cucumber, rose and eight other different botanicals that should make up the new gin. The company was convinced the product was right, but when it was first launched, Hendrick's was not an immediate success. In fact, it would take years for it to become the premium brand that they had envisaged.

What's important about this story is what the teams at William Grant's were doing during these years. They were not passively waiting for sales to improve. Instead, they were actively iterating towards a more successful product – changing the packaging to make sure it conveyed the brand's distinctiveness (eventually settling on the often surreal Victoriana imagery that we see on the Hendrick's packaging today), and designing increasingly unusual marketing campaigns (World Cucumber Day, explorations for South American botanicals and decorating a London Underground station with rose- and cucumber-scented posters, are just three such examples).

Gradually these efforts positioned Hendrick's as 'A most unusual gin' (its established tagline since 2003). After each iteration of a new packaging or marketing idea, the brand team reviewed what they had learned and how much progress the brand had made. Using this feedback, they started on another loop of improvement and learning until the brand broke through.

By 2008, the years of work were paying off: global sales exceeded 100,000 cases. By 2012, this was up to 364,000 cases and in 2017, it exceeded 1 million. I recall a conversation I had with Stella David, William Grant's CEO at the time: she described Hendrick's as 'our overnight success that took 10 years'. It's a good example of how a business can use long-term targets (they wanted a white liquid in the high-price, premium space) to shape ideas that are improved, by feedback and learning, over time. And what made this possible was having leaders with sufficient patience to see it through.

It may be that only a privately owned business such as William Grant & Sons would have been able to be *this* patient. But the essential insight from the Hendrick's story is that patience isn't passive: it takes repeated rounds of hard work, together with the insight and courage to learn from each iteration you put out into the market. It is active, hard-working patience that delivers value in the long term.

The fundamental requirement here is that leaders understand – and don't forget – that the extent of the change they've asked for will take time. This is a strategic change, after all. Provided they have taken all the essential actions during Year 1 – i.e. they've established Clarity and they've Aligned the business around the outcome they've asked for – part of the leader's job now is to wait until the results of these actions play out. My MIT colleague Peter Senge would describe this as the 'take two aspirin and wait' rule – i.e. if you believe in the medicine, you do actually have to wait until it takes effect, rather than taking more, or (even worse) different medicine before the first dose has produced results.[20]

If, on the other hand, leaders go back on their message that this will take time, and instead start pushing for quick results, then even now managers might respond by choosing to spend time and budget on some cosmetic 'quick wins' to give progress a bit of a spurt. And, as is usually the case with a 'quick win', *it will work* – albeit only in the short term – providing a quick sugar-rush to the pace of change. But it will have little lasting impact and can in fact interrupt the more fundamental work of change that managers need to be focusing on at this time. So leaders need to stay both *patient and engaged* for as long as the change takes.

The second part of being patient is that leaders must balance the need to deliver the change with the need to understand and learn from the work that is being done. This is only possible if they have truly stepped up in Year 1, because it is on the foundation of Clarity and Alignment – especially by resourcing and measurement – that long-term learning is built.

Here's the logic. If there is Clarity about the outcomes being targeted and good enough data being captured to understand why projects are working (or not), then understanding and learning becomes possible. And if there are sufficient resources devoted to the project, and managers have sufficient slack in their days to have the time to understand and learn, then this makes the possibility of learning more likely. But that's still not enough. What's needed now is that leaders signal that understanding and learning are *valued*. Put simply, this means leaders giving as much time and attention to 'how' and 'why' something is working (or not), as they do to 'what' has been achieved.

This is where being prone to the Activity or Drama Delusions can do leaders, managers and their change-efforts real harm. If you expect – or want – change to be all about delivery, then you will make it all about delivery – by the questions you ask, by what you agitate for and by what you give your time to. And you will lead other people in the firm to believe the same. If, on the other hand, you believe that change is achieved and sustained by truly understanding the dynamics of your business – why customers buy from you and why they don't, why it costs X to produce a unit, rather than 0.8X – then you will start behaving as if learning matters just as much as delivering. And that will impact the work that people do. Because as scholars such as Peter Senge have argued (see the Science Spotlight below), it is only by developing this *learning* orientation within your organization that you make delivering more likely *and* less risky.

Science Spotlight: Building a Learning Orientation Within an Organization

MIT Senior Lecturer Peter Senge has long argued that one of the reasons organizations are less successful than they should be is because they focus too much on delivering (what he terms 'performance') and not enough on learning. His seminal book, *The Fifth Discipline*[21] describes how organizations need to become much more interested and invested in being 'learning organizations'.

The outcomes of dialling-up the focus on learning – and making time for it and giving leader attention to it – offer benefits for both organizations and the individuals within them. Jobs become more interesting when the point of work becomes not just to deliver something but also to learn how and why it worked. And outcomes become less random, as our understanding of how and why certain interventions have the effects they do enables us to reduce the variance in those outcomes over time. That enables the organization to move to a place where it can both deliver *and* learn, because by learning and getting better at predicting outcomes, delivery is more likely and less risky.

For most organizations, getting the balance right between performance and learning means dialling-up their orientation towards learning. And indeed the starting point for this new virtuous circle, whereby the organization can both perform *and* learn, is most definitely to focus on learning first. In other words, you can't improve learning by asking for more performance, but you can and will improve performance by asking for more learning. For leaders of businesses who face immediate performance issues, this can feel like a Faustian pact: I can just hear you saying, 'Wait, I'm worried about performance, so I should stop worrying so much about performance? How does *that* work?'

The answer lies in understanding *why* performance isn't happening. In other words, why is there a variance between what you are predicting will happen, because of a certain intervention, and what actually happens? Only by properly understanding variance can you hope to reduce it. And the only way to understand variance is to devote time to learning about the linkages between inputs (such as activities) and outcomes.

What that means in practice – as I have argued in this chapter in the context of strategic change – is leaders spending more time talking about what's being learned from the work being done, rather than simply just asking about what's been delivered. This doesn't mean that there is *no* focus on what's being delivered – you absolutely need to know how the change is tracking against the target outcomes in order to identify the variance you need to explain. But describing the outcome isn't enough: you need to *understand* it. That requires leaders to signal the importance of this 'learning' work by asking as many questions about 'how' and 'why' outcomes have happened as they do about what's been delivered. Leaders also need to be genuinely interested in the answers to these questions.

Generating high-quality answers to these 'how' and 'why' questions is the job of managers and so, again, this requires them to have sufficient slack in their working week. They won't be able to understand 'how' and 'why' something happened if they're working flat out just to deliver the 'what'.

It also requires leaders to have the expectation that, within the long-term time frame of the change, the activities being worked on at any given time will be refined until they are working as a *process* – i.e. just another business-as-usual way of doing things – rather than remaining as a series of unintegrated projects, which is typically how they will have started off. That is how change becomes the new normal, so that it can continue without the need for ongoing heroics from either managers or leaders. And all of that depends on how much of a learning orientation leaders have shaped within their organization.

What the Ideal Case got right

First of all, the CEO in the Ideal Case stressed that this change would take time, evidencing this by having a big, long-dated, outcome-based target together with some shorter-term milestones to help track progress. As his Head of Change remembered:

> So right from the start, he had been clear that this would take time. I mean, we all knew you couldn't do 30 per cent in a year! That was always

there as that big, long-term target. So the time frame we had in mind was a long one and every message we'd had – from what he said, to the targets and the new KPIs – supported that view.

The Ideal Case was also giving as much time and attention to learning from their efforts ('how' and 'why' has this happened?) as to describing what had been delivered. As the Head of Change told me:

We had freedom to play around and experiment and try things out. But what made that meaningful was the fact we had time. Time in the day-to-day to understand how and why things turned out as they did. And time in the longer term because of the big, long-term target. So we had time to try things, fail at some of them, hopefully improve and still be able to make the big, multi-year target, because it was a while away. Of course, we had milestones for each quarter but we'd often not hit them. The important thing was working out why we hadn't hit them because the really important thing was hitting the big 30 per cent target. The conversations [with the CEO] focused on 'What's going on here and why?' If you couldn't answer that question, then he had an issue. But if you really understood why, then he trusted us that progress would come.

An example of how to use both long-term targets and shorter-term milestones to good effect is given in the Practice Spotlight below – Balancing Performance and Learning.

Practice Spotlight: Balancing Performance and Learning by Understanding How to Use Long-term Targets and Short-term Milestones

When Arm was acquired by the Japanese technology conglomerate, SoftBank, in 2016, it became a private company. No longer did CEO Simon Segars and his CFO have to troop off to the City to explain to public markets or their institutional investors why a particular quarter's numbers had turned out higher or lower than expectations. Many within Arm, including Segars himself, felt liberated by the change.

However, the external pressure of markets – and the discipline that this brought to the business – was replaced by a new pressure: SoftBank's CEO, Masayoshi Son, had big ambitions for Arm. He was looking for exponential growth and he wanted to see progress. So although the visits to investors were no longer public, they would still take place, albeit now behind closed doors in Tokyo, and with a much bigger, longer-term target in mind.

Segars and his team re-designed Arm's internal processes and disciplines to reflect these new demands. Ahead of every trip to Tokyo to update Masa-san (as he is known within Arm), Segars would meet with his senior team to understand what progress had been made and whether the business was on track. Early on during these meetings, Segars detected that people were focusing more on meeting the short-term milestones than understanding what these told them about their business. This was partly because the business was still in the habit of making its quarterly numbers; this habit survived even the change of ownership structure, which meant quarterly numbers no longer mattered.

So Segars spent considerable time emphasizing to Arm's senior leaders that what they needed to focus on was the big, multi-year target, rather than the individual short-term milestones. As he said in one of his early Senior Leadership Team meetings ahead of a Tokyo update:

The milestones are important only because they help us gauge our progress. And if we are not progressing as we expected, then they force us to understand and explain to ourselves and each other why not. But they are *not* the things we need to hit: what we need to hit is the five-year target.

Another aspect that was important in focusing people on the long-term target rather than the short-term milestones was paying attention to language. In several of the early meetings to report on progress, people often used the terms 'milestones' and 'targets' interchangeably, when actually these terms meant very different things. The 'target' was the large, multi-year goal to grow exponentially; 'milestones' related to the short-term metrics used to track progress towards this goal. As someone familiar with these early conversations remembered:

> It sounds like semantics but when you call everything a target, then you give equal status to all the numbers, short-term and long-term, inputs and outputs. That's clearly not legitimate. But when you're lazy with language, that's what can happen. So we needed to get much more deliberate about the terms we used, so we could be clear about what really mattered.

It's important to notice that there were two aspects to Segars' work here. First, he spent time emphasizing that it was the long-term target that really mattered. The milestones were important but only because of what they could tell us about progress. The second, and critical, aspect was how much time and effort he spent pushing the people who were reporting on these milestones to explain the variance between what they had expected and what they had delivered. As one of his senior leaders, responsible for a significant part of the business, put it:

> It's not the end of the world if you don't make a milestone. It *is* the end of the world if you can't explain why. We all know that to deliver the kind of growth we're going for, many of the things we're working on won't work the first n times you

try them. Things won't turn out as you expect, because you don't really know what to expect. But if you don't understand *why* things have turned out differently, if you can't explain it and what it means for how you should re-calibrate your expectations going forward, then that suggests you're not improving. And if you're not improving, your chances of success next time round are no better. That's not acceptable.

These two aspects – focusing on the long-term target and then using short-term milestones to understand and explain any variance between what was expected and what was achieved – have been critical to Arm's success in transforming from being a quoted company delivering decent growth to a privately held company capable of delivering exponential growth.

What the other cases got wrong

Patience, and a focus on what was being learned, were much less evident in the other cases. The CEO in the Early Momentum Case hadn't asked for a big improvement at the start, or communicated that this would take a long time: these managers only had annual targets (rather than milestones) and so these were what they focused on. As one of their change team put it:

There was never a sense that this was a big, multi-year effort. It was always focus on the quarter, there's the target, let's make sure we hit it. And if the numbers went down at all, there was pressure to do more to get them back up again.

This focus here on short-term milestones rather than long-term, outcome-based targets was of course partly what had led them to choose so many 'quick wins' in Year 1. This had crowded out the time and effort that could have gone into working on data, processes and more fundamental improvements. And this now made it harder to focus managers on learning rather than just delivering. Whereas the Ideal Case was balancing the need to deliver with the need to learn – and starting to see that it was by focusing more on learning that you were better able to deliver – things were different in the Early Momentum Case. Their profusion of projects meant that virtually all of the team's time was taken up with just delivering those. They had almost no time to analyze what was happening or to work out patterns between certain combinations of activities and certain outcomes:

> So even though we had decent data by now, we didn't really have the time to analyze it and learn from it. Not least because that wasn't what we were being asked about. There was definitely more of an emphasis on achieving the numbers. We were a lot less concerned about how or why we achieved them.

Things were even worse in the Under The Radar and Road Runner Cases. Their CEOs hadn't stressed that the change would take time either, nor had they introduced big, multi-year, outcome-based targets requiring large, long-term improvements. With too many short-term 'priorities' being pursued, managers in these cases still needed leaders to arbitrate on which of these short-term 'priorities' was more urgent. These two CEOs had also failed to revise KPIs for leaders across the firm. This meant managers still needed leader help to secure air-time with other departments on whom their work depended. By failing to step up in Year 1, these leaders had made it harder for themselves to step back in Year 2, because managers still needed them to be involved. And by the end of Year 2, there was a sense that these managers were running just to stand still:

> We didn't spend a lot of time understanding why things were happening. It was all about getting it done. We had so much on by now, and the

To-do list seemed to be growing every day, we were just focusing on getting the work done that was in front of our nose. And we needed the CEO's help to work out what was most important – or at least most urgent – on that To-do list. (The Under The Radar Case)

We had an annual objective by now. But it wasn't shared by the other departments so we very often needed [the CEO's] help to knock heads together. (The Road Runner Case)

In all three cases, having too little emphasis on learning (Element 2 of Focus) is worsened by the lack of slack (Element 1). But, even without adequate slack, leaders could have changed the balance in the conversations they were having with managers: they could have asked a bit more about learning and a bit less about delivery, a bit more about 'how' and 'why' and a bit less about 'what'. (As we saw in the Practice Spotlight, Balancing Performance and Learning, on page 217.)

Had they done so, it would have become clear that managers needed more slack if they were to have the time to understand and therefore be able to answer leaders' 'how' and 'why' questions. And maybe then the vicious cycle that we see in these 'non-Ideal' cases – not enough slack means not enough learning means not enough prioritization means even less slack – could have been reversed.

	Ideal	EM	UTR	RR
Element 2: Leaders need to show patience by:				
a) focusing the work on the long-dated, multi-year target, rather than the shorter-term milestones; and	☑	☒	☒	☒
b) balancing the need to deliver with the need to understand and learn	☑	☒	☒	☒

Diagram 6.1: Summary of how the Cases delivered Focus

	Ideal	EM	UTR	RR
Element 1: Leaders need to make sure managers have 'slack'. This means:				
a) they need to help them create slack by making sure managers don't have too much on; and	☑	☒	☒	☒
b) they need to help them protect their slack by actively encouraging managers to refine or cull projects, rather than add to them.	☑	☒	☒	☒
Element 2: Leaders need to show patience by:				
a) focusing the work on the long-dated, multi-year target, rather than the shorter-term milestones; and	☑	☒	☒	☒
b) balancing the need to deliver with the need to understand and learn.	☑	☒	☒	☒

Leadership lessons from Ask #3

The first lesson for leaders is that, again, the type of leadership required to help deliver Focus is both transformational *and* transactional. When it comes to helping managers create and protect sufficient slack in their working lives, leaders first need to encourage a disciplined link between activities (which managers choose) and outcomes (set at the start). This is very much in the domain of transactional leadership, requiring as it does, a focus on targets and the process by which they are delivered.

Meantime, leaders also need to coach managers to form a view about how their projects are going and why. Managers need to be the ones coming up with recommendations about whether to persevere with these initiatives – albeit with tweaks at each iteration – or to pivot, and choose different projects instead. The coaching skills that this requires from leaders (they are not *telling* their managers whether to persevere or pivot, but rather *coaching* them to come to a view); and the empowerment that they give managers as a result, both appear to be more closely related to the definition of transformational leadership. So, as was true for both Clarity and Alignment, leaders need to deploy *both* types of leadership – albeit in different ways – to deliver what managers need as the change enters its second year.

The second lesson we can take from what enables Focus in Years 2–3 is that the mid- to late-stage work of change is highly dependent on the early-stage work that was (or wasn't) done. If leaders fail to deliver the four Elements of Clarity, then their work on Focus will be harder than it needed to be. That difficulty will be compounded if even one of the four Elements of Alignment is missing by the end of Year 1.

But we know also that there are some Elements of both Clarity and Alignment that are more important than others when it comes to enabling Focus. And it turns out, the most important ones are the ones delivered by transactional, rather than purely transformational, leadership. For example, if the new change isn't explained in the context of the current strategy, so that existing initiatives can be culled; or if the outcomes being targeted aren't clear; or if leaders haven't messaged that this is a long-term effort and signalled this clearly with a large, long-term target, together with some short-term milestones embedded in revised metrics and KPIs – if any or all of these transactional Elements of Clarity are missing, then Focus is almost impossible to deliver, however much you are doing the two 'Focus' activities (i.e. slack and patience) that we've talked about in this chapter. And that's because there's little point in having slack if you don't know how to use it – and how can you, if you didn't have Clarity about outcomes right from the start? And there's little point in being patient if you don't know what you're being patient for – again, caused by a lack of Clarity, primarily in the outcome being targeted.

Thus, it is only if leaders have stepped up in the early stages – by doing more than you might expect, and in different ways than you might believe necessary – that they make it possible for themselves to step back now in these later stages. Focus is the first way in which you step back, but you'll see this theme come up again when we turn to Consistency in the next chapter.

And what do you do if you get to Year 2 and you realize that you didn't step up sufficiently in the early stages? If you realize that the outcomes you set as targets weren't specific enough, or if you didn't make it clear that this was a long-term effort; or if you didn't make the connections between this change and the past clear enough? The best advice I can give you is to go back and re-do the 'step up' work. You know what that work is now, so go back and do it properly. It really is a case of better late than never.

Of course, you can't re-do this work without making it clear that you're going back to make amends. Recognize your omissions, own up to what you didn't do and describe the ways in which this is holding back managers, the change and yourself. And then explain what you're going to do instead – now that you know what needs to be done.

The 'work' of Focus

When I talk to leaders about this new approach, I can see that they are intuitively more drawn to the two 'stepping up' stages – Clarity and Alignment – than to the 'stepping back' dimensions, the first one of which we've covered in this chapter. I have asked a number of them why that is. The answer is nearly always some version of the following: that they believe stepping up is what leaders *should* do, so they have no problem with that part. But this stepping back part, isn't that just a bit lazy? It doesn't feel right. Isn't it tantamount to letting people down?

So, I am going to reiterate here that achieving Focus takes *work*. It may be a different *type* of work from the kind we saw in the first two stages, and different also from the type of work many leaders are used to doing, but it is work nevertheless. And it will take as much discipline and effort and self-awareness from you as anything that you did in the Clarity or Alignment stages. Because, again, stepping back does not mean stepping out.

The work of Focus is the work by which leaders help managers not only to *stay in* the 'blue zone', but to *thrive* in it. That's why, as a leader, you shouldn't worry that 'stepping back' is in some way letting managers down. It's just the opposite. This 'stepping back' work requires leaders to coach managers to make 'blue zone' decisions on their own. The leader's role is to provide 'green zone' context about why we're doing this, what it will deliver and how we should be behaving. And so that managers can truly thrive in their 'blue zones', leaders need to be coaching them to make choices that create and protect slack, so that managers have the time and capacity to do that 'blue zone' role to the best of their ability. One of the main ways to do that is to coach managers to refine, rather than add to, the projects they have on their plate. And if new projects do need to be added – because the existing portfolio of work isn't getting the job done – then leaders need to push managers to cull those projects that aren't working so their total activity level does not increase.

I think of this as the equivalent of having your change programme managed by the American Tea Party. They're the fiscally conservative,

Republican group in the US that believes in small government and low taxes. They have also advocated that every time a new law is passed by Congress, an old law should be revoked, so that the total number of rules that govern citizens doesn't passively accumulate over time. Whatever you think of their politics, I think they might be onto something when it comes to managing projects to maintain slack. The idea of culling projects to make room for new ones so that the total amount of work doesn't passively accumulate over time is a good one. And the way to do it, whether you're a leader or a manager, is to ask yourself and your teams the same questions that the CEO in the Ideal Case asked – what I term the *Tea Party Test*:

1) Do you think your current set of activities is working? If so, why? (And you need to be honest and credible in this explanation.)

2) If they are, then focus on making them progressively better by learning from each iteration you go through and incorporating these insights into the next version.[22] This might be less exciting than trying something new, but if the answer to the first question really is 'yes', and the reasons why it's 'yes' are credible, then persevering with it – albeit with some tweaks based on the last iteration – really is what you should do.

3) Equally, if the answer to the first question is 'no' – i.e. you don't think the current set of activities is working – then what should we be doing *instead*? Scope out these new activities, clarifying why they will be better.

4) Work on these new, better activities, *instead* – not as well as. Cut the previous activities to free up bandwidth (and budget) for the new activities you've chosen instead, so that slack is preserved.

5) And then, once you've got some data on how these new activities are working, ask Questions 1–3 again about the progress you're making with this revised set of activities.

6) Repeat stages 1–5 until results appear.

This was precisely the process that the CEO in the Ideal Case was driving – and managers were gaining and maintaining slack as a result. That gave them time to stand back and reflect, time to improve and refine projects and time to make connections with other parts of the business. And it's only when managers are thriving in the 'blue zone' that leaders are able to stay firmly in the 'green zone' (where they, their managers and their organizations need them to be) without worrying that outcomes might be at risk.

Notice also that leaders are not *telling* their managers whether to persevere or pivot on any particular activity: rather, they are *coaching* them to come to a view and testing whether that view is credible. This requires leaders to have the right level of coaching skills and also to be comfortable asking questions rather than giving answers. This is a role with which not all leaders are comfortable. If you're one of those leaders who still needs to be the one who has all the answers, then this will definitely be a mindset shift for you. But know that coaching managers to be the ones with the answers and the ones who can make these decisions about what to work on (i.e. 'blue zone' work) is one of the most effective ways you can grow capability to whom you can safely delegate.

Assuming you *are* comfortable with asking questions rather than giving answers, then it's worth mentioning the skills that this requires:

- **First, you need to be able to ask genuinely open questions.** That doesn't just mean asking questions that don't have a yes/no answer. It also means asking questions that don't 'lead the witness' by implying that you already have the answer. 'Leading the witness' questions are what I call 'fake questions'. You know the ones I mean: the ones that aren't really questions at all, but rather are statements of your opinion, albeit with a slightly upwards intonation towards the end of the sentence. Fake questions are never a good idea but they are especially unhelpful in the coaching process because they communicate to managers that you're not really interested in the quality of their answer because you think you've already got the answer. In other words, fake questions signal to managers that you're not really 'stepping back'. And until and unless you step back, they won't properly step up and occupy the 'blue zone' – as you need them to do;

- **Second, you need to keep asking these open questions – questions that push managers to do the thinking for themselves – until they come to a view.** It might be tempting, especially when you sense that a manager may be struggling to come to a view, to 'help them out' by providing your view. But, believe me, this is not helping them out: this is short-changing them, and the process you've started. So stick with it: keep coaching rather than telling – and make sure you don't 'accidentally' give them the answer.

David Rock has termed these kinds of conversations 'thinking conversations' and the questions that facilitate them 'thinking questions'.[23] Imagine a manager comes to you with concerns about the progress she and her team are making. She starts by describing what isn't happening and then asks you to suggest what the team should do instead. It would be tempting to 'help' her by telling her your view– i.e. to enter the 'blue zone'. But to ensure she thrives in the 'blue zone' herself, you truly help her by asking questions that push her to think through the issue and come to her own view. Examples of questions you could use in this scenario might be:

- What most concerns you about progress so far?
- Why do you think this has happened?
- What's your view about the resources you've allocated to this?
- What do you think the options are now, given where we are?
- What's your favourite option right now?
- If we do that, what are you expecting to see?
- How can I best help you going forward?

By asking these questions of managers, leaders move away from being the provider of solutions (a distinctly 'blue zone' role which they ought not to be playing) and instead become a thinking partner for managers. This has three really helpful outcomes.

First, managers (rightly) maintain responsibility and accountability for determining the activities or solutions they work on. They don't give that work back to leaders. Indeed, by asking these 'thinking questions', leaders are actively giving the work (of choosing activities and finding solutions) back to managers – the people best placed to know which activities will have most impact. As a result, managers stay in the 'blue zone' and leaders stay in the 'green zone'.

Second, as a result of leaders staying in the 'green zone', they develop their 'green zone' muscles and preserve time for 'green zone' work, because the 'blue zone' doesn't encroach on them. And virtually every leader I know could use some strengthening of their 'green zone' muscles – so give yourself the opportunity to improve.

The third major benefit of having conversations where you coach, rather than conversations where you just tell, is that managers also develop their capability to develop solutions – they develop their 'blue zone' muscles, if you like. And so they should. Because this really is the manager's job now and it's their turn to excel in this role. So giving them every opportunity to do so – by pushing them to do more of the thinking and take more of the responsibility – is precisely what leaders should be doing. *This* is what stepping back looks like – and, as we said, there's nothing passive or disconnected about it. It's just a different type of work.

There is one call-out worth making about these kinds of conversations, ones that use 'thinking questions' to coach managers to come to their own answers. These conversations will take longer than conversations where leaders join managers in the 'blue zone' and just tell them what to do. Actually, these teaching and coaching conversations will typically take two to three times as long as a conversation where you just tell them what to do. Also, you might need to have several of these conversations, rather than it being one-and-done. This is just a fact of life and leaders need to bite the bullet and give these conversations the extra time they will require – *at least initially*. Because while a coaching conversation might take more time, the advantage is, once the manager leaves the conversation, it is the *manager* who owns the work and all the follow-up – not the leader. So having invested some time (stepped up) in the conversation itself, the result is that the leader gets more time back because they are not required for the follow-up work. And of course over time, these coaching conversations will take less time, and will need to happen less frequently, because the capability that you're building in managers means they need less and less input from you. So invest time and skill up-front and reap the rewards later on – a classic example of the 'step up, step back' philosophy.

To summarize what Focus requires in practice, I am including in the pages that follow some tips and watch-outs for both leaders and managers. As before, leaders and managers will need to judge whether they have sufficient Focus or not. If you haven't, the fix might be to double-down on the Focusing activities – slack and patience – that we've talked about in this chapter. Or it might be to look back at the earlier stages of the change because it may be that omissions in either the Clarity or Alignment stages – right at the start – are the reasons why managers are unable to Focus – and leaders unable to step back – now. So you may need to go back to those stages and 're-do' certain Elements from them in order to lay the foundations for delivering Focus. Sometimes that doesn't make it a quick fix, but it is the *best* fix.

Tips and Watch-outs to Help You Focus

Tips and Watch-outs for Leaders

- **Make sure you're really stepping back at this stage**. This means doing less and supporting more. While you're still talking about the new strategy at every opportunity and role-modelling the new actions and behaviours you've asked for, the main focus of your work now is to make sure your managers' 'blue zones' are kept as clear as possible;
- **Because stepping back doesn't mean stepping out**. While you're putting more of the onus – and accountability – for the work onto managers, you are still giving them the time and attention they need. You're still available when they need to see you, especially if they have issues. And you're still actively doing those things that promote their ability to focus on the change;
- **The activities that promote Focus**. You need to make sure that managers have enough slack. This means the time and capacity to stand back and reflect on what's working, to refine projects as they need to and to make connections with other parts of (and people in) the organization;
- **You need to help managers create slack**. First, make sure they don't have too much on. This means pushing them to choose the 'biggest bang for your buck' projects, bearing in mind the long-term target outcome. And if these target outcomes aren't clear or long-term enough to help them make these choices, go back and clarify them now. Better late than never;
- **You also need to help managers protect their slack**. You do this by ensuring they don't add in too many new projects as the change progresses. This may mean helping them say 'no' to new projects – or even saying 'no' for them. Use the *Tea Party Test* (page 227). If managers want to do something new, then the default position is that something has to go. Coach them to choose;
- **Focus them on the long-term targets and use milestones to track progress**. The short-term milestones aren't targets in themselves, but ways to help the team gauge progress. Make this distinction clear to managers. And if they don't hit a milestone, push them to understand why, so that it doesn't endanger the longer-term target;
- **Be as interested in what your managers are learning as in what they're delivering**. Whatever the status of the projects, keep asking about what they're learning. Understanding success is as important as understanding failure – so ask 'how' and 'why' questions about both of these outcomes. Encourage managers to ask themselves and their teams these questions, so this just becomes how they work, without you needing to be involved.

Tips and Watch-outs for Managers

- **Create slack for yourself and your team**. Make sure you agree to work on only the most impactful projects at the start of the change. Choose fewer than your instinct tells you that you can do – even if you have the resources for more. Make sure each project is directly linked to the long-term outcome being targeted. If the target outcomes aren't clear or long-term enough to help you choose what to work on, push leaders for greater Clarity;
- **Then make sure you protect it**. This means you can't add in too many new projects or other work as the change progresses. Keep being choosy about what you work on, discriminating on the basis of what will create the biggest impact on the outcome being targeted. If you find that you're getting pressure from leaders or other stakeholders in the business to add to your To-do list, know that you have to resist. Build coalitions to help you ward off these additional asks so that when you say 'no', people understand why;
- **Show the value of having thinking time** by always having smart, considered explanations of 'how' and 'why' things are working the way they are. This also helps leaders be patient. If you always come with thoughtful explanations of what's going on in the projects you're working on, this makes it easier for leaders to step back and let you get on with it;
- **Keep linking all the work your teams do to the long-term target**. Make this the focus of team conversations: why are we doing this and how should it impact outcomes? And use the same frame when you speak with leaders – focus on how what you're working on rolls up to deliver the target outcome. If you can't explain that, then you can expect them to start micromanaging more and focusing instead on the shorter-term milestones – because you're giving them no choice;
- **Talk about what you're learning as well as what you're delivering**. We're asking leaders to do this with you, but you need to do it too – with them and with your teams. Many of you will be in your roles because you're extremely good at delivering so you may need to actively reorient yourself to have more of a learning focus by asking and being interested in questions about 'how', 'why' and 'why not'. Don't just pay lip-service to this either: cultivate a genuine interest in this and use it to fuel better and less risky delivery;
- **Capture data on learning as well as on delivery** to improve the quality of your 'learning' and 'thinking' conversations. And just because the projects are going well, don't ease up on this: you need to learn from success as well as from failure because you never know when one might become the other. Only data can help you understand this and therefore give you a better chance of predicting.

CHAPTER SEVEN

Ask #4: Consistency

Now leave it alone until it's done

The second way in which leaders need to step back from Year 2 onwards is by providing managers with Consistency. What I mean by Consistency is that nothing should happen at this stage that is incompatible with the new strategy or change. In other words, leaders need to stick with the strategy until it is implemented.

Although the need for Consistency arises at the same time as the need for Focus (i.e. from Year 2 onwards), Consistency is needed for a different reason. Whereas a lack of Focus is *dilutive* to the change – because it distracts you into other activities and means you don't have time to learn – a lack of Consistency is *corrosive* to the change because it can introduce conflict into the organization. That said, as we will see in this chapter, Focus and Consistency are in many ways mutually dependent: Focus helps Consistency and Consistency helps Focus. The negative is also true: a lack of Focus threatens your ability to be Consistent and a lack of Consistency hurts your ability to Focus.

As was true for Focus, delivering Consistency is not a passive endeavour. The leadership work required for Consistency (for example, choosing to *not* back-track on the change, now that it's underway) shows that leaders need to step back, but not out: they remain engaged. But it should take much less work than the stepping up phases – and less work also than many leaders are typically having to do, at this stage in a strategic change. If you recall the 'Time Use' graphs from Chapter 3 (page 71), the CEO of the Ideal Case was spending much less time on the change in the second and third years than he'd spent during Year 1. Less time also than his peers in the other three cases. The 'stepping back' effort should take less *time* – even if it still requires deliberate and thoughtful *work*.

At this stage of the change, managers will be looking to leaders very carefully to see whether they're serious: to see whether they're going to stick with the new strategy or possibly change their minds. And even if they don't explicitly change their minds, leaders might inadvertently corrupt the change – and thereby erode whatever Clarity and Alignment they may have achieved in Year 1 – by adding in some 'additional priorities' for managers. In my experience, 'additional priorities' is an oxymoron for stuff that will mess up whatever good work has already been done. So be on the lookout for that kind of corruption – whether it's accidental or deliberate, creeping or explicit. Because this is not the time to undo the hard work that's been done to date – by both leaders and managers. Now is the time to stick with it and see it through.

As was true of the work required for Focus, the work required for Consistency will be hard for some leaders. Consistency, like Focus, requires effort, discipline and self-awareness – as leaders push themselves to really step back and avoid tinkering too much with the change. And from managers, there is now the need to use the time and capacity that Focus has given them to not only properly step up into the 'blue zone' of delivering this change, but also to really pay attention and notice what's going on in the wider business, beyond the specific change projects they're working on.

If what managers notice are inconsistencies – in either the strategy or in the messaging – then they will need to call these out. That will take skill, preparation and, sometimes, bravery. But that's what helps deliver Consistency at this stage. That's the contract now, between leaders and managers – that leaders are Consistent and that managers notice and call out if they are not. Enacting this contract is only possible if the first three 'asks' – Clarity, Alignment and Focus – are already in place. But assuming they are, then it's Consistency that's now required if leaders, managers and their organization are to achieve the change they want.

The two elements required for Consistency

Leaders need to be Consistent from the beginning of Year 2 and for as long as the original change lasts. So how can they deliver Consistency? There are **two elements** leaders need to get right in order to be consistent in these middle years.

Element 1 of Consistency: Maintain the changes

Leaders need to maintain all the changes they made – both personally *and* structurally – in Year 1. This means they are continuing to target the same outcomes, continuing to talk about the change in the same way, still role-modelling it and still making time for it. In terms of their ongoing *personal* 'work', this requires no new effort or thinking or decisions from leaders – and, as a result, it should take less time. The narrative of why this strategy is necessary and what it should produce is already established: it doesn't need additional thought, but it does need you to keep telling it. (For a good example of the impact this can have, see the Practice Spotlight 'Keep Telling the Story', opposite.)

In many ways, the 'work' of Consistency should by now be almost automatic for leaders, because they've been practising their new habits, behaviours and actions for more than a year already. It should, by now, have become their new routine – just part of the 'new normal' that is this new strategy. It still requires leaders to remember to do it, though – to keep telling the story about why the change is necessary and what it will produce, and to manage themselves so that they have the right impact on those around them. (A good example of this is the Practice Spotlight 'The Need to "Manage" Yourself', page 238.)

In terms of leaders' ongoing *structural* 'work', they need to continue to resource the change properly – so the same dedicated people are still working on it, with no reduction in headcount and with the same commitment to budgets and investment. Leaders also need to stick with the revised KPIs and metrics they introduced to support the change they asked for; and they should still be paying attention to the new data and metrics that are informing and driving the change. These structural Elements of Alignment need to all still be in place and therefore still be signalling to managers that this change matters. The message here is stick with it, don't change it and don't undo whatever good work you did in Year 1.

Practice Spotlight: Maintain the Changes – Keep Telling the Story

You'll remember that when Arm was first acquired by Japan's technology group, SoftBank, Arm's CEO, Simon Segars, had clearly stated he believed that this was the best strategy for Arm and one to which he, as a long-standing Arm employee, was personally committed. That was what Segars was saying in June 2016.

And it was still what he was saying in June 2019. Three years on from the acquisition, Segars was still taking every opportunity to evangelize about why having SoftBank as Arm's owner gave the company the best possible opportunity to win in the capital-intensive IoT and AI development markets. As one Arm-er recalled from a town hall held in Arm's large San Jose office in mid-2019:

> Simon got up and, along with all the usual updates about revenue and margins, what I remember most was him saying – again – how much he believed in the SoftBank ownership. He talked about all the advantages we had because of this, that we would never have had without it. He talked about how he hadn't regretted for a single day in the past three years recommending that we accept the offer. It's funny that this made such an impression on me – because this wasn't new, after all. But the fact that he said it, three years on, and has kept saying it all the way through, that's important. Especially for those of us who, in the day-to-day, might see the business change in ways that, let's face it, not all of us like. But when you keep hearing that it's still the best possible option – in fact, it's the only option if we're serious about winning in this space – then that really helps put the little, annoying stuff into the bigger perspective.

Practice Spotlight: Maintain the Changes – The Need to 'Manage' Yourself

Michael Chavez, the Global CEO of Duke CE, tells a great story of why managing yourself to always be consistent in the signals you send is so important – even long after you've first announced a new strategy:

> I was coming out of a meeting in our London office, and I was starting to feel like I was coming down with something. To make it worse, I was jet-lagged: I'd been in four time zones in six days and it was starting to take its toll. The meeting – about how the new strategy was playing out in this particular market and how people were feeling about it in this office – had gone well. And now I was looking forward to heading back to my hotel room around the corner and having an early night.

The local senior team who'd been in the meeting with him were all very busy, so they came out of the meeting – behind him, as it happened – and rushed back to their desks to do client calls or to work on pitches.

Three relatively junior people saw the group come out of the meeting. They interpreted Chavez's tired, ill exterior as anger and frustration. And his colleagues rushing back to their desks as them having been given a dressing-down about that quarter's numbers. Busy and not paying attention to how they were managing the signals they were sending, and failing also to give any explicit messages to people, the senior leaders came out of their meeting that afternoon and each went their separate ways, leaving the observers who hadn't been in the meeting to come to their own conclusions.

The next day, one of those people asked Chavez about the meeting. A testament to Duke's open culture, many Global CEOs may not have ever been asked this question. Chavez therefore had the opportunity to explain why people looked the way they did as they left the meeting – and how it had nothing to do with the meeting itself, which had gone well. As he remembers:

> It made me realize that, as a senior leader, I'm always 'on' – or at least I need to be. Because there might always be someone looking at me and trying to make sense of what my demeanour means for them.

So, as well as maintaining the personal and structural changes you've made at the start of the change, leaders also need to manage themselves in the moment to make sure they are not inadvertently sending mixed (or downright wrong) signals to people who are looking at them.

And if you think you might have sent a mixed or erroneous signal? The best thing to do is to own it: apologize for the confusion you've caused and explain what actually happened and any implications this has for those in question. And because you may not be as lucky as Chavez in getting the question asked of you by the people whom you've confused or worried, be proactive. At the end of every senior team meeting, for the duration of the change, agree the message that you'll all communicate about what you talked about and the decisions you made. Then go and communicate that agreed message *explicitly* to people, so that the potential for inconsistency is reduced and managers don't waste critical bandwidth trying to make sense of puzzles that you've inadvertently created for them.

What the Ideal Case got right

As you might expect, in the Ideal Case, senior leaders kept to both the personal and the structural changes they'd made in Year 1:

> They were all still role-modelling the change, still talking about it, still asking about and making time for it. And nothing had changed, either,

in the budget – if anything, we now had more resources available to us because we were getting better at proving the value we were adding. And of course we still had the KPIs that had been introduced at the end of the first year.

You'll notice from this quote that the modes of achieving Consistency are effectively mirrors of the earlier four Elements of Alignment – namely senior leader conversations and actions; and the structural changes they made, such as resource allocation and KPIs. By continuing with these four Elements of Alignment for the duration of the change, and not reversing or downgrading any of the actions or decisions they had taken in Year 1, leaders support their managers as *they* deliver the change and, as a consequence, leaders make it easier for themselves to step back.

It was a similar story in the Early Momentum Case:

Nothing changed in this respect. [The senior leaders] were all still doing what they'd done in Year 1. And we had all the same levels of budget and headcount. And the same KPIs.

And while the Under The Radar Case hadn't delivered all the Elements of Clarity or Alignment, the bits it had delivered – including leaders role-modelling the change and making time for it, allocating dedicated resource to the change, revising KPIs for managers and making sure that work was being done on the data and metrics needed to understand their initiatives – all of *these* changes were maintained:

So, however much I would have liked more by way of resources and to have had proper KPIs that rewarded outcomes, it is still true to say that the things that had shifted in our favour in that first year were maintained. No one went back on any of those in Years 2 or 3.

It's worth emphasizing again that the activities required for Consistency (actively deciding not to undo Year 1 decisions) require leaders to step *back* but not step *out*. Stepping out would mean leaders disengaging from the change, not asking about it or showing they care about it. That would actually be the *opposite* of being Consistent, because this first Element of Consistency requires leaders to *maintain* commitment to all the initial actions and behaviours they had used to kick off the change. So, as we saw when we talked about Focus in the last chapter, stepping *back* does not mean stepping *out*. Rather, it means leaders remain engaged but patient for the long-term change that is now underway.

What the other cases got wrong

Actually, in all four of the cases in this study, leaders maintained the *personal* changes they had made. They were, after all, conscientious leaders who understood the important role they played in keeping the change going – and so they did that part of their job. But when it came to maintaining the *structural* changes they had made, not all of our leaders ticked the box.

The Road Runner Case had achieved a similar level of Alignment during Year 1 as in the Under The Radar Case – worse only in that they weren't working on the data and metrics needed to understand their projects, and they didn't have dedicated people working on the change. But the situation for these Road Runner managers was to become noticeably worse during Year 2. Because while the senior leaders in this business continued with the *personal* aspects required for Consistency – talking about and role-modelling the change – they went back even on the relatively few structural Elements of Alignment they'd delivered in Year 1. As the Head of Change recalled:

Looking back, we hadn't done enough to get the business behind the change at the start. The most glaring problem was the lack of resources. But because we didn't have clear outcomes, just a list of things to work on, and because we weren't even capturing the data we needed to show the difference we were starting to make, it was hard to make the case now that what we needed was more budget. Or more people to work on it. And maybe that was why we were a relatively soft option when it came to looking for savings. Because by halfway through that second year, we were facing a cut, even to the already inadequate budget we had. And a bit later that year, we lost one of our headcount.

The ongoing result of this worsening in structural Alignment in the Road Runner Case was two-fold. First, at no point did these projects become automated into routine business processes – the critical element which the Ideal Case was achieving at around this time. Instead, in the Road Runner Case, any progress they made towards the target still required a heroic personal effort from managers. There was just as much brokering, negotiating and doing favours for other departments required now in this case as there had been in Year 1:

> So all of the change projects we were doing, they never became a *process*. They never got to a point where they happened *on their own*. And so the work still took as much effort from me and the team as it had right at the start.

Second, and because of this, managers in the Road Runner Case found working on the change much more difficult and much more stressful than in the other cases – even though they actually had less ambitious, and mainly activity-based KPIs, to deliver. In contrast, managers in the Ideal Case had to deliver a 30 per cent improvement in their numbers over three years. That sounds a lot more challenging than just working on some projects. So why was it that the managers in the Road Runner Case were more stressed and frustrated than those in the Ideal Case?

The reasons lay in the first year of the change. Their activity-based KPIs, coupled with an inadequate budget and too few dedicated resources, meant that these high-performing managers were not set up to succeed. Even without a large, outcome-based target to deliver, they feared they would fail. On top of this, they knew their hard work was not being recognized: it wasn't discussed regularly at the Board and there were no revised, firm-wide KPIs in place to support their efforts. As managers, they had nothing to point to, to help them justify the hard work or to keep their teams motivated. In the absence of structural support (i.e. revised KPIs, budgets), progress was made because of personal relationships and loyalty – loyalty to the CEO from the Head of Change, and loyalty to the Head of Change from her team members. It was a personal currency that paid for all this hard work and commitment – because that was the only currency they had.

When asked what it was like in the later stages of the change, the Head of Change's recollection gave the case its name:

> It was very difficult. Month after month, you're just left doing it on your own. Not high-profile, not being resourced. You feel a bit like the guy in that Road Runner cartoon. He's running as fast as he can and then all of a sudden, there's nothing below him. Nothing supporting him. All that effort and now nothing to help him keep going. He's over the cliff, out on a limb, on his own. I felt like that a lot.

This failure by the Road Runner Case to maintain the structural changes of Year 1 was, however, the only gap in Element 1 of Consistency across our four cases:

	Ideal	EM	UTR	RR
Element 1: Leaders need to be maintaining all the changes that they made in Year 1, both:				
a) personal and	☑	☑	☑	☑
b) structural	☑	☑	☑	☒

But worse was to come. Because just maintaining all the changes you made in Year 1 isn't quite enough: you also need to check that you don't muddy the waters – or the managers' new 'blue zone' domain – by creating any conflicting demands upon them. And that is the critical *second* Element needed for Consistency.

Element 2 of Consistency: No conflicting strategies or messages

The second Element of Consistency – and this will be the more difficult part of Consistency for many leaders – is that they also need to stick to the same strategy until it's done. This means no conflicting choices being made, and no conflicting messages or new 'priorities' being introduced, while the original change continues.

Every new initiative or strategy chosen after the original change has been announced has the potential to design conflict into the organization. So if leaders decide they want to pursue some new initiatives, they must be sure that these aren't conflicting with the original change they've asked for. They must also explain how any additional initiatives fit into this change – just as they needed to explain how the new change fitted with existing strategies when they first introduced *it*.

The logic is this: either the original strategic change is still the best course of action, in which case leaders need to make an active choice to stick with it and not to deviate; *or* it isn't still the best course of action, in which case leaders need to actively choose a different strategy, fully cognisant that this will mean the original strategy won't now get delivered. Either choice is legitimate. The market, competitive or consumer contexts may have changed in the past two years and it is right that leaders are regularly paying attention to what's going on 'outside the window' and assessing what an altered context might mean for the strategy they are currently pursuing.

What they *can't* do, though, is to choose another, conflicting, strategy – or communicate another, conflicting, message – while still expecting that the original strategy will be delivered. Organizations cannot – and shouldn't have to – deal with conflicting strategic choices simultaneously. (For more on why this is the case, see the Science Spotlight below.) So, leaders need to choose: either stick with the existing priority or choose a new one. If leaders want a different strategy instead, they can choose to have one, but they can't choose a new, conflicting strategy and still expect managers to continue delivering the original one they asked for. The strategy you originally asked for cannot withstand that level of inconsistency from you now.

This is where the strategic nature of the change being attempted becomes important. Obviously, were it a small, tactical or incremental change, the potential for conflict would be much less and the organization would have capacity to undertake several of these tactical, incremental changes at the same time. But this is a *strategic* change – i.e. a fundamental shift in what the business does or in the culture and/or capabilities by which it does it. The nature of a strategic change means that you can only have one such change happening at any one time.

Science Spotlight: Why Organizations Can't – and Shouldn't Have to – Deal with Conflicting Strategic Choices Simultaneously

Because strategy is about making choices, it follows that the choices you make need to fit together if they are to work. You can't make two choices that conflict with each other and still expect your organization to be able to deliver both of them. Yet in my experience, senior leaders often like to do just that. They often justify having two conflicting strategies by arguing that this helps them to hedge the company's position. The company isn't betting the farm on any one single outcome – and this, they argue, is a good thing.

Bringing both strategy and organizational behaviour research to bear on this claim, we can see that there are three things wrong with this view. The first is the fact that the company shouldn't ever need to bet the farm at all, because things should never have got to the stage where the farm is at risk. Rather, the company should have been engaging in regular horizon-scanning activity – paying attention to changes in consumer behaviour, customer preferences, regulations and competitors – and then adjusting its strategy as necessary. If you take this activity sufficiently seriously, by giving it the time and attention it needs, then at no point should the need for a new strategy be so grave or immediate that the farm is ever on the line. The stakes should never be that high.

Companies who change early, change with less urgency, and therefore less risk, than those who leave it later. But recognizing the need to change sufficiently early requires companies to build skills in, and devote time and attention to, generating insights about future market and customer demand. For most businesses, this is non-urgent work that rarely gets prioritized until it's too late. And even if insights are generated from this kind of work, making the case to change early – before the proverbial 'burning platform' has appeared – is hard, costing leaders time and political will as they try to disrupt the cosy world of colleagues happy with their lot.

The second issue with senior leaders' desire to fudge their position so that they are more comfortable with the strategic 'choices' they've made is that, as Roger Martin has argued, the business of choosing (which is what proper strategy requires) means that leaders shouldn't expect to ever be completely comfortable about the choices they've made.[1] If they are real choices – i.e. not only what we *will* do, but also what we *won't* do[2] – then leaders ought to be at least a bit worried that they might have made the wrong choice. As Martin has argued, if you're not at least a bit worried about the strategic choice you've made, chances are you're either unjustifiably confident or (probably more likely), you haven't really chosen at all. You've fudged it and kept a foot in both camps. And that's a fundamental problem if you want your strategy is to be sufficiently clear to the people tasked with implementing it.

The third problem with having two conflicting strategies in play at the same time is what it does to the people who work in the business. As Heidi Gardner and Mark Mortensen have shown,[3] when individuals are allocated to multiple projects – what they term 'overcommitted' – and especially where the multiple projects they are working on are targeting potentially different outcomes (and so the work they do on one project cannot be leveraged for the benefit of the other projects), this puts an enormous strain on these individuals. They are often left to manage this strain on their own, since as this research has shown, the fact these individuals are working on multiple, conflicting projects is often invisible to senior leaders. Having multiple and potentially conflicting 'priorities' is therefore not good for individuals – especially your high performers who are keen to do well.

Nearly 40 years ago, Peters and Waterman, in their bestseller, *In Search of Excellence*,[4] argued strongly that having multiple and potentially conflicting 'priorities' is also not good for the organization – especially if that organization is aiming to deliver long-term value. Looking at the eight attributes that made organizations excellent, they discerned that one of the behaviours of such companies was that they focused on doing a few things really well. They termed this 'sticking to the knitting' – and it's actually more akin to what I am calling Focus in this book. But, to help these companies focus on these relatively few important things, their leaders continued on the same strategic direction for longer than the other CEOs they studied. These leaders weren't changing direction all the time: in other words, they were being Consistent in their strategy until either that strategy was delivered, or (perhaps because of changes in markets or customer preferences, or because of competitor actions), they actively chose to pursue a different strategy instead.

Peters and Waterman admit that this could be perceived as a relatively simple way to run a business: indeed, as they put it, 'the people who lead the excellent companies *are* a bit simplistic,'[5] in the sense that they choose where they wanted to be and stuck with that course until either it's delivered or until another one is chosen. Sticking with that course can also sound like a relatively passive way to 'lead'. But in practice, sticking to the same course requires considerable leadership work. It's the work of actively scanning the environment to see what's coming at you and thinking through what that means for the strategy you've chosen. And after you've judged whether to stick or to switch, it's the work of either reiterating the old narrative for why you're sticking, or crafting a new narrative that explains the switch.

And if your call is to stick, then it's the leadership work of saying 'no' to the people in your organization who wanted to go with the shiny new ideas or the fresh alternative strategy – the grass is usually greener, after all. It's the work of reminding them why the current strategy still makes sense and what it will deliver (the 'green zone' revisited). And it's the work of reinvigorating the people tasked with delivering the existing strategy, who may have felt their efforts were in vain while the strategy re-look was going on (it's not as though they won't pick that up on the grapevine, so don't kid yourself!). All of that most definitely takes work: there is nothing passive or lazy about choosing to stay the course, if that's the active choice you've made in the context of an ever-shifting environment.

All four of the businesses studied for this research, and many others that I have worked with since, were in fast-moving, high-growth markets, facing new market entrants, increasing regulation and changing customer preferences. Given these conditions, there were many plausible reasons why a change in direction might have been warranted at any time during the nearly four-year change period. But what distinguishes the most successful CEOs at this stage of a strategic change is that they regularly review the landscape and then actively make a choice either to stick to the original strategy or to choose an alternative. If their choice is to switch, then they do so explicitly – essentially starting the Clarity, Alignment, Focus and Consistency process all over again, for the new strategy they've chosen. But if their choice is to stick with the original strategy, then they make sure that all communications and messaging remain consistent with that decision, so that no conflict is designed into their organization. (For a good example of how to do this, see Practice Spotlight: 'Being Consistent So Clarity is Preserved', below.)

Practice Spotlight: Being Consistent So Clarity is Preserved

One of my favourite examples of an organization that stuck to its strategy – and a leader who helped make this happen – is the US airline, Southwest Airlines. Started by the late Herb Kelleher in 1967, Southwest has grown to become the world's largest low-cost airline based not just on cheap fares, but also a great passenger experience and on-time stats. It's a low-cost, high-margin airline – and almost unique as a result.

From the start, Southwest positioned itself as a low-cost airline – this was at the heart of its strategy and all its decisions supported this positioning. But even in an organization as clear in its strategy as Southwest, inconsistency is a possibility – unless leaders guard against it. Here's how the situation arose at Southwest.

Southwest operated a number of longer-haul internal flights within the US and, on one of these routes, the airline was losing market share to a competitor. The marketing manager in charge of the route (her name was Tracy, as the story goes) did her homework and saw that these passengers would appreciate a proper meal during these longer flights, rather than just the peanuts and snacks that Southwest was used to serving. After working up some proposals, including moving budget around so that this additional service would be cost-neutral, she walked into Kelleher's office to present her idea.

His response was a definite no. The reason *why* is the interesting bit and his response has been quoted widely.[6] He is reported as saying: 'I can teach you the secret of running this airline in 30 seconds. This is it: we are THE low-cost airline. Once you understand that fact, you can make any decision about this company's future as well as I can.' Faced with a motivated manager looking to improve customer satisfaction, he knew why it had to be a 'no' – because to say 'yes' to this idea would be to compromise the consistency of Southwest's positioning. Kelleher reportedly continued: 'Will adding that chicken Caesar salad make us THE low-cost airline? Because if it doesn't help us become the unchallenged low-fare airline, we're not serving any damn Caesar salad.'

Kelleher said no to the idea of adding a meal not because it was a bad idea for his passengers, but because it was off-strategy for Southwest. After all, even if the meal was cost-neutral, that suggested the business could cut the cost of the fare – and *that* was what they ought to have done, given their positioning as THE low-cost airline. If Southwest passengers wanted a meal more than a low-cost fare, they shouldn't be Southwest passengers because that wasn't Southwest's offer.

This is a great example of what Consistency looks like in practice – and how hard it is to do. It is not just making sure no changes are made to the big macro-level strategy of a firm. It's also navigating (and clearly communicating) the myriad choices that companies face every day. Many of these choices arise because companies are striving to respond to customers' demands – as was the case here. Well-meaning requests to add more – and often conflicting – activities into the mix will come up. Leaders need to be thoughtful, active and disciplined in how they respond. It would be tempting (and, to be honest, not uncommon) to say 'yes' to such requests. If, however, you're serious about Consistency, then you need to lead by saying 'no' – so that the initial Clarity and Alignment, which your strategy had at the start, isn't compromised now.

What the Ideal Case got right

The leaders in the Ideal Case did just that – as one of the managers recalled:

There was nothing new that came at us – nothing that was conflicting.

This created a virtuous cycle for the Ideal Case, as their Focus helped them be Consistent and their Consistency in turn helped them continue to Focus. Their Head of Change remembered:

We knew what we needed to focus on – we'd been clear about that from the start and we were getting better at making those calls as we got better and better data as the projects went on. That meant we could focus on fewer things and I think that really helped us in Years 2 and 3. I mean, the more things you have on, the more chance there is that, at least some of those activities won't be completely on-point, and that can mean the overall message about what you're doing is lost, or – not so much lost, as watered down. Whereas when there's only a few things on the To-do list, it's less likely that there'll be confusion about what's being done and what it stands for. And that means everybody can be on the same page.

And, this time, the Under The Radar Case also achieved the same kind of Consistency:

> This was always the priority for us. There were no new strategies during this time, so the message to me and the team – remember, this was all done very much on the quiet – was that this was still important.

Ironically, it was at this point that being 'under the radar' actually helped this case. Although this status had undoubtedly cost the change some early momentum in Year 1, the fact that nobody other than the CEO was paying attention to the change or even knew what outcome the team was targeting meant that the team working on the change now faced much less pressure to justify their numbers than the teams in the other cases, and so they were essentially just left to get on with it. The additional time that this bought them (notably towards the end of Year 2 and into Year 3) would pay dividends over the long term. Although they were still under-resourced, their lack of visibility gave the Under The Radar team a grace period during which they could work out some of the linkages between what they were doing and what was being produced. They started to make smarter choices about what to work on. By Year 3, they had reduced the number of projects they were working on and their numbers were improving. As one of the team members put it:

> It helped that this remained a priority for the CEO. And so that gave us time and some breathing space. But in some ways, it also helped that no one was looking at us. So whatever had been lacking in the early days, we started to make up for, I think. We got better at capturing the right data and understanding the projects and that meant we chose what to work on more effectively. We never did get all the budget we wanted, but we started getting some, because now we were able to make the case to [the CEO]. It wasn't fast or dramatic, but we improved over the years.

I said right at the start of this chapter that Focus helps Consistency and Consistency helps Focus. The Under The Radar Case suggests that having Consistency can even help *create* Focus, when you have none to start off with. And this is a major factor in explaining the difference in long-term performance between the Under The Radar and the Road Runner Cases in particular – given that, otherwise, these two cases were very similar.

What the other cases got wrong

In the other two cases – the Road Runner Case and the Early Momentum Case – things were very different. Here, the strategic priority of the business changed towards the end of Year 2 and into Year 3.

The seeds of inconsistency were sown much earlier, though. By spending too much time during the first year on 'quick wins' and too little time on the more fundamental, 'zero glam' work, whatever change had been delivered in these two cases was fragile. The reasons for this erroneous early choice might have been different – the absence of an outcome-based target in the Road Runner Case; and because fundamental change didn't seem necessary in the absence of a big, multi-year target, in the Early Momentum Case. But the impact was the same – worsening performance of the change projects and a sense, therefore, that this change just wasn't working.

We know of course that the reasons the change didn't appear to be working now (around 30 months in) were not because the new strategy had suddenly become a bad idea, nor because performance on the activities chosen was actually worsening. But rather because the consequences of the decisions these cases had made back at the start of the change were now becoming apparent. Not enough stepping up (Clarity and Alignment) in the early stages, followed by not enough stepping back (Focus) during Year 2 made it harder to be Consistent now. The chickens were coming home to roost.

Now, as I said at the start of this chapter, it is perfectly legitimate to change your mind about a change and to choose a different strategy instead. What *isn't* valid is to do what these two cases did – which was to change their minds, introduce a conflicting new strategy, but nevertheless expect the original change to still be delivered.

Specifically, there were three things wrong with how the 'change of mind' played out in these cases. First, leaders failed to explicitly acknowledge their 'change of mind' – in other words, there was a failure to deliver the Elements of Clarity on the new strategy they were choosing. In particular, the leaders in these two cases failed to explain how their new strategy impacted on the existing one. It was almost as if two parallel universes opened up in these businesses. As a result, managers were now less clear about what to do, meaning they relied on leaders even more to make decisions for them.

Second, managers were still expected to deliver on the original strategy: it hadn't gone away, despite a new and conflicting strategy also being asked for. Not only did this increase the workload for managers, meaning they had even less slack than before; but they now had to compete for resources and senior leader time with the latest strategy. Managers were now even less likely to succeed than before.

And third, and most insidious of all, managers hadn't actually noticed that there was even a new conflicting strategy at the time it was first introduced. Leaders were of course partly to blame – had they been explicit about the new strategy and clear in their communication, this may have flagged up the change in direction. But the real culprit here was the lack of slack these managers had. They hadn't had the time or opportunity to look up and see what was going on in the rest of the business. And that meant that leaders weren't challenged about the new strategy until it was too late.

All three of these issues came up in the Road Runner Case. As their Head of Change remembered:

> So there were statements and at least one town hall about the [new] strategy, but it wasn't clear that this was a different direction. That only became clear to us much later. And in the meantime, nothing changed for our team – we still had to work on the old priority – only now there was even less budget.

It was a similar story at this point in the Early Momentum Case. As one of their team told me:

> Honestly, no, we didn't notice it [the change in priorities] at the time. I mean, we were snowed under. By the time I was realizing that things had changed, it was already too late. That ship had sailed and we couldn't have a conversation with the CEO or the senior leaders about whether this was a good thing to do. The only conversation left for us to have with them was, what shall we work on now?

This isn't just an example of how a lack of Focus (too many projects on, not enough slack) enables inconsistency to creep in unnoticed. This is also an example of how, by failing to fully step up to deliver sufficient Clarity and Alignment in the early stages, coupled with a failure to step back now to deliver both Focus and Consistency, leaders create a situation where the conversations they are being pulled into by managers are 'blue zone' ones – in this case, what projects to work on – when leaders ought not to be needed for that kind of conversation at this stage in the change.

In fact, arguably even more depressing than the Road Runner Case's poor performance was what was happening now in the Early Momentum Case. The Early Momentum leaders had done so much good work in stepping up in the early days, achieving many of the Elements of Clarity and all the Elements of Alignment. But that early effort – all that stepping up – was now undermined because, from Year 2 onwards, these leaders failed to properly step back: they had little or no Focus and now they changed their minds and introduced a new strategy. This served to compromise much of the successful early work. As the Head of Change told me:

> Actually, there was alignment initially. But over time, it got compromised and we lost it. I put that down to having too many things on. And of course, to there being another priority that crept in.

So, stepping up is essential, but not enough. Leaders must follow it up by active, disciplined stepping back – by being Consistent and by helping managers Focus. If they don't, they could be back at square one, as the return on all their early work evaporates. Which is exactly what happened in the Early Momentum and Road Runner cases:

	Ideal	EM	UTR	RR
Element 2: **Leaders need to have introduced no conflicting strategies or messaging since they asked for this change**	☑	☒	☑	☒

And if leaders are worried that stepping back is somehow a 'lazy' option, believe me, the lazy option I see leaders most often take is what the leaders of the Early Momentum and Road Runner Cases did. They fail to actively choose to stick with the strategy when it's running into difficulties, or perhaps because something more interesting comes along instead. They fail also to diagnose why the change is failing – something that's often due to errors or omissions in the stepping up stages. And then when they do choose another strategy, they fail to explain how their old and new strategies fit together and, specifically, what of the existing work can be stopped. Instead, they just leave managers to make sense of it on their own. This is of course also an example of leaders stepping *out* of the original change, by simply stepping into another, when what they need to do is step *back* from the original change, but still have it as the priority, so that managers can continue to deliver on it.

Leaving managers to make sense of it on their own, or not being prepared to own and explain decisions, is lazy leadership as far as I'm concerned. And whenever we allow leaders to be lazy, we make it more likely that managers will need to be heroic. Equally, when leaders don't allow themselves to be lazy, but instead use their skill and will to step back rather than step out, there is no need for heroic managers. They can instead get on with the job they have, because leaders have done theirs.

To help us see how these cases scored on both Elements of Consistency, see Diagram 7.1 opposite.

Diagram 7.1: Summary of how the Cases delivered Consistency

	Ideal	EM	UTR	RR
Element 1: Leaders need to be maintaining all the changes that they made in Year 1, both:				
a) personal and	☑	☑	☑	☑
b) structural	☑	☒	☑	☒

	Ideal	EM	UTR	RR
Element 2: Leaders need to have introduced no conflicting strategies or messaging since they asked for this change	☑	☒	☑	☒

Leadership lessons from Ask #4

The first lesson for leaders looking to deliver Consistency for their managers is, again, that they need to deploy both transformational *and* transactional leadership. They need to be transformational when it comes to continuing to talk about and role-model the change, and they need to be transactional to help maintain the resourcing and measurement that they changed in Year 1.

But notice that the second Element of Consistency – the need to not ask for any new strategy or ideas that might conflict with the original change that was asked for – requires something more from leaders. And this is where stepping back really comes into its own. In order to deliver Consistency for managers, leaders need to actively decide *not* to flip-flop or interfere.

This is precisely why this stage of the change is about stepping back. And why this way of leading change is profoundly different from the old approaches. Because, in the old approaches to change, leaders would still be keeping a close eye on *managers* at this stage. With this new approach to delivering change – that, by this time, should see the change being delivered by managers themselves with less need for input from leaders – leaders need to be keeping an eye not on managers but on *themselves*. That's because it's only when they are noticing what they are doing and making active, disciplined choices to stick with the original strategy that they are likely to be truly Consistent.

The second lesson we can take from Consistency is that, like Focus, it is highly dependent on the early stage work on Clarity and Alignment. If leaders fail to deliver any of the Elements of Clarity, how can they know what to be Consistent about? And if they are missing one of the Elements of Alignment, how can their signals be fully Consistent during this later stage, any more than they were during the first year?

As we saw in the two cases that introduced new, conflicting strategies, organizations can be susceptible to changes in strategy almost by stealth. But strategy-change by stealth is only really a danger for organizations who lack all the Elements of Clarity and Alignment. Because if you have all of those Elements in place, it's hard for you to change the strategy without people noticing. And that should mean that the resulting decision, whether to change strategy or not, is fundamentally a better one, because it will have been subject to scrutiny and challenge.

There's one Alignment Element that's particularly important when it comes to alerting people to a change in strategy – and it's one of the structural sources of Alignment, namely the introduction of revised KPIs to support the change. Because where organizations have introduced new metrics and KPIs to measure and reward the change, asking managers to work on a *new* strategy instead will lead to KPIs being missed and, over the longer term, changed. Changes in, or breaches to, existing KPIs – with implications for how people get paid – command people's attention. Therefore, businesses which embed strategy in organization-wide KPIs (i.e. for both leaders and managers) may well be less vulnerable to changes in strategy 'by stealth' because a subsequent change in strategy involves either introducing new KPIs, or breaching the existing ones. When the business's KPIs reflect its current strategy, KPIs can act as a canary in the mine on a strategy change. And that can prompt the kind of scrutiny and challenge of the proposed new strategy that invariably improves the quality of the decision being taken.

So, as was true for the Elements that made Focus easier to achieve, it turns out that the most important pre-conditions for Consistency are also those of a structural nature – the ones delivered by what we would call 'transactional' leadership. It seems like this 'poor relation' of the leadership literature is bringing quite a lot to the party.

The third leadership lesson we can take, now that I have explained both Focus and Consistency, is that these two 'asks' are fundamentally dependent on each other. Less Focus makes it harder to be Consistent ('Consistent about what?') and less Consistency makes it harder to Focus ('Focus on what?'). So, given the interdependency between these two late-stage 'asks', what can leaders do if they sense that their change is not Consistent enough? My best advice is to double-down on the work of Consistency – something I'll talk about next. And that will often require you to go back and understand where the foundations of Consistency – i.e. Clarity and Alignment – may be lacking and then shore those up. As I've said before, better late than never. You may plan, and hope, for change to be linear, but its practice is much more iterative. So accept the feedback on the lack of Consistency as potentially feedback on a lack of Clarity (or Alignment) and go fix that.

The 'work' of Consistency

As was the case with the work of Focus, when I talk to leaders about the work of Consistency, they sometimes give me the impression that I'm misleading them. That what I'm talking about here – making sure they don't make any changes, making sure they introduce no new, conflicting strategies, generally saying 'no' to new ideas and the people who want to try them – isn't really 'work'.

My response is always the same: I always say to them that Consistency is probably the hardest of the four 'asks'. It is so counter-intuitive for many leaders because it requires them to unlearn much of what they know, not just about leading change, but about leading in general. Because, in order to be Consistent, leaders really need to be managing themselves – rather than other people. And that takes work – in the shape of discipline, honesty and the setting aside of any last vestiges of attachment to the 'blue zone' and the Four Delusions of Leadership.

It also requires leaders to put up with a certain amount of boredom. After all, Consistency requires you to keep talking about the change using the same language and adhering to the same routines that you established over a year ago now. So there is very little 'newness' for leaders at this stage of the change. And there shouldn't be: rather, 'newness' is something that should be being enjoyed by the *managers* as they implement the change – learning new lessons from their efforts and tweaking their projects to get better over time. (For more on the benefits of boredom for leaders, see the Science Spotlight below.)

Science Spotlight: The Benefits of Boredom

Our novelty-hungry brains, and the chemicals they feed on, make it hard for us to deal with boredom. We crave newness as a way to keep us motivated. But this craving for newness can mean that we tend to shift our goals too quickly, not giving goals that take longer – which are often the ones that are most worthwhile – the attention and time that they need.

Leaders who refuse to be bored risk simply feeding this addiction to new ideas or strategies – and thereby failing to devote sufficient time to the existing one. This often shows up as the Activity or Drama Delusions – the idea that change should be action-packed and that it should be fast, exciting and risky when, as we now know, particularly the later stages of a successful change should be dull and routine – precisely because the change is becoming the new 'normal'. So if being prepared to be bored is an important part of successfully 'stepping back', how can we become more content with boredom?

Well, being bored – at least for short periods of time – can bring benefits. A study by Sandi Mann and Rebekah Cadman suggested that enduring a dull task can make people more creative.[7] The researchers asked their 80 participants to complete a creative challenge (in this case, to come up with a list of alternative uses for a plastic cup – a fairly standard way to assess divergent thinking). One group of subjects did a boring activity first (for example, reading the phone book) while the control group went straight to the creative task. Those who had been bored prior to doing the creative task came up with a significantly greater number of ideas for the plastic cups.

The reason for this boost in creativity seems to be that boredom encourages people's minds to wander. This 'mind wandering' – that we first encountered in Chapter 6 as a by-product of having more slack (see page 193) – means our brains make more associations and, as a result, produce more creative ideas. And this only happens when we are sufficiently bored that our minds wander. So boredom can be good for us.

Leaders need to accept that feeling some boredom might be a consequence of leading well. Because if they have stepped up enough as leaders in the early stages of the change, and if they are following that up with some stepping back work – including deciding not to change the strategy and to say 'no' to new ideas – then they will now have less to do on the change. But recognize this as a consequence of your success as a leader. Embrace it and use the time and space it gives you for *personal* creativity and reflection – you've earned it.

But leaders might get bored with all this 'sameness'. They might seek to assuage their boredom by looking for alternative ideas to implement. As Dorothy Parker is claimed to have said: 'The cure for boredom is curiosity. There is no cure for curiosity.'[8] Looking for new ideas, or even just a new way to talk about the change, is tempting. It's also potentially derailing for the original change.

Even a variation in how the change is talked about can lead some in the business to wonder whether the change itself is being varied or deprioritized. And a new idea, however attractive on its own merits, is also a potential conflict with the change that is now firmly underway. What's important for leaders to remember at this point (in fact, the most important lesson from the Early Momentum Case) is that a single decision at this stage – whether deliberate or inadvertent – can undo the previous two years' worth of effort. So at this stage, leaders need to make sure they aren't attracted to every shiny new idea they come across.

January is, in my experience, the worst time of year for this kind of problem. The Christmas break – the only time of year when it seems everyone is out of the office for at least a week – gives leaders downtime. They may have travelled and so bought a book in an airport bookstore and read it on the plane, or been able to finally catch up with a few of the business magazines that have gone unread in the previous six months. It is also for many businesses their year-end, so the sales and operational rush of Q4 is suddenly over. It's a classic opportunity to read, reflect and think creatively about what's next for the business.

It was Paul Graham who noted that both Microsoft and Facebook were started in January, when, after the Christmas break combined with a Reading Week, entrepreneurial students had no classes for a number of weeks.[9] This is a good example of free time (or slack) producing creative, new ideas – we talked about the *upside* of that in Chapter 6 on Focus. But there's a potential *downside* too – and it's that leaders will have creative, new ideas that they decide should *also* be implemented, and which will derail the change they originally asked for, where progress is underway but not yet complete.

So, while of course I would urge leaders to spend more time reading, reflecting and thinking about what's next for the business, I also want them to understand the implications of changing a strategy or the messaging around it. Because many leaders, especially those still in hock to the Activity and Drama Delusions, will be starting to enjoy the extra time that 'stepping back' frees up for them and will be looking for 'what's next?' But the reality of a long-term change effort is that the best 'what's next?' for the business might well be *exactly what you're already doing*. The right strategy might well be the *existing* strategy. And that is a completely legitimate choice – *provided it is a choice*, i.e. you make it with all the deliberateness and attention and care with which you made the choice in favour of the existing strategy in the first place.

But of course you need to be keeping a weather-eye on what's coming at you, whether opportunities or threats. Otherwise, your business is in danger of stagnating rather than gradually, incrementally improving. So how can you strike the right balance, as a leader, between wanting to future-proof your business using attractive new ideas and remaining Consistent about the current strategy? How should leaders be using this new-found time that their stepping back work has given them?

The first thing leaders should be doing with the time they've gained by stepping back is doubling-down on their 'green zone' work. In fact, having more time for leaders to do this 'green zone' work is one of the major benefits of this new approach for the organization and the people who work in it, because most managers lack sufficient 'green zone' context to help them make their 'blue zone' decisions. As a result, they choose badly, or suck their leaders into those choices. With more time and attention being given by leaders to the 'green zone' narrative – Why are we doing this work?, What will it produce? and How will we behave with each other to get it done? – the whole organization is set up to do the right work in the right way. As I argued in Chapter 4 on Clarity, the amount of extra time that the vast majority of leaders need to be devoting to this 'green zone' is significant, so this will hoover up quite a lot of the extra time that stepping back has freed up and it is, in my experience, the first, critical thing to do with the extra time leaders now have.

Now, with the right amount of time devoted to the 'green zone' work, it's right that leaders also spend some of their new-found time thinking about what's next for the business. Several leaders I work with, who have now got their 'Step Up, Step Back' balance right, use their extra time in the following ways:

- visit and spend time with customers or clients, to better understand why they buy from you and why that might change;
- visit your own operations to check in with employees, especially those on the frontline. This is a good opportunity to sense-check how the new strategy is working and also to boost

morale, assuming these visits aren't sanitized 'state visits' but rather offer proper opportunities for employees to talk and for you to listen;

- spend time on the peripheries of your business. As Rita Gunter McGrath has pointed out, the peripheries (or 'edges') of your business (the direct interface with customers, for example) are where you're most likely to see signals from the future. So if you want to understand how to future-proof your business, go visit its 'edges' – and, critically, don't resist what you discover there, even if it comes as an unwelcome surprise to you;[10]

- check in with the brightest and best thinkers in your company. What ideas are they having and which of these deserve investment? This was what Microsoft founder Bill Gates regularly spent his 'Think Weeks' on – leading to game-changing products, such as Internet Explorer and Virtual Earth;[11]

- get to know other businesses to understand what they're up to. Choose businesses both in and out of your sector, so you don't constrain your ideas. While some of these businesses may become part of your eco-system (for example, by becoming partners or even by sharing customers with them), the main point of these connections is not to monetize them, but to learn new things from them;

- check in with opinion leaders to discover new perspectives on your market. While you may have gained some of these by talking to customers, competitors or other companies, spending some time with external, objective, often non-profit organizations can give you an additional perspective. Examples include think tanks, NGOs and academics connected to your world.

All of this time spent thinking about the business – using either the 'green zone' structure to further that thinking, or the external sources to provide new perspectives – is likely to provoke new ideas. So, what do you do with these – if the continued success of the new strategy requires you to be Consistent?

Well, as I have argued in this chapter, what you *can't* do is come back, dump all of your amazing new ideas on the business and ask for all of them to be implemented. You can certainly bring them back to the organization and think carefully about how they might fit in. My advice to leaders is to walk through what I call my *New Ideas Test*. This is a series of questions that help you judge whether the shiny new idea that you've just picked up, and which you think might help future-proof your business, really is all that. And whether it really is right for your business *right now*. Here are the questions I suggest you run through, for any new idea that you think you might want to implement:

1) Of the various ideas you've come across, whether from visiting a competitor, or from talking to a customer, or from reading something interesting in *Harvard Business Review*, which ones do you think your business needs in the next 12 to 18 months? Write that list.

2) Next, think about which ones you think your business needs over a longer time horizon, but not in the next 12 to 18 months. Write that list.

3) Give this second list to your internal 'Think Tank' team – they might already sit within your Strategy function or within R&D, but wherever they are based, their job is to horizon-scan your sector and to help future-proof your business. Ask them to explore the ideas on this second list and to come back to you with what they think; give them at least a month to do this, so that they do a decent job. If you don't have this capability internally, consider building it and, in the meantime, find an innovation consultant in your field. These often aren't the usual management consultants, but rather sector specialists with real expertise about customer and market trends in your sector. They can sometimes be found within universities or research institutions – get the big brains on your case.

4) In parallel, discuss your first list with a group of your senior leaders that, critically, includes the managers responsible for implementing the existing strategy. The questions for the series of conversations you have with this group are similar to those you would have used to achieve Clarity when you first decided on the strategy:

- Which of these ideas do we really need now and why? Agree a shorter list.
- What would *these* ideas deliver? What outcomes would improve?
- How do these ideas fit with the current strategy we are pursuing? How would we explain the linkages?
- Can these ideas be integrated into the existing strategy and the activities that are currently being worked on? If so, what additional resources would be needed, what new data would need to be captured and what new metrics or KPIs would need to be introduced to make this work?
- If the new ideas cannot be integrated into the existing strategy, are these new ideas at least compatible with it? Can we run them in parallel without designing in conflict?
- If that isn't possible (i.e. if the new idea or strategy is incompatible with the existing strategy), which of the existing work will we stop in order to do the new idea/ strategy? (Remember, this isn't just so that we don't design in conflict, but also to make sure we preserve managers' slack.)
- If the new ideas cannot be integrated and may even produce conflict with the existing strategy, are the outcomes that these new ideas would produce still worth it? If so, can we start a ring-fenced change programme, using the same Clarity-Alignment-Focus-Consistency model, which segregates the new idea from the existing strategy, to assess how well the new idea might work, but without compromising progress on the existing strategy in the meantime? This gives us some

optionality on which strategy to choose, before we finally make a decision one way or the other. But we recognize that we *will* have to make this decision, because these two strategies aren't compatible.

I wish I could tell you that all the organizations I work with go through this *New Ideas Test* with the rigour and discipline that it requires to do these questions justice. But what I can say is that those organizations that do, find it is a good way to think through the implications of a new idea in the context of their existing strategy.

It is understandable, of course, that leaders are often anxious not to miss the boat on a new idea, but it might be helpful to remember that many new ideas, especially ones specific to a sector or a tool, will turn out to be passing fads, which deliver little or no long-term value.[12] So don't be seduced by them. Instead, choose judiciously which ones might work for your business at this time – and for which you have the necessary bandwidth. Then make your choice fully cognizant of your past choices and the existing strategy you already have in play, and fully prepared to adopt the same Clarity-Alignment-Focus-Consistency approach for the new strategy you've chosen as you deployed for the old one.

As for the previous three chapters, to help summarize what Consistency requires in practice, you will find some tips and watch-outs for both leaders and managers at the end of this chapter.

Change that no longer needs leaders

Interestingly enough, it was at this stage in the change (early on in Year 3) that something fairly important happened in two of our cases: the CEOs of the Ideal and Road Runner Cases both left their roles. In the Ideal Case, the departing CEO took with him another member of the senior team, and the Head of Change who'd been tasked with delivering the new strategy. What would happen to the change now? Would progress stall? What would the impact be on the managers working on the change who were now making the choices about what projects to work on and how to make them better?

The answer was very different between these two cases. Without their departed CEO, the managers in the Road Runner Case were lost. The reason was that so much of the impetus for the change – even by Year 3 – remained personally dependent on him. As the Head of Change remembered:

> I had always gone to him for input on what we should prioritize. But I'd also gone to him for personal support. He always had time, always helped. I felt lost without him.

Not enough 'stepping up' work had been done by this leader to translate this personal support into structural support in the early days. As a result, the change team had little or no alternative support mechanisms to turn to when the CEO left. Returning to the Road Runner theme she had spoken about earlier, the Head of Change in this case told me:

> The change of leadership came when we'd been working on this for a while, so you're already off the edge by then. But there's still not really anything beneath you. It was OK when you had the CEO saying, jump, jump, go for it! But now he isn't there anymore, he isn't behind you urging you on, it feels like it's just you. And you have nothing – no structure, no KPIs, no processes – to hold you up.

In contrast, in the Ideal Case, the departure of the senior leaders had relatively little impact on the change. Progress continued on much the same trajectory. Managers continued to analyze and refine their projects and focus on delivering the long-term, outcome-based target they'd been set. Admittedly, this required a continuation of the same strategy (the new CEO did not change that) and the continued allocation of resources to the projects (he maintained that too). And it's worth calling out there is no indication that this change could have survived either a revision in strategy or a cut in resources by the new, incoming CEO. Nevertheless, it was clear that because of all the work done to step up in Year 1, followed by the work to step back (but not out) from Year 2 onwards, by now the change – and the managers working on it – *could* survive a series of resignations and the replacement of one senior leader with another. As one of the remaining managers in the change team put it:

> We knew what we were delivering and by now we knew a lot about what worked and why. So things carried on pretty much the same.

Continued progress was no longer dependent on having the same set of senior leaders in place – or, by implication, on the Magic or Agency that they personally brought to the effort. Rather, the change could now continue despite a change in leadership because this change was now being led not by leaders but by managers. This change was now part of the routine of the business.

Of course, this was made possible because of all the heavy lifting that these leaders had done in the early stages of the change. They stepped up and delivered all the Elements of Clarity in the first three months. This meant that managers knew what they needed to deliver in the long term and could scope their work appropriately. Leaders also stepped up and achieved all four Elements of Alignment during Year 1. Managers kept hearing about the change, they kept seeing it role-modelled and there was time being made for it at the highest level. More than that, there were structural changes being made to ensure it would be properly resourced, measured and rewarded. This meant that managers were set up to deliver because all the signals they were getting (including the structural ones) were pointing in the same direction. Taken together, this meant they now felt able to make their own decisions about what to work on.

And then, in the later stages of the change, these leaders had stepped back. Now leader effort was on helping managers stay focused and coaching them to refine, rather than add to, their projects. And on making sure that all the initial changes were maintained and that the initial strategy and messaging were kept consistent for the duration.

With Clarity, Alignment, Focus and Consistency in place, these leaders could safely leave the building. Literally. Because, by now, thanks to the combination of stepping up and then stepping back, their managers were now the ones delivering the change with very little input needed from them: their work here was done.

Where the four cases stand at the end of Year 2

By the end of Year 2, the progress made by each of the four cases looked very different from the last time we looked at the Progress Graph – at the end of Year 1 (see page 182).

Diagram 7.2: Progress at the end of Year 2

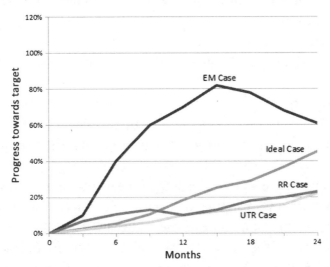

By now, the Ideal Case is starting to deliver on the change and is roughly halfway towards its target (which, remember, for each of the cases equates to 100 per cent on the y-axis). Its slow and steady progress, grounded in early, 'zero glam' work on data, processes and systems, means that whatever progress it makes is sustained. This is the period when managers in the Ideal Case report feeling less busy; and when its leaders say they are spending less time on, and making fewer and fewer decisions about, the change. They are now able to 'step back' because of all their 'stepping up' work in the early days.

In contrast, the early progress of the Early Momentum Case is now falling away. Its initial focus on 'quick wins' meant that too little work was done on data and systems in the early days. This case is paying the price for those choices now. As managers belatedly start to add in the 'zero glam' work on top of their existing projects, their workloads increase. The change in strategy at the end of Year 2 (which goes unnoticed by these busy managers) further compromises progress going forward. Managers report frustration with the reversal in their fortunes, feeling the last year has essentially been wasted; while leaders report they are now more involved during the second year of change than they had been in Year 1. Their ability to 'step back' is now constrained because not quite enough 'stepping up' work was done at the start.

The Under The Radar Case is making slower progress than the Ideal Case, but – like them – it's steady. While the 'under the radar' status of the change definitely made change harder than it needed to be in the early days – largely because of poor co-operation across silos and the inadequate budget that meant not enough work could be done on data and systems – it also meant the change team have been left to get on with it. They end Year 2 with a comparable level of progress as in the Road Runner Case – just over a fifth of the way towards their target – but with much less frustration on the part of managers. Leaders report they are spending more time on the change than they did at the start, however – again, they are unable to 'step back' because of inadequate 'stepping up' at the start of the change.

The Road Runner Case is still struggling, with results that improve only to fall back again. Their immediate focus on 'quick wins' right at the start may have produced some early success but, coupled with a lack of Clarity about outcomes and inadequate resources, this meant longer-term progress has been patchy and temporary. The change in strategy at the end of Year 2 means even less support for this change now. They end the second year of the change having only closed around a fifth of the gap between the target and their original starting point. Not much to show for the time, effort and stress expended by these managers who are now overworked and frustrated. Leaders are spending more time on the change now than they did at the start – again, there's no room to 'step back' if you haven't made this possible by 'stepping up' in Year 1.

Tips and Watch-outs to Help You Be Consistent

Tips and Watch-outs for Leaders

- **Make sure you're maintaining all the changes you made in Year 1.** You need to maintain both the personal and structural changes you made. But by now, the personal changes you've made – your communication and role-modelling efforts, making time for the change and discussing it at your SLT meetings – should be routine. And, as long as the structural changes – to resources and KPIs and metrics – are left unchanged, these require no new effort at all;
- **Stepping back doesn't mean stepping out.** With managers now doing more of the change themselves, you need to make sure you balance the need to step back with the need to remain engaged – you still have a role to play;
- **The activities that promote Consistency.** Your role is now to say 'no' to new strategies or initiatives that might conflict with the change you originally asked for. This ensures you don't design in conflict, or outcome arbitrage, into your business. This also helps keep managers – and you – focused on the change, by reducing the total amount of activities being worked on;
- **Don't get seduced by too many new ideas.** By now, you should have more time to focus on your 'green zone' work, including thinking about the long-term direction of the business. That should mean you have more time to read and think – which is great. But don't be seduced by every new idea you come across, regardless of how attractive it seems to you. Because the more new ideas you feed into the business, the more potential conflict you design in and the less slack managers have;
- **Equally, to keep your business safe from missing out on new ideas**, establish a 'think tank' within the Strategy function to scan the horizon for market, consumer and competitor changes. This means your business won't be blind-sided by external developments and therefore you can be more relaxed about remaining Consistent.
- **If you do choose another strategy, you need to explain the implications for your original ask.** It's perfectly legitimate to decide the business needs a new strategy and that the one you originally chose is no longer appropriate. But if you make that decision, you need to explain what this means for the original strategy. Is it no longer a priority at all? Are the existing projects to be stopped, or can they be integrated? To know how a new strategy fits with the current strategy, see whether it passes the *New Ideas Test* (page 266);

Tips and Watch-outs for Managers

- **Make sure you are on the lookout for inconsistencies.** Leaders need to be maintaining all the changes they made in Year 1 and you may need to help them do this – by paying attention to what they are saying, doing, resourcing and measuring, and calling out when these are inconsistent with the change they asked for;
- **Keep making the case for continuing with the change.** By now, you should have data about what the change is delivering. Use it not only to refine the projects you're working on (a key part of achieving Focus), but also to make the case internally for continuing with the change. This makes it more likely that your budget and teams will be left intact, which in turn makes it more likely that the change will succeed;
- **Push back if leaders try to add in too many new ideas.** Leaders should have more time now to think about the business. If this results in lots of new ideas coming your way, push back. You can't let them compromise the Focus and Consistency you have, or let them interfere with your 'blue zone' work;
- **Notice and then challenge if you think a new, conflicting strategy is being chosen.** The slack you need for Focus should also give you time to notice if something changes in the strategic priorities of the business. Make time to actively notice the signals leaders are sending. And if these seem to conflict with the change they originally asked you to deliver, call this out as soon as you can. Work with leaders to understand how the new strategy fits (or not) with what you are working on. Keep this conversation as 'green zone' as possible, making sure you get concrete answers to what this new strategy will deliver and how it fits with your work. It should pass the *New Ideas Test* (page 266). If it doesn't, something has to give;
- **Notice also if the messaging changes.** This can be as simple as leaders using different words or phrases to talk about the change or what it will deliver. This might be accidental, but it can also be because the change has morphed into something different, or been relegated as less of a priority. So that nothing is lost in translation, ask leaders why they're not sticking to the same language. Was it deliberate? If so, this might be a red flag that there's been a change in priorities or target outcomes, in which case this needs to be discussed and understood. Or was it accidental – in which case, they need to be more careful with the language they're using;
- **Call out also if you think leaders are stepping *out*, rather than stepping *back*.** While you should by now need much less time and input from leaders, they still need to be engaged and available when you do need them. Talk to them about the kind of input you still need from them, and about what you can do to make the best use of the time they give you. The nature of the contract between you may have changed, but it still takes both of you being involved if it is to work.

CHAPTER EIGHT

'Meaningful' Autonomy

The prize for leaders, managers and their organizations

Back in Chapter 3, I explained why I termed this new approach to leading change the 'Step Up, Step Back' model. I've now set out the first four dimensions (or leadership 'asks') of this approach – Clarity and Alignment (the two Stepping Up 'asks'); followed by Focus and Consistency (the two Stepping Back 'asks'). But there is a fifth and final dimension of this model – and it's the result if these first four dimensions have been achieved.

The final dimension is Autonomy and – along with being able to deliver successful change that sticks – it's this Autonomy that's the big prize for leaders and managers who get the first four 'asks' right. Because what the 'Step Up, Step Back' approach offers is a way to implement successful change that not only sticks, but that can be delivered by managers **without the need for ongoing input from leaders.**[1]

This is a special kind of Autonomy, one that I've termed **'meaningful' autonomy.** It's where managers are able (and willing) to take the decisions required to deliver the new strategy or change without feeling the need for leader input, support or cover. They get on with delivering the change – because they can. And they *can* because of the combination of the 'stepping up' and 'stepping back' work that leaders have done in the first two years of the change.

'Meaningful' autonomy is of course a prize for managers – at least for the ones who want to exercise their autonomy without the need to check in with those above them. For the ones who want to practise their own skills of making decisions and holding themselves accountable. And for the ones who want to learn, develop and take on opportunities for more responsibility faster than they might otherwise be able to.

It is also a prize for organizations (and the investors who fund them) because everyone within the organization is now being used to their full potential. If we were to take a purely economic view of this, we would say that using people to their maximum potential is what's required if the return on the organization's assets is to be maximized. Beyond the economics, this is also what's required if the best people are to thrive in the organization, feeling stretched but also supported; feeling they are learning while delivering; feeling they are both empowered and accountable. Higher employee retention, satisfaction and therefore productivity are the outcomes for organizations – and these have been shown to be the critical variables in achieving both high revenues and high margins.[2]

But the prize is also huge for leaders. They now have more time and capacity for the true work of leadership. For the strategic rather than the tactical; to look to the future, rather than being stuck in the present; to lead their organizations, rather than police them. In other words, to focus on what I have termed the 'green zone', rather than being sucked into the 'blue zone' in order to get things done. With time and practice, it is this 'green zone' work that delivers most value for their organizations – and which is ultimately most meaningful for them personally.

What does it mean for managers to have 'meaningful' autonomy?

'Meaningful' autonomy means that, instead of just notionally having the authority to make decisions about how to deliver the change, managers also feel able and willing to fully exercise the authority that their positions give them. In other words, that the autonomy they have is 'meaningful' to them – something they can and are willing to exercise without needing further input, support or cover from leaders. With 'meaningful' autonomy, managers can and will make choices about how to deliver the change (the 'blue zone' work) because it doesn't feel personally risky for them to do so.

But 'meaningful' autonomy doesn't just happen. Nor, as the four cases in this research show, can it simply be claimed by managers because they choose to 'lean in' to the situation. No, managers only experience 'meaningful' autonomy when leaders have laid the foundations for it. And they do *that* by delivering Clarity, Alignment, Focus and Consistency. If these four dimensions (or 'asks' of leaders) are in place, then 'meaningful' autonomy can happen. Equally, if these four dimensions are *not* in place, then it's likely that whatever autonomy managers technically have will be 'meaningless' – in other words, something they don't feel it's *possible* to exercise, or something they are not *prepared* to exercise, without further input, support or cover from leaders.

Science Spotlight: What the Empirical Research Tells us About Autonomy (or 'Empowerment')

Autonomy has been defined as 'the experience of acting with a sense of volition and having choice in pursuing an activity'.[3] In the academic research, it is very similar to the concept of 'empowerment'.

The research in this area has shown that autonomy – or empowerment – produces positive outcomes for employees (such as higher job satisfaction[4] and reduced end-of-workday fatigue[5]) and for organizations (reduced employee attrition and higher engagement and productivity).[6] What isn't understood as well are the *antecedents* of autonomy – in other words, what do leaders need to do to help employees feel autonomous?

Den Hartog and Belschak's definition of autonomy starts to unpack what might be necessary:

> Autonomy provides employees with room for self-determination. They can choose alternative ways to approach tasks, experience more ownership and have a more direct impact on outcomes.[7]

Now, of course this implies that, for employees to have autonomy, they at least need to be clear about the outcomes they have to deliver. In fact, a 2008 study of 262 middle managers across 12 organizations found that, in order for managers to have autonomy,[8] leaders needed (at a minimum) to explain the target outcomes and why these were necessary (which, in my approach, are key Elements of Clarity). Having clear expectations of what their roles required of them enabled managers to make their own decisions about *how* to deliver the outcome – what I have termed 'blue zone' work – because they were clear about the context and outcomes they needed to deliver (because leaders had done their 'green zone' job).

Ironically, it seems that having empowered, autonomous employees requires leaders to be highly prescriptive – at least about these macro-level outcomes. That is what makes it possible for employees to work out how best to deliver. Anything less than clarity about macro-level outcomes means employees – especially the *best* employees – end up flailing around in their so-called 'freedom'.

Another construct that has been extensively researched – and has, more recently, come to dominate the literature on empowerment – is what has been termed 'psychological empowerment'.[9] This term expressly acknowledges that empowerment needs to be felt and experienced, rather than merely given. In developing this concept, Gretchen Spreitzer argued that employees needed to experience four things. They needed to feel that their actions could make a difference; that they would be able to enact the key choices they wanted to make; that it is important to them personally; and that they feel they have real choice about what to do.

I wonder, though, if there might be something missing from our understanding of autonomy? Most of the empirical studies on autonomy and its related concepts are about employees enjoying *freedom from* intervention from supervisors. What's required for this to happen is that leaders step back and don't micromanage or interfere. Which is all well and good, but what about when employees feel they need to *pull leaders back into* their decisions, because they can't or won't make the decision without their input? That's what was happening in the three 'non-Ideal' cases I have set out in this book. It wasn't that micromanaging leaders were interfering where managers didn't need them. Rather, managers were pulling leaders back into 'blue zone' decisions because they felt unable or unwilling to make these decisions themselves without help or cover from the boss.

True, meaningful autonomy, then, isn't simply *freedom from* supervisor intervention: true, meaningful autonomy is freedom from *the need for* supervisor intervention. And *that's* the critical element – missing from much of the current empirical research – that the concept of 'meaningful autonomy' contains. It speaks directly to the idea that managers *want to* act independently from leaders, but they *don't always feel able to*. I call this the idea of manager 'independence' from leaders and we can contrast it with its mirror image – that of manager 'dependence' on leaders.

In fact, one study that empirically tested what can cause manager dependence on leaders suggested this can happen when leaders rely too much on purely transformational leadership.[10] Using a sample of nearly 900 bank employees who reported to 76 branch managers, the researchers found that when employees identified more with the leader personally than with the organization or its purpose (what the authors termed 'personal' rather than 'social' identification), employees became more dependent on the leader personally and experienced less empowerment. We know from a whole body of work on leadership that personal identification with the leader is a typical by-product of transformational leadership. This more recent study – one of the few studies to empirically test the impact of transformational leadership – suggests that relying too heavily on it could lead to dependent, rather than empowered, employees – ironic, given that for years, it was argued that transformational leadership would, by its very nature, cause employee empowerment.[11]

The reality is that if your managers are still dependent on you as a leader, if they cannot (or are not prepared to) make decisions independent of you, then you haven't empowered them. They may have technical autonomy (the necessary decision-rights, for example), but this autonomy is *meaningless* to them because they can't or won't use it without input, support or cover from you.

'Meaningful' autonomy requires that managers become *independent* of leaders. By 'independent', I don't mean that they go rogue and can do exactly what they want, in pursuit of their own, divergent agendas. Rather, I mean that they are capable of making decisions *without leaders* – decisions that deliver on the agreed organizational agenda. This, then, is not *limitless* autonomy: rather, it is *constrained* autonomy, used for the agreed organizational purpose.

As we have seen, this agreed, organizational purpose is created by leaders engaging in a significant amount of 'green zone' work – creating the narrative for the change, to explain why the change is needed and why now; explaining how it fits with what's gone before and what it will produce; and also how people need to behave in order to deliver these outcomes. That 'green zone' work creates the context for the change. We can think of this context as a *constraint* on people (leaders, as well as managers) within the organization. And this is the critical point: **it is this 'green zone' constraint (what the change must deliver and how people should behave in delivering it) that makes managers' 'blue zone' autonomy (what to work on and what to prioritize) 'meaningful'.**

What happens if this 'green zone' constraint is not clear for managers? In other words, if the constraint is insufficiently constraining? Well, the result for the best managers – the ones who want to make decisions and do the right thing – is that they *flail in too much freedom*. The best analogy I have for this is the mathematical concept of 'degrees of freedom'.[12] The number of degrees of freedom in any scenario is the number of ways in which a dynamic system (such as an organization) can move, without violating the constraints imposed on it. In the absence of any constraint, the degrees of freedom a manager has – and therefore the choices that she could make – would be infinite.

That might well sound attractive – at least at first. But the problem for high-performing, ambitious managers such as the ones allocated to an important strategic change is that operating without any constraints (i.e. with infinite degrees of freedom) is risky. It's the risk of not making the best possible decision, or of not performing as well as they could have done. What these best managers actually need is not infinite degrees of freedom, but rather some constraints – and, critically, constraints of the right *type* – so that their degrees of freedom are reduced. That enables them to make more effective choices, and more quickly, because they are not having to consider and second-guess every possible option.

And what *type* of constraints do the best managers need? They need leaders to specify purpose, outcomes and behaviours – the three critical component parts of 'green zone' Clarity. They need that to be backed up with the four Elements of Alignment (leader Conversations and Actions and leader-sponsored changes to Resourcing and Metrics) so they feel supported in the decisions they are making. And they need that to be augmented by Focus and Consistency during the second and third years of the change so they can continue to deliver – and improve the quality of the decisions they are making over time. This virtuous circle gives managers more and more confidence that they can exercise the autonomy they have, and so makes them more and more likely to do it – and to do it successfully.

It may seem ironic, then, but it is *only by constraining managers in this way* – and, note, *only* in this way (i.e. by specifying what to deliver but not telling them *how* to deliver it) – that leaders can empower managers to deliver the 'how' without their input or support. If, on the other hand, leaders fail to deliver this 'green zone' constraint, then managers will still have too many degrees of freedom and, as a result, they'll still need to revert to leaders for help deciding on the 'how' – pulling leaders back into the 'blue zone'.

As we first saw in Chapter 3, 'meaningful' autonomy has two Elements.

Element 1: Autonomy is possible

This first Element relates to what might technically or practically get in the way of managers exercising the authority they have. At the most basic level, of course, managers need to have the right level of authority or decision-rights in order to make the decisions leaders want them to make. But for autonomy to be possible it takes more than this: managers also need to have the right resources (people as well as budget) so that the decisions they make can be executed. And they need to have the right metrics in place to measure progress. To the extent these Elements have been delivered in the earlier stages of the change, then it will be *possible* for managers to exercise the autonomy that their roles gave them.

What the Ideal Case got right

We can immediately see how autonomy relies on the earlier dimensions of the model. Managers in the Ideal Case had all the advantages of Clarity and Alignment – delivered by their leaders stepping up – and they explained what this meant for their autonomy. As the Head of Change told me:

> We had a lot of autonomy to do things, suggest things, test things … It's easy to have autonomy when you know what you're supposed to be doing – I mean, overall, the big picture is clear, you have enough resource to get it done, and you know what's being measured and what they're asking about. Within that context, we decided what to do and we got on with it.

But Focus and Consistency – delivered by leaders stepping back – mattered too. In particular, the need for time and patience to deliver the big, multi-year outcome that had been asked for. As the same manager put it:

> This kind of change doesn't happen overnight, so even if we'd had resources and KPIs and all the autonomy in the world, without time and the ability to learn from what we were doing, we would've had to have asked leaders for input on how best to make progress. But because we had time to learn, *we* became the experts and so we could make those calls ourselves. Equally, if we'd have had inconsistent objectives, again we would've needed to check with the boss to see what was really the priority. Without time and consistent signals, you become much more of an order-taker.

Equally, although the Early Momentum Case had compromised managers' Focus by not being sufficiently Consistent, nevertheless their early work on giving Clarity and Alignment helped them feel that they could exercise the authority they had:

> I think the key thing for us was that they backed it up with resources and metrics. That meant we could actually make decisions and put them into practice. Without those things, autonomy wouldn't have been possible.

What the other cases got wrong

And so it proved in the other two cases: without sufficient budget, the ability for managers to implement the decisions they were authorized to make was compromised:

> There was too much to do and not enough to do it with. That made it hard to work out what to prioritize, so even though I didn't need anybody's actual sign-off to make the call, I would usually get [the CEO's] input, because somebody had to choose what to work on, we couldn't do it all. (The Under The Radar Case)

> It was just impossible. Even when we felt we had a good way through – a worked-up business case for a new initiative, something we believed would work – we had no budget and no prospect of getting any. It was really demoralizing. (The Road Runner Case)

The result was that in only two out of the four cases did managers feel that it was possible for them to exercise the autonomy they had – although in all four cases, they technically had all the decision-rights and authority that they needed.

	Ideal	EM	UTR	RR
Element 1: **Managers need to feel that it's possible for them to exercise their autonomy**	☑	☑	☒	☒

Element 2: Autonomy is comfortable

It's not enough that it is *possible* to exercise the autonomy you have: you also have to be *comfortable* in exercising it. And that means it mustn't feel personally risky for you to make a call on what to work on or how to act. Managers shouldn't feel like they are going out on a limb, or having to make a decision in the dark, when choosing priorities for themselves and their team. If that's the case, many managers won't exercise the autonomy they have – even if they have the authority and resources to do so. Instead, they will look to leaders to give them cover for these decisions, thereby sucking them back into these tactical, 'blue zone' decisions.

In my experience, if managers need 'cover' for a decision, and won't take it without leader input, that's a classic marker of managers not having 'meaningful' autonomy. And chances are that's because leaders haven't done a good enough job in creating the conditions for such autonomy – in other words, they haven't delivered sufficient Clarity, Alignment, Focus or Consistency.

So what enables managers to feel *comfortable* exercising their autonomy? *That* happens when all the leader's signals are pointing in the same direction. In other words, when the target outcome is clear, when all four Elements of Alignment are signalling the same way, and when these have been maintained throughout the change; when no new messages or conflicting strategies have been announced in the meantime; and when managers have time to learn from, as well as deliver, what's being asked of them. All of that – the four 'asks' of Clarity, Alignment, Focus and Consistency – makes managers comfortable in the exercise of their autonomy – and that's the second, crucial part of making it 'meaningful'.

What the Ideal Case got right

We see this in the Ideal Case – where managers were perfectly comfortable exercising the autonomy they had. As the new Head of

Change (who'd just been hired to replace the previous incumbent who'd now left the business) recalled of her first few months in the role:

> So it's having clarity on objectives and having resources and time that makes autonomy not just *possible*, but also *pleasant*. Pleasant. And that's important – because otherwise, autonomy can be *un*pleasant. I mean, if you're not quite sure what you should be delivering, then autonomy's a risk for you. You might make the wrong call or choose the wrong priority, because the signals you had weren't clear. And then it's on you. When it *shouldn't* be on you. It should be on the CEO and the senior team. And here it definitely was on them – they'd done all of that work. So I could just come in and know exactly what to do.

As a result, the conversations between leader and manager remain in the 'green zone', focusing on outcomes and 'how' and 'why' these are being delivered. The CEO does not micromanage or interfere in manager activities and is not involved in the detail of what they are working on because *he doesn't need to be* – that's 'blue zone' territory that managers are by now more than capable of occupying. He expects them to master this 'blue zone' and he recognizes that that doesn't require him to join them in it.

As you might remember from the time-analysis graphs in Chapter 3, by now the (new) CEO of the Ideal Case was spending much less time than either his predecessor had spent in Year 1, or than his peers in the other three cases were *still* spending, on this change. And, of the total amount of time he *was* spending on it, hardly any of that time was spent making decisions about the change: whatever time he was still spending on it, was spent thinking about it or talking about it.

The reason that this CEO was needed less was that, by now, the personal leadership activities – the conversations and role-modelling – that had been used to establish the change in its early days were needed less. Because by now, more and more of the heavy-lifting of keeping the change going was being done by the new routines and structures of the organization – its processes, systems and KPIs. Coupled with leaders prepared to step back – to enable managers to Focus on delivering a change about which they remained Consistent – these new routines reduced the need for leader involvement (let alone 'magic') and meant that managers could lead themselves.

What the other cases got wrong

It's worth saying that none of the leaders in the other three cases were egotistical micromanagers: they all wanted their managers to experience autonomy. But in the cases that lacked sufficient early Clarity and Alignment – the Under The Radar and the Road Runner Cases – autonomy never became 'meaningful' for managers. While inadequate resources in both cases meant that autonomy was not always possible, it was the lack of both Focus and Consistency that caused managers to be *unwilling* to take decisions:

> Because that target wasn't shared across the Senior Leadership Team, there were a lot of requests and priorities. We'd always gone to the CEO to help us adjudicate on those, and we were still doing that by Year 3. That didn't change. (The Under The Radar Case)

> By now, we had a lot of mixed messages about what was important, so I looked to the CEO not just for personal support, but also for cover. Making calls on what to work on felt way too risky otherwise. (The Road Runner Case)

As a result, these CEOs were being pulled back into 'blue zone' conversations about what to work on and which priority to give most time to.

But autonomy was also compromised to some extent for managers in the Early Momentum Case. Despite this CEO's early work that had partly delivered Clarity and fully delivered Alignment, by Year 2, this case had too many things on and not enough slack. This, in turn, meant managers were susceptible to a change in strategy by stealth, so that when leader inconsistency occurred, it went unnoticed and unchallenged. And, having occurred, the inconsistency in strategy meant that whatever Clarity and Alignment they'd had initially was now corroded, causing managers' autonomy to go from 'meaningful' to 'meaningless'. Or, as the Head of Change termed it, 'horrible':

> Empowerment is fine if you know exactly what you need to deliver and if everything's consistent. But if some of that is not clear or it's not consistent, then empowerment just means people ending up doing the wrong things. We had real empowerment early on, when we could make decisions without ever worrying whether this was the right thing to do. But with the change in strategy and no real explanation about what this meant for us, that's when being empowered was horrible. And what I mean by that is, we were still expected to deliver all of that original change but we just couldn't do it now without checking in. And of course that made us feel pretty useless. But we didn't have a choice. It was just too uncertain and too risky to make those decisions by ourselves.

Facing the reality of 'horrible' empowerment, these managers gave their power back – in the form of reverting to senior leaders to make decisions for them, or at least asking them for cover on the decisions they were still prepared to make. This meant senior leaders still being needed to make decisions, in a way that wasn't true for the Ideal Case. And this despite the Early Momentum senior leaders putting in a comparable level of effort and involvement in the early stages of the change – they had definitely stepped up. But their failure to step back in the right way – the lapse in Consistency, aided and abetted by the lack of Focus – meant their return on this early investment was negligible. The result was that it was only in the Ideal Case that managers felt comfortable to exercise the autonomy they had, without the need for input or cover from senior leaders:

	Ideal	EM	UTR	RR
Element 2: **Managers need to feel comfortable in exercising their** **autonomy and this does not entail personal risk for them**	☑	☒	☒	☒

Diagram 8.1: Summary of how the Cases delivered 'Meaningful' Autonomy

	Ideal	EM	UTR	RR
Element 1: Managers need to feel that it's possible for them to exercise their autonomy	☑	☑	☒	☒
Element 2: Managers need to feel comfortable in exercising their autonomy and this does not entail personal risk for them	☑	☒	☒	☒

Change – and 'meaningful' autonomy – delivered?

Returning to the combined progress graph, we can now view progress over the full duration of the change programme.

Diagram 8.2: Progress over three and a half years

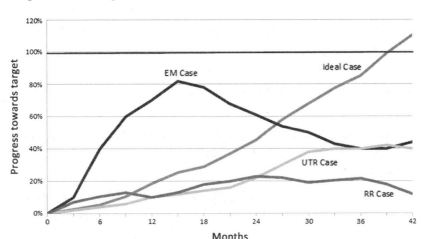

Helped by a glut of resources and by only doing the cosmetic 'quick wins' in the first year, the Early Momentum Case made stellar early progress. But these highs were not sustained – partly because the fundamental work on data and systems, on which further progress depended, hadn't been done in Year 1; but also because of a change in strategy which went unchallenged by over-worked managers in Year 2. Life for them became hard, as they had to contend with more and more 'priorities' against a background of falling numbers. And autonomy for them was now relatively meaningless, as they checked in regularly with senior leaders, unsure of what really was a priority in their business.

Meanwhile, for the Under The Radar Case, they had started off very slowly, hampered by a lack of resources and no clear argument having been made for fundamental change. But they kept going, gradually building up data about which projects were working and why. Despite no additional resources coming their way, they were blessed with at least a consistent strategy. This helped them sustain the progress they made. Although they would not improve significantly – because too little of the fundamental work had been done, largely because whatever *was* done had to be low-key and 'under the radar' – the numbers did not worsen, meaning managers never faced the demoralizing downward slide on progress. Feeling gradually more able to predict results and deliver targets, autonomy became slightly more meaningful for these managers over time, even if the gap between target and output was still disappointing. They ended up with a comparable level of improvement over the three and a half years as in the Early Momentum Case – an ironic result, given the amount of time, effort and money that the latter had invested.

In the Road Runner Case, progress was more erratic. The progress that was made was down to the personal effort and commitment of both leaders and managers. They made decent early progress because they immediately started working on 'quick wins' – without even agreeing the outcome being targeted. But this early progress evaporated as inadequate resourcing and no structural support took its toll. Coupled with a change in strategy which, as in the Early Momentum Case, went unnoticed and unchallenged by overworked managers, this meant that the numbers took a downward turn in Year 3. Tired, frustrated and now demoralized by poor results, these managers needed more from leaders than any of the other cases – not just guidance and input as to what to work on (as in the Early Momentum Case), but also personal support, coaching and empathy as they dealt with the pressure they were under.

For the Ideal Case, it was a different, and happier, story. In the early days, this business appeared less successful than the Early Momentum and Road Runner Cases. That's because its early results were being dampened by the time and effort it was investing in the 'zero glam' work – work it knew needed to be done because of the Clarity given about the outcome being targeted. The return on this investment became apparent only in the middle years of the change, as these long-dated efforts came to fruition and as projects were gradually refined to produce better, less risky outcomes by managers who now truly understood the dynamics of the business, thanks to the data and systems changes put through during Year 1.

This business was also set up to succeed because of the Alignment efforts that leaders made. By talking about and role-modelling the change, by resourcing it properly and by changing the metrics used to measure and reward it, managers were able to do what they did best – i.e. work out how to deliver the change that had been asked for, rather than having to second-guess the signals leaders were sending.

Helped in the second and third years by an unchanging strategy (giving them Consistency) and by having sufficient time and resources (giving them the patience and slack required for Focus), managers in the Ideal Case were able to deliver a large, multi-year uplift in performance. They were also able to do this without needing ongoing input, support or cover from leaders. In fact, several of the most critical change-leaders, including the CEO, left the business during Year 3 – with no impact on progress, because progress was now no longer dependent on their ongoing personal involvement. In other words, the autonomy the Ideal Case managers had was 'meaningful' – and, as a result, the change they delivered was successful and sustainable.

One final watch-out: the stories people tell themselves

Virginia Woolf once noted in her diary: 'One never realizes an emotion at the time. It expands later, and thus we don't have complete emotions about the present, only about the past.'[13] It's clear from the four cases I have set out in this book that only one of them – the Ideal Case – delivered its target outcomes. We know now why that was – because leaders delivered Clarity, Alignment, Focus and Consistency, enabling managers to have 'meaningful' Autonomy that meant they could deliver the change that had been asked for. But while it was only the Ideal Case that had this happy ending, nevertheless the managers in the three other cases *all told happy, hopeful stories* during the change they were working so hard on.

One of the things you notice when you do the kind of research on which this book is based – i.e. collecting people's stories about how something unfolded for them over time – is that they very often tell positive stories (to themselves and to each other) at the time, even when, with hindsight, they are disappointed with how things turned out. At the time, all the managers in these four cases were looking on the bright side and believing that what they were doing (and what their leaders had done) would be enough.

Evolutionary biologists have speculated that human beings developed this tendency to focus on the positive partly as a way of dealing with crises in their lives, especially when these events felt out of control. The people who looked on the bright side and maintained a positive frame of mind were more likely to be hopeful enough to reproduce – which was, in evolutionary terms, our critical purpose.[14] And so those positive 'look on the bright side' genes were reproduced and are still with us today.

But whatever its genesis, this human tendency to look on the bright side and see the positives is one way that human beings make sense of things being harder than they'd hoped, and over time not turning out quite as they had intended. We see this particularly in the stories we tell ourselves when things go *very* badly wrong. When empirical researchers investigate (i.e. collect stories about) disasters, what they find are people making sense of bad things happening by telling themselves more hopeful stories about these events than the researchers might have expected.

One of the best examples of this are the stories told by the survivors of a famous air-crash in the early 1970s. The plane had been on its way from Montevideo in Uruguay to the Chilean capital, Santiago. It crashed high up in the Andes Mountains. Of the 45 passengers and crew on board, twelve were killed in the crash itself. Stranded on a glacier and with no way of contacting the outside world – they had a makeshift transistor radio that could pick up signals, but no way of transmitting – the survivors would wait 10 weeks before they were found. By the time they were, only 16 of them were still alive.

How they survived – and the lengths they had to resort to – are well-documented.[15] But more recently, the academic Spencer Harrison (now a Professor at INSEAD) investigated how and why they were able to survive. He met with the survivors of the crash, studied their diaries from the time and asked them how they had made sense of the dire situation in which they found themselves. What he found was that invariably these survivors had told themselves, and each other, positive stories of hope. They had believed they would be rescued, and because of this, they made decisions that were likely to increase their chances of this happening. It was hope – that they would survive long enough to be found – that made it possible for them to continue.[16] As Harrison put it in the Academy of Management session when he first presented his paper: 'They had hope. That made them believe they would be OK. And that meant they continued to try.'[17]

And so it was in the four cases in this book. Even though for three of them the results of the change were disappointing relative to the outcomes they had targeted, managers remembered at the time being full of hope that things would work, and therefore motivated to keep going. In fact, it was only with hindsight that they looked back and saw what had been missing in the change and what had made their lives harder than they needed to be. At the time, the managers involved in the day-to-day activities of the change were all motivated, positive and convinced their approach would work in the end.

To help us see what this positive, look-on-the-bright-side attitude looks like in practice, in the section that follows, we'll walk through the narratives that the managers in each of the four cases were telling themselves at the time. Note that – other than the final sentence (shown in bold), which is a direct, verbatim quote – each of the stories that follow is a compilation of stories from all the managers I spoke to in each case, written using *my words and phrases.* By putting their combined stories into the phrasing and framework of the model that emerged, it is easier to see how these four stories contrast with each other. It is easier also to see how these managers' positive spin on the failings and inadequacies of leaders helped them keep up their pretence of hope. I'm including them here as a final watch-out – so you can see the contrast between what the managers were telling themselves at the time, with what they later came to believe about the change and the progress they made. Because it is only when we're able to recognize these overly positive, and ultimately misguided, narratives *in real time,* that we will be able to intervene quickly enough to course-correct and thereby produce a different outcome.

Let's take the Ideal Case first. Here (as I say, in my words, not theirs) is the story these managers were telling themselves about the work they were doing:

Because this new strategy is important and something our leaders are committed to, because it's needed now, and because we understand how this relates to previous and current strategies – i.e. what we'll keep and what we'll stop – we understand the relative priority of this new strategy.

And because we also understand the outcome metrics being targeted by this new strategy and the full extent (and it's big!) of the improvement we need to deliver over the coming years, we can see that this change will take a long time, and will require fundamental change to the way we do things, including some new behaviours from all of us. Therefore, while we might have some 'quick wins' in there for political or motivational reasons (to get people on side and to make them feel like this is doable), the real early work at this stage is boring, mundane and decidedly unglamorous – because that's what we need to be focusing on if we're going to make this deep, fundamental change to how we do things. This work is critical and we give time and attention to it.

Having established Clarity right at the start, leaders follow this up by Aligning the business around the change they've asked for. They spend time and attention talking about the change in ordinary conversations, and role-modelling it at every opportunity. They're also making time for it: they're always there if we need help. They've given us the power we need to make the decisions and it's on the agenda of their SLT meetings, so it's being talked about at the highest level of the organization.

They've allocated sufficient budget to help us achieve what we need to, as well as the right people to work on this. And, for most of them, this is the main thing they're working on. We're collecting all the data we need to understand why things are working or not, and we're measuring the impact. Leaders have also changed the KPIs to support the change. By the start of Year 2, both leaders and managers have these revised KPIs in place. All of which means, we're set up to succeed.

We also need time to deliver the big ask – and leaders are giving us that. They're patient for the big improvement. They're also pushing us to learn what's going on in these projects rather than to just 'deliver' them. That means they're encouraging us to tweak rather than add to the projects we're working on, and they often say 'no' to the new ideas we have so that we are focusing on a smaller number of activities. Iterative improvements to projects means we're getting better and more focused over time.

Leaders are also staying really consistent about what they want. They've maintained all the changes they made – personal and structural – in Year 1. And the change has remained the priority – there have been no conflicting strategies or messages communicated. That's meant we've been able to stay the course and stay focused on delivering the change they originally asked for.

And all of that has meant we knew what to do – what to work on and how to use the budget and our own time – and we were able and willing to make decisions on our own. We need much less help from the leaders than at the start. We don't need input from them (because we know what to do) and we don't feel we need cover from them either (because making these calls doesn't feel risky for us). **Leaders gave us autonomy to do this and we've run with it. We've done a great job.**

This was the narrative that the managers in the Ideal Case told themselves – and it was true! If your managers can say the same about the change you've asked them to deliver – and critically, if they're not kidding themselves – then you're in good shape. The danger is that they might kid themselves – because of those inherited human predispositions to 'look on the bright side'. Because, as we'll see, the narrative being told by the managers in the Early Momentum Case was very positive too. It was certainly a much more exciting story early on. And although that excitement would dissipate as progress slowed, nevertheless the managers in the Early Momentum Case stayed positive:

Because this new strategy is important and something our leaders are committed to, because it's needed now, because we understand how this relates to previous and current strategies – i.e. what we'll keep and what we'll stop – we understand the relative priority of this new strategy. We also understand the outcome metrics being targeted by this new strategy, so we have a good idea about the sorts of initiatives to work on. We also know the new behaviours expected from us.

The best bit is that, because we don't have a big, multi-year target, and the target we have for Year 1 isn't so big, we're spending most of the first year harvesting some of the low-hanging fruit. These 'quick wins' are easy and exciting and they're more than enough to meet our Year 1 target. It doesn't seem like we need to change our systems that much, actually. And it seems like it would be a waste of time and effort to be doing much on data or systems right now, so we're not prioritizing that. Sure, there might be bigger targets coming down the track, but we're smart and hard-working and so we'll be able to deliver. At this rate, this change won't take us that long.

Leaders are spending time and attention talking about the change in ordinary conversations and role-modelling it at every opportunity. They've given us the power we need to make the decisions and it's on the agenda of their SLT meetings, so it's being talked about at the highest level of the organization.

They've allocated sufficient budget to help us achieve what we need to, as well as the right people to work on this. And, for most of them, this is the main thing they're working on. We're collecting all the data we need to understand why things are working or not, and we're measuring the impact. Leaders have also changed the KPIs to support the change. By the start of Year 2, both leaders and managers have these revised KPIs in place. All of which means we're set up to succeed. And, like we said, our initial targets weren't that big, so it feels really doable.

More recently, things have got harder for us, but I guess that's true for most change initiatives. By Year 2, we have lots of projects on – all the stuff we'd been working on in Year 1, plus some pretty boring stuff (like data cleansing and systems change) that we've more recently turned our attention to. This is definitely less fun – and it's a lot slower. But we've still got the resources we need and a lot of senior leader support and we're keen to work hard, so it's all good.

We can also run with whatever new ideas we have – no one says 'no' to anything, which is great. What's also exciting is the sheer number of new ideas we get to bring forward – rather than just tweaking existing stuff. And there's a real focus on delivering – we don't have to spend too much time analyzing why things were happening. It's exciting work!

More recently still – I'd say Year 3 – things feel like they've changed for us. It doesn't feel like this is quite such a priority for the business. This means it's harder for us to know what decisions we should be making. But leaders have kept up with all the changes they've made, personally and structurally, early on, so we're just continuing to work on our projects. And leaders are still there if we need help. In fact, I'd say they're giving us even more specific input than at the start.

I guess by the end of Year 3 it feels like we've gone backwards but I've read that most change runs into difficulties about this stage. And whenever we need senior guidance – because, to be honest, recently, we haven't always known what to prioritize – or because we feel we'd like them to make the decision rather than us risk making it on our own – they're there for us. We have all the authority we need and lots of resources so it's fine. **Actually, they've been great leaders and we've done a pretty good job.**

Of course, we now know the flaws in this narrative: it is short-sighted and naïve. And it is, especially in the later stages of the change, far more positive than the outcome data could justify. But that may be just the human condition – at least of high-performing, driven, ambitious managers, keen to do well.

This positive spin was evident in the two other cases too. Take the Under The Radar Case. Its managers were still looking on the bright side, however hard the work was:

This new strategy is important, it's something the CEO is personally committed to, and it's something we need to do now. But it's not really that different from our previous strategies, so we're keeping all the current strategic initiatives that we had on and we've just added this onto them. We don't think this will take that long either or require that much fundamental change, so it isn't worth doing too much work on data or systems right now. Instead, we're getting some activities going to show that this can be done.

We can also think about metrics later – once we know what we can achieve. So while we've agreed the outcomes we're targeting with the CEO, and talked about the new behaviours expected from us, we haven't publicized those too widely. These targets aren't long-term and they aren't that big either, so we'll be OK.

Leaders are helping us by spending time and attention talking about the change in ordinary conversations and role-modelling it at every opportunity. They're also making time for it and they've given us the power we need to make decisions. They haven't been able to give us sufficient budget as yet, but as I say, it may not be so big a change, so that might be OK. We're also collecting some data on this, which is good.

The change team have revised KPIs, which is a real motivator. Leaders haven't changed the KPIs for anyone else, or for leaders, but that can come later. They have definitely devoted the right people to the change, though – and for most of them, it's the main thing they were working on. So it feels doable.

More recently, things have got harder for us, but I guess that's true for most change initiatives. By Year 2, we had lots of projects on – all the stuff we'd been working on, plus some extra stuff that our CEO has added in. He really cares about this change and so he's very involved, which is fantastic. We have some data on why certain things are working, but we're still managing to avoid too many of the boring projects that other businesses are working on. We still don't have enough budget, but we're hugely motivated to do this, largely because of the extent to which it's still personally supported by the CEO.

The middle period of this change has been busy! We have more and more projects on our plate which, given that we started with too little budget, has definitely made life harder. We need help a lot – simple things like deciding what to work on, given these pressures. But we keep going.

One of the things that's made it possible to make some progress is that leaders have been really consistent. Not only have they kept up all the changes they'd made in the first year – personal as well as structural – but there's also been no conflicting strategies or messages. The fact that this is still a priority has really helped us stay the course. That and the fact that this whole thing was 'under the radar' has given us the time and space we needed to start making some real progress. That was a blessing in disguise.

And even if we still need to go to senior leaders for guidance (to help us make choices about what's really important, given the number of 'priority' projects and the lack of resources) at least they're always there to help. We also don't want to take the risk of making decisions about whose project *should get priority, so we go to them for cover on those calls. But, like I said, they're always there to help. We haven't achieved our target but that's not their fault. **They've been great leaders. I guess we've done a pretty good job – we've certainly worked hard!***

We now understand the gaps in the thinking – and, notably, in the work chosen. Outcome metrics need to come before activities, so they can help shape the choices made about them. And the extent of the change, and its fundamental nature, are best communicated early rather than late – if you are to give such fundamental change the kind of investment and time it invariably needs.

But it was the work and effort in the Road Runner Case that was most compromised. Lacking most of the dimensions we now know are important, nevertheless managers told a positive story:

This new strategy is important and something our leaders are committed to. It's not so different from what we're doing anyway though, so we can simply add this new strategy and its initiatives onto the existing work that we already have on. We haven't spelled out how long this will take, or what we're aiming for as a result. But that's OK – the main thing is to take personal responsibility for getting some activities going. And to get those started as soon as possible. So we've agreed which activities we'll work on. Once they are up and running, then we can put some metrics in place to measure what we're achieving. It would be a waste of time and effort to put those in place this early – and I'm not sure we have time or resource to do that work right now.

Leaders are helping us by spending time and attention talking about the change in ordinary conversations and role-modelling it at every opportunity. They're also making time for it and they've given us the power we need to make decisions. They haven't been able to give us sufficient budget as yet, but as I say, it may not be so big a change, so that might be OK. It helps that we're focusing very much on getting on with the projects rather than collecting data or doing tons of analysis. And we don't have to worry about revised KPIs or anything like that, so that's a massive help.

More recently, things have got harder for us, but I guess that's true for most change initiatives. By Year 2, we had lots of projects on – all the stuff we'd been working on, plus some extra stuff that our CEO has added in. And we needed to deliver quickly on those. He really cares about this change and so he's very involved, which is fantastic. We still don't have enough budget, but we're hugely motivated to do this largely because of the extent to which it's still personally supported by the CEO. And because we're still very focused on delivering immediate activities to make a difference quickly – we're not slowing ourselves down by analyzing why things are working or not and we have hardly any data anyway – it feels really exciting.

It's hard work, though – and that's been especially true in this middle period. We have more and more projects on our plate which, given that we started with too little budget, has definitely made life harder. We need help a lot – simple things like deciding what to work on, given these pressures. But we keep going.

More recently still – I'd say Year 3 – things feel like they've changed for us. It doesn't feel like this is quite such a priority for the business. This means it's harder for us to know what decisions we should be making. But leaders have kept up with the personal changes they'd made early on, so we're just continuing to work on our projects. We've seen a cut to resources recently, but the CEO says he's still totally behind us. And they're always there if we need help. In fact, I'd say they're giving us more help now than they did in the early days. And that means we keep going.

I guess by the end of Year 3 it feels like we're not really making progress at all. I've read that this is when most change programmes run into difficulties and it's certainly hard for us. We go to leaders a lot. Partly because we need guidance about what to prioritize – given the number of 'priority' projects and the lack of resources, we don't want to take the risk of making these decisions on our own. And partly because we just need support. The work is exhausting, we don't feel that we're making progress and we don't really know why. The fact that leaders are always available to us makes all the difference. We haven't succeeded but that's not their fault: they were there for us. **Actually, they've been great leaders but we just haven't been able to deliver.**

Notice that all of these narratives retain a positive spin all the way through, even as managers were starting to realize that their change was failing relative to the outcomes being targeted, and certainly relative to the performance of the Ideal Case. But regardless of the reality at the time, all of these managers were looking on the bright side and believing the best of their leaders and themselves.

And the lesson for leaders in these stories? It is that, as a leader, you can't always rely on managers to be the canary in the mine on whether you're failing to lead. Managers might just be hoping that things will work out, or get better. So instead, *you* need to look honestly at how you're leading at each of four dimensions – Clarity, Alignment, Focus and Consistency. Ask managers for specific feedback on each of the Elements you need to put in place, so you can identify weak spots and then fix them, whether by stepping up more on the first two 'asks' (Clarity and Alignment), or by stepping back more on the second two (Focus and Consistency).

And the lesson for managers here? Look hard at each of the four 'asks' of leaders to help identify what your leaders aren't doing well enough. Compare what you delivered with what you were targeting and understand the variance between them. And by 'understand', I don't mean 'explain away' or 'pretend it's better than it is'. I mean properly understand so you know what you need to change in your approach. And then, having thought carefully about the gaps and how you can close them:

- First, talk with leaders about where they haven't stepped up enough. Perhaps there's still insufficient Clarity about what the change will deliver or how it fits with what's gone before? Or not enough Alignment, especially in resourcing and metrics, to support the change they've asked for? In which case, they should go back and re-do these Clarity and Alignment stages to re-lay the foundations for success.

- Then talk with leaders about where they aren't stepping back enough – perhaps not helping you Focus, by interfering too much, or adding in too many other 'priorities'; or perhaps not giving you the time and slack you need to deliver. Or by not delivering Consistency, perhaps by being inconsistent about whether this strategy is actually the priority or by being undisciplined in the language they use and how they manage themselves. If leaders are doing any of these, raise this with them. As part of that conversation, take the time to understand why they haven't been able to step back and how you could make this easier for them.

Writing more than 2,500 years ago, the Chinese philosopher Lao Tzu made a distinction between good leaders and the best leaders. While good leaders are revered by the people they lead, the work done by the *best* leaders enables the people they lead to say, 'We did it ourselves.' The sentences (shown in bold) that end each of the narratives above are direct quotes from the managers in these cases and they perfectly exemplify this bit of ancient wisdom. Notice also what these sentences tell us about where the locus of power now lies in each organization. Only in the Ideal Case is power with managers. Their narrative ends with the reflection, '*Leaders gave us autonomy to do this and we've run with it. We've done a great job.*' Good leadership enables managers to do, and be at, their best.

In contrast, the other three cases end with managers claiming their leaders were 'great' because they supported them personally and reflecting that it was *they themselves* who hadn't done a good enough job in delivering the change. These quotes make me really sad. They show how forgiving managers can be of inadequate leadership; and how rarely managers speak up at the time and in the moment, to call out leadership inadequacy above them. They show also how deep-seated is our attachment to leaders working merely as champions and coaches, rather than also working to re-shape the organization's structure to support strategic change, and the managers whom they've tasked with delivering it.

The 'Step Up, Step Back' approach I've presented in this book tells a different story and therefore offers us a different way to lead strategic change. It tells us that if you fail to sort out the structure and instead rely only on your agency to get change done, you make life harder for your managers, your organization and yourself. But if you use both – initially by stepping up and then by stepping back – everybody wins. Which helps us not only understand how leaders can *really* lead successful change that sticks, but also how we can reconceive of the 'Hollywood' version of leadership itself. That's what I'll cover in the next, and final, chapter.

Tips and Watch-outs to Help You Make Managers' Autonomy 'Meaningful'

Tips and Watch-outs for Leaders

- **Is their autonomy possible?** If not, then look again at the decision-rights managers have, the resources allocated to the work and the metrics by which progress is being measured. Hear from them what more they need in these areas to help them make decisions without your input. If this first Element is in place, then move on to the second Element;

- **Are managers comfortable exercising the autonomy they have?** If not, find out why, because the reasons are likely to be down to you. Ask a wide range of managers which of the four 'asks' (Clarity, Alignment, Focus or Consistency) they feel have been short-changed and then be prepared to focus time and attention fixing these until they're sorted;

- **Be prepared to step up again** – to make sure that whatever Clarity and Alignment you may have had in the early days hasn't been corroded over time. Start with Clarity. Are people still clear why this strategy is needed and why now? Are they clear about the outcome metrics and the distinction between the long-term target and the shorter-term milestones? And what about the data being collected: is this enough to help them understand how and why some projects work and others fail?

- **If you need to, re-do the signalling**. Often the reason that autonomy isn't comfortable is because the signals you've sent (or at least, that they've received) haven't pointed in the same direction. If some of your signals were mixed, look again at all four Elements of Alignment and be prepared to re-do the ones that are missing;

- **Are you really stepping back?** Most leaders know they ought not to micromanage, but their own conceptions of 'work' in organizations, including the Magic and Activity Delusions, mean they often stray into the 'blue zone' even when their managers are more than capable of occupying it. Get them to manage you by getting feedback on whether you are accidentally doing too much. Get feedback also on how consistent you really are. And if you need to, step up to clarify again that this really is the priority strategy;

- **Check on their slack**. If you're serious about creating an organization where managers feel confident enough to act on their own, they need slack so they can learn what works. You help this by creating an environment where the emphasis is as much on learning from projects as on delivering them. Check that the slack they had early on in the change is being maintained. If not, then coach them to reduce the number of activities they're working on, and manage yourself to say 'no' to other 'priorities'.

Tips and Watch-outs for Managers

- **Is your autonomy possible?** If not, then ask for the decision-rights, or resources or metrics you need to be able to exercise the authority that your position gives you. You shouldn't have to make do without these things. Nor should you believe that, if only you worked harder or smarter, you could make up for the lack of them. You shouldn't be succumbing to the Activity or Magic Delusions any more than leaders;

- **Are you comfortable exercising the autonomy you have?** If you have the right structures in place, why is it that you're not comfortable making these decisions without input or cover? Be honest about this. Walk through the Elements of each 'ask' (Clarity, Alignment, Focus and Consistency) to see what's missing. And then ask leaders to close the gap, either by stepping up, or by stepping back;

- **Coach leaders if they need to step up again.** If what's missing – perhaps it was never there, or perhaps it has become corroded – is Clarity about what the strategy will deliver, or Alignment around the change that was asked for, then coach leaders to devote time and attention to this now. Use whatever infrastructure you have (the annual budgeting process or the strategic planning process, or your own performance appraisal) to push for Clarity and Alignment. Each of these tools can help force a conversation – about resources and outcomes and KPIs, respectively – without you needing to create a new forum;

- **Are they really stepping back?** If you have sufficient Clarity and Alignment, it may be that leaders are not stepping back enough. Where are they straying into your 'blue zone', or where are they not being quite as consistent as you need? Where have they sown seeds of confusion by choices they've made and perhaps not explained, or ways they have behaved? This may be accidental, so ask them to clarify. And if it's not accidental, and suggests a change in priority instead, then ask them to re-do the 'Step Up, Step Back' process for the new strategy they're choosing instead, so that neither of you wastes your efforts;

- **Create and maintain your own slack**. If you're serious about getting smarter at what you do, you need to become the keeper of your own learning time. Find it, ring-fence it and keep it as sacred as you can. Show the return on this time by using it to generate insights – about what's working or not, about what customers really value – that means slack is also valued by others. But it will only be valued by others if it is first valued by you.

CHAPTER NINE

A Different Way to Think About Organizations

Re-writing the 'Hollywood' version of leadership

Right at the start of this book, I introduced the flawed philosophy on which the existing approaches to leading strategic change are based. This philosophy is anchored in what I call the Four Delusions of Leadership – i.e. that leadership is all about magic, activity, drama and agency – and it has fostered the 'Hollywood' version of leadership that has dominated the advice given to leaders about how to lead change. Fundamentally, this philosophy assumes that individuals are more important than the structures within which they operate; and therefore that heroic, charismatic leadership is sufficient to produce strategic change.

This book argues a different case, based on very different empirical research. But as well as offering a different way to lead strategic change, this approach also offers us a different way to think about organizations.

Organizations as systems

We can think of organizations – or indeed, any other entity that involves human beings, be it an organization, a team, a family or a whole society – as being a *system*. The system is made up of two elements – people (endowed with agency) and structure. [1]

People + Structure

People use their agency to create structure. This helps give their endeavours shape and scale. The structure they create can be either:

- **procedural (or 'hard') structure** – such as the organization's KPIs and metrics, the org chart with roles and job descriptions, budgets and resourcing, processes and IT systems; or
- **social (or 'soft') structure** – things like the culture of the organization or group, the habits and behaviours of the people within it and the unwritten rules by which they all live.

People use their agency to create structure – both 'hard' (or 'procedural') structure such as org charts, roles and KPIs; and 'soft' (or 'social') structure, such as the organization's culture and routines

People   Structure

Once these structures are created, however, they in turn start impacting the people – including even the individuals who created them. The structures (both hard and soft) of the organization now either *enable* or *constrain* how people will choose to behave and what, and how much they – no doubt all talented, driven, high-performing individuals – will be able to achieve.

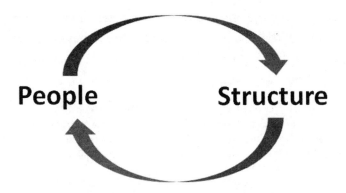

People   **Structure**

The structures that people create in turn impact people – either enabling or constraining them from acting in the way they may want to

'Agency' (i.e. people) may have originally created structure, but now the structure they have created becomes independent of them[2] and gradually comes to either enable or constrain their future agentic choices.

Using both people and structure to effect lasting change

There are two main complaints that I hear from change veterans. The first is that change doesn't stick. The second is that leaders get pulled in to too many of the implementation decisions during the change (the Tom and Sue problem from right at the start of this book).

The 'Step Up, Step Back' approach that this book outlines aims to deal with both of these issues, by making sure that the people and the structure within an organization are *both* used as vehicles of change. If we only focus on people (whether leaders or managers), chances are the change will never become routine – putting its long-term success at risk. Equally, it's unlikely we'll ever free leaders from being pulled into the detail, regardless of how able managers are.[3] It is only by making the structure work for you – and for the change you've asked for – that we can start relying on it to continue and embed the change, because it's only when the structure is working in support of the change that people (whether leaders or managers) have an easier time.

Of course it requires people to *make* the necessary changes to the structure so that the changed structure can now help make the change happen, rather than work against it. As a result, the **people–structure** endeavour is now a virtuous, rather than a vicious circle:

People impact Structure: People use their agency to create structure – both 'hard' and 'soft' structure – that supports the change that they are asking for. Examples might be changes in job roles, reporting lines, resourcing or KPIs and metrics

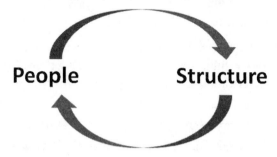

People   Structure

Structure impacts People: These new structures that have been created now support the change, rather than work against it. People are now supported when they make a decision in favour of the new way of working because the structure – be it their budget, or their new headcount, or their revised KPIs – supports them in making that choice

The 'Rock Star' and the 'Nerd'

You'll recall that in the old 'Hollywood' version of leading change, the charismatic leader – we called him 'Steve' – thought transformational leadership was sufficient (page 16). My research shows that leaders do need some of this type of leadership – using the purely agentic tools they have at their disposal. But they also need to honour, care about and give time and attention to the more mundane, 'zero glam' work of how organizations are changed – by also using the structural tools that every system has.

So as a leader, you need to not only be the 'rock star', you also need to be (or at least honour) the 'nerd'.[4] Which is actually why most of the *best* leaders I know are a skilful combination of these two things – they can do the 'rock star' bit when they need to, but they also give time and attention to the nerdier aspects when they need to do *that*, too. And,

critically, they know *how* and *when* to deploy both of these capabilities –
at the different times and in the different ways we've seen in the 'Step
Up, Step Back' approach – to effect the change they want to see. They
do this not only to give their new strategies and change efforts more
of a chance, nor even so that their managers have more opportunity to
occupy the 'blue zone' and feel that the autonomy they have is meaningful.
They do this also because it's easier *on them, as leaders.*

Because there are a few issues with choosing to try to *only* be a 'rock
star', without giving time and attention also to the less glamorous and
structural sides of the change effort. The first issue is that this is risky.
Because if you don't quite manage to pull off the 'rock star' role – and
actually, most leaders aren't quite as charismatic as they think they are –
then what are you left with? More importantly, what are the people following you left with, if you can't quite deliver on the 'rock star' rhetoric?

The second issue with relying solely on being a charismatic 'rock
star' leader is that it's exhausting – even for leaders who are naturally
charismatic. Why? Because it's all on you. There's no help coming from
any of the structural elements of the firm – from new metrics, or revised
KPIs or a new org chart – because you haven't devoted sufficient time
and attention to getting those things sorted out. So that leaves it all
on you to campaign for the change, to galvanize people that it can be
done, and to persuade them to keep going when momentum stalls.

Now, as we've said, it's up to you, as a leader, to judge when you need
to be the 'rock star' and when you need to be (or, at least, when you
need to honour) the 'nerd'. But this book should help you see which
type of leadership to use and when – by guiding you through what each
of the four 'asks' (Clarity, Alignment, Focus and Consistency) requires
from leaders. In the early stages of the change, there will be times when
charismatic leadership will be needed – when you're evangelizing for
the change and why it's needed now; when you're interacting with
people in individual conversations; and when you're role-modelling
the change through your own behaviours. These Elements of Clarity
and Alignment do indeed rely on good old-fashioned transformational
leadership. But as we've seen, this isn't enough. Leaders also need to

engage in some transactional work – when specifying the outcomes being targeted, when re-shaping the organization, its budgets and decision-rights, and when re-designing the metrics and KPIs that will calibrate and reward success.

This combination of transformational and transactional leadership – a combination of being both a 'rock star' and a 'nerd' – is, as we've seen, the secret to having successful, sustainable change delivered by empowered managers exercising their 'meaningful' autonomy. And remember those Four Delusions of Leadership we talked about in Chapter 1? This new way of leading strategic change helps us challenge those too.

How this new way of leading change helps counter the Four Delusions of Leadership

We talked about what I term the Four Delusions of Leadership back at the start of this book. I argued that these Delusions are dangerous for leaders, managers and organizations alike, not least because they give succour to the Hollywood version of how to lead change and, in particular, to the myth of the charismatic, 'rock star' leader. These Delusions cause three pernicious outcomes. First, for leaders, they keep you down in the detail of the change, because managers continue to need input, support and cover from you. Second, for managers, they prevent you being empowered to do this on your own, and thereby stop you from learning and developing into leaders in your own right. And for the organization, they reduce the chances of the change being successful and sustained.

Now that we have a different – and, I would argue, *better* – way to lead change, what different advice can we give leaders to help them counter these Four Delusions?

1. The Magic Delusion
This Delusion meant leaders believed that the change they wanted to see could be affected largely by their own charisma – their 'magic'. This would be enough. They didn't need to re-work the less glamorous aspects of the organization, such as KPIs and metrics, or budgets and

resourcing. So what's the lesson for leaders of the 'Step Up, Step Back' approach? **It's less about the magic and more about the mundane.**

The truth – as told by the managers in the Ideal Case – is that, while having a charismatic leader is good, strategic change takes much more than mere charisma or 'magic'. It requires the less glamorous, more mundane details of the change to be worked out – the new roles people will play, how progress will be measured and rewarded, how the structure and reporting lines of the business need to change in order to drive accountability for outcomes. This boring stuff is often seen as the stuff *managers* rather than leaders do – it is the essence of the three-decade-long split between 'leadership' and 'management', after all. I'm not suggesting leaders be the ones to *do* this work, but if they are to lead strategic change effectively, they need to give time and attention to these mundane issues – even if they're not actually *doing* the work of it themselves – rather than believing their 'magic' is all that's required.

So, by all means, be charismatic and inspiring; paint a picture of the bright new future and lead people up to the top of the hill; tell people you believe that they'll succeed in this effort and that you're there to support them. But then sweat the boring, mundane details that will set them up to succeed in this effort too. Worry about the org chart and the job descriptions, so people understand their role; worry about the KPIs and the metrics so they know how they'll be measured and rewarded; make sure the resourcing is sorted, so they believe what you're asking them to do is actually doable. And then make sure you are managing yourself so that – however 'magical' you are – you aren't sending mixed signals about how important this change is to you and the business.

2. The Activity Delusion

As you'll recall, this Delusion meant leaders focused too much on the detail of which activities or projects people should be working on, and too little on the outcomes that all of these activities should produce. The lesson for leaders of the 'Step Up, Step Back' approach? **It's not about activities, it's about outcomes.**

Deciding on activities too early and in the absence of clear, agreed target outcomes; and spending valuable leadership time on choosing activities rather than choosing outcomes, is a huge mistake. Without clear and agreed outcomes (mandated by leaders), managers can't make smart choices about which activities to work on. And that ought to be the division of labour: for leaders to decide the outcomes and for managers to decide the activities that will deliver them.

Without clear, agreed outcomes, it's also easy for the organization to default into working on 'quick wins' or 'low-hanging fruit'. But such 'quick wins', chosen without a clear target outcome in mind, are not usually a sustainable source of momentum, so don't focus on them. And especially don't waste the unique opportunity of the early stages of the change – when the spotlight and the air-time of the organization is focused on the change in a way it may never be again – to talk about something as micro and potentially toxic as 'quick wins'.

Instead, focus on getting, and then giving, sufficient Clarity about the outcomes you want. What will change as a result of this new strategy? What outcomes will get better, by how much, and by when? This is what enables managers to make the decisions about which initiatives to work on.

Having Clarity about the outcomes being targeted also means that the hard grind of data and metrics can be kicked off early because, by knowing the outcomes being targeted, you know what data you need to capture and what you need to measure. This early work on data and metrics lays the foundations for proper Alignment (through revised KPIs for both leaders and managers) and, from there, for Focus and Consistency. And from all of these, for managers to have 'meaningful' Autonomy and a strategic change that is delivered and sustained without the need for ongoing leader involvement.

3. The Drama Delusion

This Delusion meant leaders believed that the change needed to be fast, exciting, action-packed and risky. The result was, first, that leaders expected fundamental change to happen faster than was realistic, and second, that they paid too little attention to the need to embed the new way of doing things so that it becomes routine. The lesson for leaders of the 'Step Up, Step Back' approach? **It's not fast, it's slow. And it's less about drama and more about routine**.

Of course, speed and agility in organizations are assets in certain circumstances, but the truth in a strategic change situation is, as ever, more nuanced. The reality is that strategic change is a serious business which, as we have seen, requires the fundamental re-shaping of an organization. Fundamental change is not fast and yet the Drama-deluded leaders expect – and also signal – that a new strategy or change can be implemented quickly. This is as flawed as a dieter believing he can lose 12 lbs in a week: the reality is it's unlikely to happen and, even if it did, he wouldn't be able to sustain it.

Instead, accept that fundamental change will take time and then signal that you are giving the change – and the managers tasked with delivering it – the time you all agree it needs. Only when managers feel they have the time needed to make a meaningful difference will they invest in the deep, fundamental, long-dated work – to systems and capabilities – that this kind of change requires, rather than defaulting into choosing cosmetic 'quick wins' that, as we've seen, can be so toxic to fundamental, long-term, strategic change.

It is undoubtedly true that leaders need to demonstrate, in a way that is visible to people, that they believe in the change and are personally committed to it – we see that in *all* the successful change cases. But they need to do more than that. So while some early 'drama' might be effective in kicking off the change (perhaps alongside a little bit of leader 'magic'), actually if the change is going to get implemented, let alone stick, it needs to become the new 'way of doing things around here'.[5]

In other words, it needs to become routine. Because once the change is implemented, it isn't 'change' any more. It's the new normal. This sounds counter-intuitive. But if change is going to stick, it needs to get baked into the ordinary, everyday processes, systems and routines of the business and its people. And, *for a while at least*, these new processes, systems and routines will be stable and unchanging, producing value for the business without the need for any further change or another new strategy – at least for now.

Leaders must also accept the fact that change will not always be exciting or action-packed or risky. Indeed, to properly deliver Focus and Consistency in the later stages of the change, leaders need to embrace the duller, less eventful, frankly more boring (and therefore much easier!) nature of their 'change' programme. After all, the main reason that change *ever* becomes risky for a business is when that change has been left too late and is now overdue, perhaps because changing customer demands have gone unnoticed or maybe competitors have stolen a march on you. So don't wait for a 'burning platform' to trigger a change. Instead, always be keeping a weather eye on what's coming at you, and pre-empting any such threat – even when it's as yet no more than the smell of smoke in the air.[6]

To do this, leaders need to pay as much attention to the low-profile parts of their work as they do to the more visible. And we need them to protect the change by opting, not for continuously new activity, but for *inactivity* (*no* change to the strategy, *no* new, potentially conflicting initiatives) until the change has bedded down. Of course, for most leaders, it was precisely their ability to visibly engage in high-profile activity that got them to their leadership role in the first place. So this call to choose *in*activity and to focus on the *in*visible can seem very counter-intuitive. Indeed, to some, this might not seem like the work of leadership at all. But choosing and actually embracing the value of boredom and inactivity is essential if leaders are to help this new strategy or change bed down. That is how to make your change the new routine, rather than just another change initiative that didn't work.

4. The Agency Delusion

This Delusion meant leaders believed that it was people alone (albeit both leaders and managers) who make change happen. Therefore, the success or failure of a change was down to how capable people were, how hard they worked and how resilient they proved. The result was that leaders viewed any problems with the change as exclusively a 'people problem' rather than perhaps also a problem with the structural aspects of the organization. The lesson for leaders of the 'Step Up, Step Back' approach? **It's not just about 'fixing' the people, it's about re-making the whole system.**

This research tells us that, if all the elements which make up the 'system' of the organization – i.e. both people and structure – aren't changed to help support the new strategy or change being asked for, then the current structures will slowly defeat the change. The reason is simple: the existing structures require no new input from individuals to make them work. They just work, delivering the old strategy or way of doing things. Meanwhile at least initially the *new* strategy or change needs regular, active input from individuals (i.e. their effort and willpower and resilience) to push it forward – until these individuals have re-made the structures to support the new strategy or way of working.

And if the old structures aren't changed to support the new strategy, eventually these individuals will give up, perhaps moving jobs or even organizations, and the existing structures (and the old strategy that they support) will win – in large part because they didn't need to expend any effort to beat the change. So, if you don't change the existing structures and you rely solely on people – as those in thrall to the Agency Delusion are prone to do – the system can't work properly and, despite all the efforts and willpower and resilience of people, the structure will win out and the change will die.

So, if you want this change to stick, leaders need to re-make the structures of their organizations rather than merely 'fixing' the people within them. And because they are in positions of authority and power – which gives them greater leverage within the system – it is leaders who are best-placed to make such structural changes, because it is disproportionately easy for them to do so.

If you do this, then as a leader, you shouldn't ever have to 'fix' it personally – and nor should anyone else. Because in a system that's working well, that's supporting the change you've asked for, the need for individual heroics or 'above and beyond' effort should be minimal. Instead, you should have re-structured the system so that personal 'fixes' or individual heroics are no longer necessary. Therefore, your job as a leader is not just to engage in leadership *behaviours* – though these are important. Rather, you need to think more about leadership *endeavours*. In other words, think more widely about the range of things for which you can use your power. And, in particular, choose to use the power you have (your agency) to make changes to the structures of the organization, so that the *system* is re-made (and can work properly) to support the change.

That means that other people – especially those lower down the organization – when they're trying to decide what to do, or how to behave, can now look to the *system*, rather than to you personally, as the prompt to help them work out what to do or how they need to act. It's no longer a personal (or agentic) solution; it's a structural and therefore systemic one. And that means the change is inherently less fragile and more sustainable because at this point, you no longer need leaders (or any other individuals, for that matter) to continue, by deploying their effort and willpower and resilience, to push the change forward or keep it going. Instead, the *structures* of the organization – and the entire system that these create – are now doing the heavy-lifting for you.

Armed with these specific ways to challenge the Four Delusions of Leadership, we can start to view leadership differently. And to see more clearly the benefits this kind of leadership has for leaders, for managers and for organizations.

The benefits for leaders, for managers and for organizations

Right at the start of this book, we tried to imagine a world where, as a leader, the change you wanted was delivered as you intended, and without you having to be involved in every detail of it. A world where, as a manager, you understood the change that leaders wanted so that you could fully use your autonomy to deliver it. And where, as an organization, you could build a track record for successful, sustainable change that galvanized people rather than frustrated them.

If, as a leader, you lead strategic change using the 'Step Up, Step Back' approach, and if, as a manager, you hold your leaders accountable for delivering the four 'asks' at the three critical stages, then you can expect three outcomes from a change that is led in this way.

1) **For leaders: more time for the true work of leadership – the 'Green Zone'.**

   Having invested time and effort being clear and re-aligning the organization in the early stages of the change, direct leader involvement is increasingly unnecessary – because the whole system is now doing the heavy-lifting required for the change. That early effort – time and attention given to the 'zero glam' work and the people who were doing it – frees up leaders to spend the later stages of the change, not on the detail of that change – because they're not needed for that now – but rather, for the more strategic, 'green zone' work of leadership that focuses instead on:

   - why we're doing this, and why now;
   - what it will deliver (the key outcomes of this endeavour);
   - how we'll behave – with all those needed to effect the change.

   This may take a certain bravery from leaders – as well as a re-learning of much that we currently believe 'leadership' to be. But the prize is huge: to work in the 'green zone' on issues of strategy rather than on questions of tactics; to successfully re-shape organizations for the benefit of investors and the people who work in them; and to steward the next generation of leaders who come after them to see what great leadership really takes.

2) **For managers: 'meaningful' autonomy – real empowerment in the 'Blue Zone'.**

Managers are able and willing to get on with the implementation (choosing activities and managing them to successful, sustained outcomes) without having to check in with, or seek input, support or cover from, leaders. The 'blue zone' is now fully theirs. Which means they are able to truly excel, thereby taking on more responsibility and learning to lead in their own right.

And, as well as getting on with implementing the new strategy, managers also now have time to stand back, reflect and learn. First, about how their own 'blue zone' work is going (what's working and what's not). This makes their current job more interesting and less risky. And second, about the effectiveness and consistency of their leaders' 'green zone' work to make sure leaders do this job properly. This means they can keep leaders honest about the amount of time and effort they are giving to the 'green zone', meaning the green/blue split continues to work – for the benefit of leaders, managers and the organization as a whole. It also means managers learn the right lessons now about what leadership takes, so they are better able to lead when they're in that role themselves.

3) **For the organization: successful, sustainable change.**

The new strategy or change is successfully implemented and, because this is achieved as much by remaking the structure as by using pure agency (the willpower, effort and resilience of individuals), this change stands much more chance of being sustained, because it has been designed into the structures of the organization and doesn't need ongoing input (even more willpower, effort and resilience) from leaders or managers to sustain it. Leaders and managers have played their respective parts to make this happen, but now the system of the organization – via its structures, processes and routines – can keep it going.

Acknowledgements

This book began life – a while ago now – as a doctoral thesis. And so my first thanks must go to those who helped shape that work. The expertise, criticism and support of my supervisors (Professor Chahrazad Abdallah, Dr Richard Tacon and Emeritus Professor Chris Voss), and my viva-examiners (Professor Julia Balogun and Professor Michael Smets) made this a much better piece of research than it would otherwise have been. And to Birkbeck, University of London, for the excellent research training and support, as well as a Scholarship that helped fund it.

To my informants, who gave so generously of their time: thank you for meeting me as often as I needed to, so I could properly understand your stories; thanks for searching for the old presentations and documents you remembered but couldn't find the first time you looked; and thanks for checking my write-ups of the stories that resulted. I can only admire the dedication and resilience with which you tried to change your organizations.

When it came to turning the research into a book, I knew I needed a good literary agent. And, thanks to my always-generous friend Dr Rebecca Newton, I found one in Giles Anderson. Thank you, Giles, for your help in turning my initial idea into a book proposal and then, with the help of an introduction from my friend and networking goddess Julia Hobsbawm, in finding the right home for it. That home was Bloomsbury Business. My thanks especially to Ian Hallsworth, Publisher, who seemed to love this book right from the start; and to the brilliant Allie Collins, who managed the process of turning the manuscript into an actual book.

Thank you also to the people who read it before submission – to Philip Collins, Dr Heidi Gardner, Adrian Bettridge, Professor Fiona Murray and Meghan Oates. Your all-quite-different comments drove me crazy at the time but made the book so much better. I am honoured to have 'help' of this calibre. Thank you also to my former HBR editor, the amazing Sarah Greene Carmichael, who provided superb comments on the close-to-final manuscript and who – not for the first time – made my writing clearer and tighter than it was before.

My most important editor, though, was undoubtedly Spencer Livermore who read the book several times. Spencer, your insights about how to structure (and restructure!) the book were astonishingly smart. Your ability to cut to the point of a paragraph and help me get out of my own way linguistically was something I couldn't have done without. And your dedication in reading the final manuscript through, in full, one last time – and the quality and detail of your red pen comments – was what gave me the confidence to actually submit it. So now, to the various titles you already hold (including Peer of the Realm and my closest friend), I now need to add 'editor extraordinaire'. Thank you.

The opportunity to teach and work with smart, committed people is an everyday privilege for me. In the context of this book, it has also given me the opportunity to try out, and improve upon, my ideas. So to the thousands of students and executives at London Business School, the London School of Economics and now at MIT, to whom I have taught parts of this new approach over the years, thank you for all the smart questions you asked and all the doubts that these provoked. You made my thinking better.

And finally to my clients: many of you will recognize some of the concepts in this book and, again, they are better and sharper because of the discussions we had. You also provided virtually all the practical examples in the book – for which I am extremely grateful. I'm sure your stories will inspire others, as they have inspired me.

Endnotes

Introduction: Why this book is needed

1   The much-quoted myth that 70 per cent of change efforts fail appears to be exactly that – a myth. There is little or no empirical research to support it. One early source of this stat may have been Hammer & Champy's 1993 book *Reengineering the Corporation*, where they make what they call an 'unscientific estimate … that as many as 50 per cent to 70 per cent' of re-engineering efforts fail to achieve their intended results (1993:200). This 'unscientific estimate' was gradually assimilated into mainstream and even some peer-reviewed articles apparently without anyone ever going back to validate it. Examples include Beer and Nohria's well-known *Harvard Business Review* article in which they claim 'the brutal fact is that about 70% of change initiatives fail' (2000:113) but provide no evidence of this; and John Kotter's book, *A Sense of Urgency*, where this 70 per cent failure rate is again claimed but not substantiated (2008:12). A 2006 McKinsey & Company study sought to provide some evidence: they asked 1,536 leaders about their experience of change. Only 38 per cent said their change efforts had been 'completely' or 'mostly' successful. While this still leaves a lot of room for partial success – in the same study, only 11 per cent said their change efforts were 'completely' or 'mostly' *unsuccessful* – this does suggest something is being lost in translation between the change that leaders are asking for and the change that's being delivered. (For more on this, see Hughes, 2011, 'Do 70 Per Cent of All Organizational Change Initiatives Really Fail?', *Journal of Change Management*, 11(4), 451–465; Hammer and Champy, 1993, *Reengineering the Corporation: A Manifesto for Business Revolution*, HarperCollins; Beer and Nohria, 2002, 'Cracking the Code of Change', *Harvard Business Review*, 78(3), 133–141; Kotter, 2008, *A Sense of Urgency*, Harvard Business School Press; and McKinsey & Company, 2006, 'Organizing for successful change management: A McKinsey Global Survey', *McKinsey Quarterly*, June 2006.)

2   We know that there are often material differences in how leaders and managers perceive the relative success of the same change activities. For example, in a study of 28 organizations going through change, there were significant differences in how well senior leaders believed the change was going, versus their middle managers. The specific items which showed the greatest disparities in perception were: 'the change has increased empowerment in the organization' with which 71 per cent of senior leaders agreed, compared with just 44 per cent of middle managers; and 'the pace of change is "burning out" many middle managers in the organization', with which 54 per cent of middle managers agreed, compared with only 29 per cent of their senior leaders. Interestingly, the areas of greatest disparity between leaders and managers related to middle-manager autonomy, stress and frustration. See Doyle, Claydon and Buchanan, 2000, 'Mixed results, lousy process: the management experience of organizational change', *British Journal of Management*, 11(Special Issue), S59–S80.

Chapter 1: The Problem

1   Bass, 1990, 'From Transactional to Transformational Leadership: Learning to Share the Vision', *Organizational Dynamics*, 18, 19–31 at p. 21

2   Shamir, House and Arthur, 1993, 'The Motivational Effects of Charismatic Leadership: A Self-Concept Based Theory', *Organization Science*, 4(4), 577–594

3   For more on the academic background to transformational leadership, see the likes of Bass, 1985, *Leadership and performance beyond expectations*, Free Press; Bass, 1999, 'On the taming of charisma: a reply to Janice Beyer', *The Leadership Quarterly*, 10(4), 541–553; Bass and Avolio, 1990, 'Multifactor Leadership Questionnaire', Consulting Psychologists Press; Bass and Avolio (Eds.), 1994, *Improving organizational effectiveness through transformational leadership*, Sage; Bass, and Riggio, 2006, *Transformational Leadership*, 2nd Ed., Lawrence Erlbaum

4   Dionne, Gupta, Sotak, Shirreffs, Serban, Hao, Kim and Yammarino, 2014, 'A 25-year perspective on levels of analysis in leadership research', *The Leadership Quarterly*, 25, 6–35; and see also Lowe and Gardner, 2001, 'Ten years of the Leadership Quarterly: Contributions and challenges for the future', *The Leadership Quarterly*, 11(4), 459–514

5   Kotter, 1995, 'Leading Change: why transformation efforts fail', *Harvard Business Review*, 73, 59–67; and in his 1996 book, *Leading Change*, Harvard Business School Press

6   Bass, 1990, *op. cit.*, pp. 19–20

7   Van Knippenberg and Sitkin, 2013, 'A critical assessment of charismatic-transformational leadership research: back to the drawing board?', The Academy of Management Annals, 7(1), 1–60, at p. 12. This article is one of the best critiques of the concept of transformational leadership and essential reading for anyone who wants ammunition to combat the received wisdom that transformational leadership is even an empirically robust construct, let alone sufficient on its own for the complex, nuanced business of leading strategic change

8   Bass, 1990, *op. cit.*, p. 20

9   One notable exception is Vera and Crossan's (2004) paper, 'Strategic Leadership and Organizational Learning', Academy of Management Review, 29(2), 222–240

10   Again, there are a few exceptions, notably Nadler and Tushman's (1990) excellent examination of whether transformational leadership is sufficient, especially for the later stages of a change. See Nadler and Tushman, 1990, 'Beyond the charismatic leader: leadership and organizational change', *California Management Review*, Winter, 77–97

11   See Alvesson and Spicer, 2012, 'Critical leadership studies: the case for critical performativity', Human Relations, 65(3), 367–390 at p. 384; and also O'Reilly and Reed, 2010, 'Leaderism: An evolution of managerialism in UK public service reform', *Public Administration*, 88(4), 960–978

12   What Nadler and Tushman called 'the need for continuing magic' – see Nadler and Tushman, 1990, 'Beyond the charismatic leader: leadership and organizational change', *California Management Review*, Winter, 77–97, at p. 84

13   Report by PwC, reported in the *Financial Times*, 15 May 2017 – see https://www.ft.com/content/ded1823a-370e-11e7-99bd-13beb0903fa3. See also Jeffrey Sonnenfeld in *Fortune Magazine*, 6 May 2015, which suggested the average tenure of a S&P 500 CEO was 4.9 years – see http://fortune.com/2015/05/06/ceo-tenure-cisco/

14   It was the great James March who talked about the 'search for drama' that has coloured much of our understanding of organizational change. See James March, 1981, 'Footnotes to Organizational Change', *Administrative Science Quarterly*, 26, 563–577

15   Quentin Skinner, the former Regius Professor of History at Cambridge, has made the point that 'The question of the relative weight to be assigned to agents and structure' became a preoccupying question for social scientists and historians from the early 1980s onwards. See Skinner, 1985, *The Return of Grand Theory in the Human Sciences*, Canto Books, at p. 18

16   Some evidence suggests that particular parts of the world may be more susceptible than others to an overly agentic focus. Professors Richard Nisbett and Takahiko Masuda have conducted a number of empirical studies investigating how people from different cultures interpret certain visual prompts. In one study, the researchers showed a short video of fish swimming underwater to two groups of people – the first, a group of 41 Japanese, and the other, a group of 36 Americans. When asked to describe what they had seen, the Americans talked mainly about the fish (clearly the protagonists of the video), whereas the Japanese group talked much more about the environment in which the fish were swimming,

including the plants they swam around, the other creatures they encountered and the relationships between these elements. In another study, American and Japanese students were asked to take a photo of a person. The results were very different: the Americans tended to take a photo of the person's face, whereas the photos the Japanese students took showed the whole person, as well as the environment they were in. In the Japanese photos, the person took up a much smaller proportion of the total view. And being able to notice the environment someone is in is a critical first step in understanding the impact that that environment can have on the person's decisions, actions or achievements. (For more on this research, see Richard Nisbett, 2003, *The Geography of Thought: How Asians and Westerners Think Differently – and Why*, Nicholas Brealey Publishing; as well as Masuda and Nisbett, 2001, 'Attending holistically vs analytically: Comparing the context sensitivity of Japanese and Americans', *Journal of Personality and Social Psychology*, 81, 922-934; and Nisbett and Masuda, 2003, 'Culture and Point of View', PNAS, 100(19), 11163-11170; https://doi.org/10.1073/pnas.1934527100.) I have certainly experienced resistance from groups of American students and executives when I have challenged the power of agency. But in my more recent work with Asian audiences and groups, I am also finding an increasing focus on the individual as an agent of change, regardless of their environment. Might this be the influence of an increasingly 'Hollywood' version of leadership on Asian business, whether through trade (meeting and working with 'Hollywood' leaders), education (reading case studies about 'Hollywood' leaders) or media (watching 'Hollywood' leaders in movies and shows now syndicated worldwide)?

17   One expression of this idea is Anthony Giddens' Structuration Theory. This theory seeks to understand any human activity in terms of both agency and structure, where primacy is given to neither but rather a balance sought between the two. See Giddens, 1984, *The constitution of society: outline of the theory of structuration*, Polity Press

18   The distinction I make here between 'hard' and 'soft' structure has been called other things by other people. Ranson, Hinings and Greenwood used the terms 'structural' and 'interactionist' (Ranson, Hinings and Greenwood, 1980, 'The structuring of organizational structures', *Administrative Science Quarterly*, 25, 1–17) while Paula Jarzabkowski made the distinction between 'procedural' and 'interactive' structure (Jarzabkowski, 2008, 'Shaping strategy as a structuration process', *Academy of Management Journal*, 51(4), 621–650). Either way, the point is structure isn't just the hard, processual elements like KPIs and org charts: it's also the soft, social elements such as the habits, routines and culture of the organization and the people within it.

19   Deal and Kennedy's (1982:4) definition of culture – see Deal and Kennedy, 1982, *Corporate Cultures: The Rites and Rituals of Corporate Life*, Perseus Books

20   Stephen Barley memorably described structure as 'patterned action' (1986: 79) – in other words, the accumulated (or, to use his term 'congealed' (1986: 81)) actions of individuals which, over time, become the accepted ways of working within the organization. See Barley, 1986, 'Technology as an occasion for structuring: Evidence from observations of CT scanners and the social order of radiology departments', *Administrative Science Quarterly*, 31(1), 78–108

21   This is true even in the most rigorous and frequently-cited published research: for example, Gioia & Chittipeddi (1991) where the duration of the change studied was 12 months – see Gioia and Chittipeddi, 1991, 'Sensemaking and sensegiving in strategic change initiation', *Strategic Management Journal*, 12(6), 433–448; or Balogun and Johnson (2004), where the duration of the change studied was 11 months – see Balogun and Johnson, 2004, 'Organizational restructuring and middle manager sensemaking', *Academy of Management Journal*, 47(4), 523–549; or Hope (2010), where the change studied last only four months – see Hope, 2010, 'The politics of middle management sensemaking and sensegiving', *Journal of Change Management*, 10(2), 195–215

22   Excerpted from Morris and Raben, 1995, 'The fundamentals of change management' in Nadler, Shaw & Walton (Eds.), *Discontinuous change leading organizational transformation*, Jossey-Bass, at p. 64; Kanter, Stein and Todd, 1992, 'Implementing Change' in *The Challenge of Organizational Change*, Free Press, First Edition, at p. 383; Cummings and Worley, 1993,

Organizational Development and Change, West Publishing Company; and Kotter, 1996, *Leading Change,* Harvard Business School Press, at p. 21

23   Among my favourites are Stephen Barley's 1986 paper exploring how scanning technicians adapted to the introduction of new CT scanning technology (see Barley, 1986, 'Technology as an occasion for structuring: evidence from observations of CT scanners and the social order of radiology departments', *Administrative Science Quarterly,* 31, 78–108); and Stensaker and Falkenberg's 2007 exploration of how managers in a large Norwegian oil company responded to a new, four-year strategic change initiative (see Stensaker and Falkenberg, 2007, 'Making sense of different responses to corporate change', *Human Relations,* 60(1), 137–177)

24   It is for this reason, i.e. to de-position this Agentic Bias, that I sometimes prefer to use the term leadership 'endeavours' rather than leadership 'actions' or 'behaviours'. The latter terms can imply that leaders remain solely agentic in what they choose to do, whereas 'endeavours' implies that they may also deploy their agency to effect structural changes

25   In addition to the work on Structuration Theory (e.g. Giddens, 1984; Ranson et al., 1980), the well-established field of Systems Dynamics has shown in numerous empirical studies that it is the system, rather than the agent, that is the main driver of organizational outcomes. The famous Beer Game, designed by MIT's Jay Forester in the 1960s and played with thousands of MIT students since, has demonstrated time and again that the structure and context of an organization is more important than the decisions made by the individuals within it. The Beer Game is a simulation where participants play different roles to produce, distribute and sell beer over a 24-week period. Their only objective is to maximize their own profits and they will each take decisions at various times during the game to try to do that. The problem is that, because they are part of a system, the results of these individual decisions will be shaped by the system; they may also cause some unintended consequences. One of the interesting things about facilitating the Beer Game is how confident participants are at the start of the simulation that they will be different, that they will beat the system and prove the power of agency. Ninety minutes later, when the results are on the walls, and those results look essentially exactly like all the other results produced every other time we've played the Beer Game, the truth starts to dawn on them. That, whatever the literature on leadership and change might have told you, actually it is the *system* that creates behaviour (and, in turn, largely determines outcomes), by either enabling or constraining the choices that individuals feel able and willing to make. For more details on the Beer Game, see Peter Senge, 2006, *The Fifth Discipline,* 2nd Ed., Random House, at pp. 27–54. And if you fancy playing it for yourself, join us at MIT for any of our courses that includes a session on Systems Dynamics

26   It's worth noting that the research questions in so-called 'process studies' do indeed usually start with the words 'how' and 'why'. For more on the value of such studies, see Langley, Smallman, Tsoukas and Van de Ven, 2013, 'Process studies of change in organization and management: unveiling temporality, activity and flow', *Academy of Management Journal,* 56(1), 1–13; and Pettigrew, 1997, 'What is a processual analysis?', *Journal of Management,* 13(4), 337–348. And for an excellent example of the deep and very practical insights that such a study can produce, see Ann Langley's 1989 paper, 'In search of rationality: the purposes behind the use of formal analysis in organizations', *Administrative Science Quarterly,* 34, 598–631

Chapter 2: The Research

1   For more on the benefits and methodology of theoretical sampling, see Kathleen Eisenhardt's seminal 1989 paper, 'Building theories from case study research', *Academy of Management Review,* 14(4), 532–550 and also Eisenhardt and Graebner, 2007, 'Theory building from cases: opportunities and challenges', *Academy of Management Journal,* 50(1), 25–32

2   The benefits of using outcome metrics when assessing the relative success of change programmes is well established, especially when the outcomes are chosen by the business itself. Andrew Pettigrew (1990) argued that empirical change researchers must 'define what change means in their research design' (1990: 273), ideally in outcome terms because, as

Pettigrew et al. (2001) noted: 'the outcome provides a focal point, an anchor for the whole investigation' (2001:701). See Pettigrew, 1990, 'Longitudinal field research on change: theory and practice', *Organization Science*, 1(3), 267–292; Pettigrew, Woodman and Cameron, 2001, 'Studying organizational change and development: challenges for future research', *Academy of Management Journal*, 44(4), 697–713; as well as Hiller, DeChurch, Murase and Doty, 2011, 'Searching for outcomes of leadership: a 25-year review', *Journal of Management*, 37(4), 1137–1177

3   For more on why so-called 'polar cases' are especially useful in case study research, see Eisenhardt, 1989, 'Building theories from case study research', *Academy of Management Review*, 14(4), 532–550; and Pettigrew, 1990, 'Longitudinal field research on change: theory and practice', *Organization Science*, 1(3), 267–292

4   Barley, 2006, 'When I write my masterpiece: thoughts on what makes a paper interesting', *Academy of Management Journal*, 46(1), 16–20, at p. 16

5   Elrod and Tippett, 2002, 'The "Death Valley" of Change', *Journal of Organizational Change Management*, 15(3), 273–291

6   Report by PwC, reported in the *Financial Times*, 15 May 2017 – see https://www.ft.com/content/ded1823a-370e-11e7-99bd-13beb0903fa3. See also Jeffrey Sonnenfeld in *Fortune Magazine*, 6 May 2015, which suggested the average tenure of a S&P 500 CEO was 4.9 years – see http://fortune.com/2015/05/06/ceo-tenure-cisco/

7   As Emeritus Professor Chris Voss and colleagues have noted 'retrospective cases allow for more controlled case selection [because] it is possible to identify cases that reflect either success or failure only in retrospect.' See Voss, Tsikriktsis and Frohlich, 2002, 'Case research in operations management', *International Journal of Operations and Production Management*, 22(2), 195–219, at p. 202

8   For more on the benefits of this kind of case study design, see Leonard-Barton, 1990, 'A dual methodology for case studies: synergistic use of a longitudinal single site with replicated multiple sites', *Organization Science*, 1(3), 248–266; Eisenhardt and Graebner, 2007, 'Theory building from cases: opportunities and challenges', *Academy of Management Journal*, 50(1), 25–32; and Noda and Bower, 1996, 'Strategy making as iterated processes of resource allocation', *Strategic Management Journal*, 17, 159–192. For a more general introduction to using case study research designs, see Robert Yin, 2009, *Case study research: design and methods*, 4th Edition, Sage Publications. And for more on the importance of including time as a key aspect of research design, see Shamir's 2011 paper, 'Leadership takes time: some implications of (not) taking time seriously in leadership research', *The Leadership Quarterly*, 22(2), 307–315; and Langley, Smallman, Tsoukas and Van de Ven, 2013, 'Process studies of change in organization and management: unveiling temporality, activity and flow', *Academy of Management Journal*, 56(1), 1–13

9   Or, as one of the masters of this kind of research has commented: it is 'only when people focus on the past from some point behind it' that they can 'look back over the episode to sort out what happened' – the great Karl Weick, 1995, *Sensemaking in Organizations*, Sage Publications, at pp. 43 and 306

10   Process researchers such as Stephen Barley, Ann Langley and Julia Balogun show how analyzing the likes of meeting notes, strategy presentations and diary entries made and used at the time of the change that's being studied can help counter any hindsight bias that may still be present in what informants recall from this time. For great examples of their work, see Barley, 1986, 'Technology as an occasion for structuring: evidence from observations of CT scanners and the social order of radiology departments', *Administrative Science Quarterly*, 31, 78–108; Langley, 1989, 'In search of rationality: the purposes behind the use of formal analysis in organizations', *Administrative Science Quarterly*, 34, 598–631; and Balogun and Johnson, 2004, 'Organizational restructuring and middle manager sensemaking', *Academy of Management Journal*, 47(4), 523–549

11   As Langley, et al. (2013) put it, process research questions 'focus on how things unfold and change over time' (see Langley, Smallman, Tsoukas and Van de Ven, 2013, 'Process studies of change in organization and management: unveiling temporality, activity and flow', *Academy of Management Journal*, 56(1), 1–13, at p. 9). As such, 'history and

context are central to this approach' (see Dawson and Buchanan, 2005, 'The way it *really* happened: competing narratives in the political process of technological change', *Human Relations*, 58(7), 845–865, at p. 847), requiring the researcher to 'interrogat[e] phenomena over time using language of what, who, where, why, when and how' (Pettigrew, Woodman and Cameron, 2001, 'Studying organizational change and development: challenges for future research', *Academy of Management Journal*, 44(4), 697–713, at p. 700)

12 Jeffrey Fear, 'Mining the Past: Historicizing Organizational Learning and Change' in Bucheli and Wadhwani (Eds.), 2014, *Organizations in Time: History, Theory, Methods*, Oxford University Press, at p. 173

13 For more on how historians select and interpret sources from the past, see Kipping, Wadhwani and Bucheli, 'Analyzing and Interpreting Historical Sources: A Basic Methodology' in Bucheli and Wadhwani (Eds.), 2014, *Organizations in Time: History, Theory, Methods, ibid.*

14 For more on the historian's methodology, see E.H. Carr, 1961, *What Is History?*, Penguin; and Geoffrey Elton, 2002, *The Practice of History*, 2nd Edition, Blackwell Publishing; and for more on how historical methods can be used to improve the quality of organizational research, see Gaddis, 2002, *The Landscape of History: How Historians Map the Past*, Oxford University Press; Burgelman, 2009, 'Combining grounded theorizing and historical methods: a proposal to strengthen the power of qualitative research', *Stanford Research Paper Series*, Paper No. 2045, 1–23; and also Bucheli and Wadhwani (Eds.), 2014, *Organizations in Time: History, Theory, Methods, ibid.*

15 Eisenhardt (1989), Pettigrew (1988 and 1990), Flyvbjerg (2006), Yin (2009) and Jarzabkowski (2008) all make strong arguments about why this kind of 'compare and contrast' research design can produce high-quality insights. See Eisenhardt, 1989, 'Building theories from case study research', *Academy of Management Review*, 14(4), 532–550; Pettigrew, 1988, 'Longitudinal field research on change: theory and practice', paper presented at the National Science Foundation Conference on Longitudinal Research Methods in Organizations; Pettigrew, 1990, 'Longitudinal field research on change: theory and practice', *Organization Science*, 1(3), 267–292; Flyvbjerg, 2006, 'Five misunderstandings about case-study research', *Qualitative Inquiry*, 12(2), 219–245; Yin, 2009, *Case study research: design and methods*, 4th Edition, Sage Publications, and Jarzabkowski, 2008, 'Shaping strategy as a structuration process', *Academy of Management Journal*, 51(4), 621–650. Both Stensaker and Falkenberg (2007) and Kaplan and Orlikowski (2013) provide excellent examples of the quality of the insights that such a design can generate – see Stensaker and Falkenberg, 2007, 'Making sense of different responses to corporate change', *Human Relations*, 60(1), 137–177; and Kaplan and Orlikowski, 2013, 'Temporal work in strategy making', *Organization Science*, 24(4), 965–995

16 For a classic explanation of how inductive research can produce new theory, see Kathleen Eisenhardt's 1989 paper 'Building theories from case study research', *Academy of Management Review*, 14(4), 532–550. The specific methodology I used to code the data and then induce and present the theoretical model in this study is known as the 'Gioia Methodology' after its creator, Professor Dennis Gioia. For more detail on this methodology, see Gioia, Corley and Hamilton, 2012, 'Seeking qualitative rigor in inductive research: notes on the Gioia methodology', *Organizational Research Methods*, 16(1), 1–17. And for examples of how this methodology is used, see the likes of Corley and Gioia, 2004, 'Identity ambiguity and change in the wake of a corporate spin-off', *Administrative Science Quarterly*, 49, 173–208; Nag, Corley and Gioia, 2007, 'The intersection of organizational identity, knowledge and practice: attempting strategic change via knowledge grafting', *Academy of Management Journal*, 50(4), 821–847; Gioia et al., 2010, 'Forging an identity: an insider-outsider study of processes involved in the formation of organizational identity', *Administrative Science Quarterly*, 55 (March), 1–46; Sonenshein et al., 2014, 'It's not easy being green: the role of self-evaluations in explaining support of environmental issues', *Academy of Management Journal*, 57(1), 7–37; and Patvardhan et al., 2015, 'Weathering a meta-level identity crisis: a coherent collective identity for an emerging field', *Academy of Management Journal*, 58(2), 405–435

17 See March's 2000 Plenary Address at the 16th EGOS Conference in Helsinki. Warren Bennis and James O'Toole made a similar point in their 2005 HBR article, 'How Business Schools Lost Their Way' (Harvard Business Review, May Issue, https://hbr.org/2005/05/how-business-schools-lost-their-way), arguing that the over-emphasis on the scientific model in Business Schools and the under-emphasis on the ontology and skills of the humanities has often blinded students to the messy complexity of the real world: 'When applied to business—essentially a human activity in which judgments are made with messy, incomplete, and incoherent data—statistical and methodological wizardry can blind rather than illuminate.' (Bennis and O'Toole, 2005: 96)

18 Dr. Antara Haldar from the University of Cambridge, writing in *The Atlantic*, 14 December 2018. See https://www.theatlantic.com/education/archive/2018/12/why-do-econ-classes-barely-mention-behavioral-economics/578092/

19 As Eisenhardt (1989) reminds us, when seeking to build theory from cases, any knowledge you have gleaned from whatever extant literature there is should be placed as far to the back of our minds as possible, in what Professor Dennis Gioia has described as an act of 'enforced ignorance of the literature' (Gioia et al., 2012, *op. cit.* at p. 7):

> Theory-building research is begun as close as possible to the ideal of no theory under consideration and no hypotheses to test. Admittedly, it is impossible to achieve this ideal of a clean theoretical slate. Nonetheless, attempting to approach this ideal is important because preordained theoretical perspectives or propositions may bias and limit the findings.

Eisenhardt, 1989, *op. cit.*, at p. 536

20 Gioia et al. 2012 *Op cit.* at p. 15

21 This is what Edmondson and McManus described as 'openness to input from the field' (Edmondson and McManus, 2007, 'Methodological Fit in Management Field Research', *Academy of Management Review*, 32(4), 1155–1179 at p. 1162). See also Gioia and Thomas, 1996, 'Identity, image and issue interpretation: sensemaking during strategic change in academia', *Administrative Science Quarterly*, 1, 370–403; Gioia et al. 2012, *op. cit.*

22 'Buckets' is a less technical term for the data structure used in the Gioia Methodology. Under this coding and analysis method, you group individual data (i.e. quotes) into First Order Categories, then into more abstract Second Order Themes (using the researcher's own terms) and finally, into what they term Aggregate Dimensions. These final, large 'buckets' – into which all the data now fits – will become the *dimensions* of the model – in this case, Clarity, Alignment, Focus, Consistency and Autonomy. These dimensions (and their sub-attributes) could then be tested for validity using Structural Equations Modelling in a mixed methods study. For more detail on the analysis of qualitative data, see Miles and Huberman, 1994, *Qualitative data analysis* 2nd Edition, Sage Publications

23 Or what my friend and colleague Professor John van Maanen termed 'close, trusting contact with the studied', 1988, *Tales of the Field: On Writing Ethnography*, University of Chicago Press, at pp. 21–22

24 Langley, A., 1989, 'In search of rationality: the purposes behind the use of formal analysis in organizations', *Administrative Science Quarterly*, 34, 598–631 at p. 691

25 Langley, 1989, *ibid.*, at p. 693

26 For more on this, see Ann Langley's 1999 paper on the benefits of what she terms 'temporal bracketing' in process study research designs – Langley, 1999, 'Strategies for theorising from process data', *Academy of Management Review*, 24(4), 691-710

Chapter 3: The Result

1 There is considerable research on management fads, for example the use (or, more accurately, non-use) of tools such as Total Quality Management introduced in many firms during the 1980s and 90s and specifically why these failed to become embedded within, or add value to, the firms that introduced them. See Abrahamson, 1991, 'Managerial fads and fashions: The diffusion & rejection of innovations', *Academy of Management Review*,

16(3), 586 – 612; and also Perkmann and Spicer, 2008, 'How are management fashions institutionalised? The role of institutionalised work', *Human Relations*, 61(6), 811-844. A number of scholars support the view that leaders should guard against such fads: as Gebhardt et al. (2006) argued, leaders need to show 'vigilance against management fads and fashions' (2006: 50) if their most important strategic changes are to be maintained. See Gebhardt, Carpenter and Sherry, 2006, 'Creating a market orientation: a longitudinal, multi-firm, grounded analysis of cultural transformation', *Journal of Marketing*, 70, 37-55

2   We can see the distinction between stepping back and stepping out in two recent studies. In Cheong, et al. (2016), a study of 226 pairs of leaders and followers found that 'when the managers or leaders engage in empowering behaviours toward their followers *unconditionally*, followers possibly perceive their leader as a permissive one, and feel that the leader is abdicating his or her responsibilities or duties' (2016: 610). The authors don't explain what they mean by 'unconditionally', nor do they explore how and why this finding might occur. But it may be that followers want leaders to step back, but not out – i.e. they want leaders to give them autonomy, but they still want their involvement and input when they need it. They may also want to be held to account. (For more details, see Cheong, Spain, Yammarino and Yun, 2016, 'Two Faces of Empowering Leadership', *The Leadership Quarterly*, 27, 602–616.) Also of interest is Langfred and Moye's (2004) paper which argued that autonomous employees may perform less well when they perceive that the autonomy given them is – in their words – a 'shameless attempt' to get them to take on more responsibility for the same pay or with inadequate resources (2004: 937). In other words, managers won't step up if they think the leader's attempt at stepping back is actually just a 'hospital pass' that asks managers to take responsibility for outcomes they can't control. See Langfred and Moye, 2004, 'Effects of Task Autonomy on Performance: An extended model considering motivational, informational, and structural mechanisms', *Journal of Applied Psychology*, 89(6), 934–945

Chapter 4: Ask #1: Clarity

1   As James March put it: 'there is likely to be a difference between the *maximum* clarity of goals and the *optimum* clarity'. We're going for optimum clarity here – as defined by managers, not leaders. The kind that will help managers make their own decisions about what to work on. Therefore, we need the right type of goals (outcome-based, rather than activity-based) and at the right level of specificity – i.e. clear but not micro. See James March, 'How We Talk & How We Act: Administrative Theory & Administrative Life', in Sergiovanni and Corbally (Eds.), 1986, *Leadership and Organizational Culture*, University of Illinois Press, at p. 25

2   The flow of each section in Chapters 4 to 8 – starting with what leaders should do and then explaining how this showed up in the cases – is of course exactly the opposite of the flow of the original inductive *research* which went from the case study data to abstract themes and only then to the dimensions and practical implications of the model that emerged. As JoAnne Yates has noted, this is often how inductive research ends up getting presented in its final form – even if this obscures the sequence and methods by which it was arrived at. See JoAnne Yates, 'Understanding Historical Methods in Organization Studies', in Bucheli and Wadhwani (Eds.), 2014, *Organizations in Time: History, Theory, Methods, op. cit.*, at p. 273

3   Porter, 1996, 'What is Strategy?', *Harvard Business Review*, November–December issue

4   Lafley and Martin, 2013, *Playing to Win*, Harvard Business School Press, at pp. 3 and 5. See also Martin, 2014, 'The Big Lie of Strategic Planning', *Harvard Business Review*, January–February issue

5   Bank of America Investor Relations presentations; The *FT*'s Lex column, 'Bank of America: call me responsible', 16 July 2018; John Maxwell's 'How Brian Moynihan is redefining Bank of America', published on Motley Fool, 16 March 2017

6   *Financial Times*, 16 April 2019, 'Retail banking insulates BofA from choppy markets' – by Rob Armstrong

7   London Stock Exchange Group stats

8   BofA shares traded at US$13.52 on 1 January 2016 and at US$27.50 on 1 January 2019

9   And indeed it would be hard to design the empirical research that might prove this assertion, given it would require some time-warping, counter-factual evidence – i.e. you'd have to run a change programme to its conclusion and assess its success against target outcomes at the end; and then go back in time and re-run the same change programme, with all the same conditions, but stop it prematurely and assess the gap in outcomes delivered at that point.

10   One way to do this is to embrace an ethnographer's skill set to properly understand the problems customers have that they need you to solve for them. For more on this, see Christian Madsbjerg and Mikkel Rasmussen, 2014, *The Moment of Clarity: Using the Human Sciences to Solve Your Toughest Business Problems*, Harvard Business School Press; Tim Brown, 2008, 'Design Thinking', *Harvard Business Review*, June issue; Clay Christensen, Scott Cook and Taddy Hall, 2005, 'Marketing Malpractice: The Cause and the Cure', *Harvard Business Review*, December issue

11   For great ideas about how to break down silos, see Gillian Tett, 2015, *The Silo Effect*, Simon & Schuster. And for the research behind why collaboration increases margin, especially in professional services firms, see Heidi Gardner, 2017, *Smart Collaboration*, Harvard Business School Press

12   This example is reproduced from Johnson, 2017, 'How to Communicate Clearly During Organizational Change', *Harvard Business Review* – see https://hbr.org/2017/06/how-to-communicate-clearly-during-organizational-change

13   See Teresa Amabile and Steven Kramer, 2011, 'The Power of Small Wins', *Harvard Business Review*, May issue, for how leaders can help employees stay motivated by helping them see progress in small wins. But note that small wins aren't 'quick wins'. In fact, Amabile and Kramer's argument that leaders can help employees stay motivated by helping them see the value of the work is borne out in the four cases here. As they argue, the role of leaders is to help employees see how their particular work is contributing to the whole, and in particular, to make sure that nothing undermines the value of the work they are doing. The work that needed to be done to effect fundamental change in the four cases was technical, long-term work – and it needed to happen in the early days of the change. That was what the CEO of the Ideal Case championed and made time for – thereby signalling to managers that this work was important

14   One famous proponent of the value of 'quick wins' is Harvard Business School's John Kotter – in fact, using 'short-term wins' is one of the steps in his well-known 8-Step Change Model – see 'Leading Change', 1996, *op. cit.*

15   An example of this human bias is the Planning Fallacy. This term was coined by Nobel-winner Daniel Kahneman and his colleague Amos Tversky: their work describes how humans systemically underestimate how long it will take them to do certain tasks – whether it's a project at work or completing their tax return. See Kahneman and Tversky, 1979, 'Intuitive prediction: biases and corrective procedures', *TIMS Studies in Management Science*, 12, 313–327; and also Buehler, Griffin and Ross, 2002, 'Inside the planning fallacy: The causes and consequences of optimistic time predictions' in Gilovich, Griffin and Kahneman (Eds.), *Heuristics and Biases: The Psychology of Intuitive Judgment*, Cambridge University Press, pp. 250–270

16   Nelson Repenning and John Sterman, 2002, 'Capability Traps and Self Confirming Attribution Errors in the Dynamics of Process Improvement', *Administrative Science Quarterly*, 47, 265–295

17   Wharton Professor Adam Grant has shown how when jobs that might otherwise be relatively mundane are given context and meaning because of how these roles are structured, employee satisfaction and performance improves. He studied employees working in a US-based customer call centre: those who spent time meeting customers and understanding how their individual work fitted into the company's mission had higher productivity and job satisfaction, as well as improved revenue per employee. As

Grant made clear in this study, leader rhetoric (or transformational leadership) was not enough to achieve these outcomes: rather it required employees' roles to be restructured to contain these additional work elements. See Grant, 2012, 'Leading with meaning: beneficiary contact, prosocial impact and the performance effects of transformational leadership', *Academy of Management Journal*, 55(2), 458–476. See also Teresa Amabile and Steven Kramer, 2011, 'The Power of Small Wins', *Harvard Business Review*, May issue on how leaders can give work meaning

18   David Rock has termed such questions 'Thinking Questions', precisely because they push the other person to do more of the thinking for themselves. See Rock, 2007, *Quiet Leadership: Six Steps to Transforming Performance at Work*, HarperCollins

19   I have borrowed this phrase from Hiefetz and Laurie's 2001 *Harvard Business Review* article, 'The Work of Leadership' (December issue) in which they call on leaders to 'give the work back'. But I think this may confuse some leaders: actually, the *only* work you need to give back is the 'blue-zone' stuff. The 'green-zone' work – *and it is still work!* – is most definitely the realm of leadership and, to some extent, can only be done by leaders.

20   Berger and Luckmann, 1967, *The Social Construction of Reality*, Penguin, p. 56

Chapter 5: Ask #2: Alignment

1   Camerer, Loewenstein and Weber, 1989, 'The Curse of Knowledge in Economic Settings: An Experimental Analysis', *Journal of Political Economy*, 97, 1232–1254

2   For more detail on this, see Newton, 1990, 'The Rocky Road from Actions to Intentions', PhD dissertation, Stanford University

3   Newton, 1990, *op. cit*, p. 44

4   Mortensen and Gardner, 2017, 'The Overcommitted Organization', *Harvard Business Review*, September–October issue

5   John Doerr, the billionaire investor and early-stage supporter of the likes of Google, terms such tools 'OKRs' – 'Outcomes and Key Results'. In his book, *Measure What Matters* (2017, Portfolio Penguin), he makes the case that OKRs are what helped drive 10x growth at Google. But whatever term you prefer, the important point is that having *outcome-based* metrics or KPIs is a critical part of driving performance.

6   Goodale, Koerner, and Roney, 1997, 'Analyzing the impact of service provider empowerment on perceptions of service quality inside an organization', *Journal of Quality Management*, 2(2), 191–215, at p. 198

7   Such so-called 'shared fate rewards' (Jansen et al., 2008: 999) have been shown to drive cross-functional and cross-level alignment. See Jansen, George, Van den Bosch and Volberda, 2008, 'Senior team attributes and organizational ambidexterity: the moderating role of transformational leadership', *Journal of Management Studies*, 45(5), 982–1007; also O'Reilly, Caldwell, Chatman, Lapiz and Self, 2010, 'How leadership matters: the effects of alignment on strategy implementation', *The Leadership Quarterly*, 21, 104–113

8   Ariely, 2010, 'You Are What You Measure', *Harvard Business Review*, June issue

9   Collins, 2001, *Great to Good*, William Collins Publishing

10   Robinson, Gallus, Lee and Rogers, 2018, 'The Demotivating Effect (and Unintended Message) of Awards' – *Harvard Kennedy School Working Paper*, unpublished, at the time of writing in the revise and re-submit process

11   Gneezy and Rustichini, 2000, 'A Fine is a Price', *Journal of Legal Studies*, 29(1), 1–17

12   And there is considerable evidence that paying people properly for the work they do does generate feelings of worth and satisfaction – see David Levine's study of more than 8,000 employees in nearly 100 manufacturing plants in the US and Japan. The workers receiving higher wages for a given job reported they were less likely to quit, more likely to work hard and felt happier in their jobs. See Levine, 1983, 'What Do Wages Buy?', *Administrative Science Quarterly*, 38, 462–483

13   Banker, Lee, Potter and Srinivasan, 1996, 'Contextual Analysis of Performance Impacts of Outcome-Based Incentive Compensation', *Academy of Management Journal*, 39(4), 920–948

14   Kerr, 1975, 'On the Folly of Rewarding A, While Hoping for B', *Academy of Management Journal*, 18(4), 769–782

15   Fong and Tosi, 2007, 'Effort, Performance and Conscientiousness: An Agency Theory Perspective', *Journal of Management*, 33(2), 161–179

16   John van Maanen, 1988, *Tales of the Field: On Writing Ethnography*, University of Chicago Press, at p. 26

Chapter 6: Ask #3: Focus

1   Teresa Amabile and Steven Kramer, 2011, 'The Power of Small Wins', *Harvard Business Review*, May issue

2   Elrod and Tippett, 2002, 'The "Death Valley" of Change', *Journal of Organizational Change Management*, 15(3), 273–291

3   Bougeois, 1981, 'On the Measurement of Organizational Slack', *Academy of Management Review*, 6(1), 29–39; borrowing from James March – see March and Simon, *Organizations*, Wiley; and also, Cyert and March, 1963, *A Behavioural Theory of the Firm*, Prentice-Hall

4   As Bazerman notes, it was Warren Bennis who first said that the best leaders are 'first-class noticers' (a term actually borrowed from Saul Bellow's novel, *The Actual*). See Bazerman, 2014, 'Becoming a First-Class Noticer', *Harvard Business Review*, July–August issue

5   For more on the value of slack to organizations, see Cyert and March, 1963, *A Behavioral Theory of the Firm*, Prentice-Hall; Bourgeois, 1981, 'On the Measurement of Organizational Slack', *Academy of Management Review*, 6(1), 29–39; and Leventhal and March, 1981, 'A Model of Adaptive Organizational Search', *Journal of Economic Behavior & Organization*, 2(4), 307–333

6   Clegg, Kornberger and Rhodes, 2005, 'Learning/Becoming/Organizing', *Organization*, 12(2), 147–167 at p. 157

7   Agrawal, Catalini, Goldfarb and Luo, 2018, 'Slack Time and Innovation', Working Paper – see https://papers.ssrn.com/sol3/papers.cfm?abstract_id=2599004

8   Manoush Zomorodi, 2018, *Bored and Brilliant: How Time Spent Doing Nothing Changes Everything*, Macmillan USA

9   Agrawal, Catalini et al., 2018, *op. cit.*

10   The value of sabbaticals is well-established, for both individuals and their organizations. In a study of 258 academics, half of whom were given a sabbatical and half of whom were not, those who had time away reported feeling refreshed personally and more productive when they returned to work. See Davidson, et al., 2010, 'Sabbatical leave: who gains and how much?', *Journal of Applied Psychology*, 95(5), 953-964. Similarly, in a study of 70 medical school faculty members, three quarters of them 'accomplished something substantial, such as writing books or reorganizing teaching programs, following the sabbaticals' – see Jarecky and Sandifer, 1986, 'Faculty members' evaluations of sabbaticals, *Journal of Medical Education*, 61(10), 803-807 at p. 803

11   A well-known example of this is the author Jonathan Franzen, who advised authors to turn off the Internet if they wanted to write good fiction (his eighth rule – see 'Ten Rules for Writing Fiction', published in the *Guardian*, 10 February 2010 (https://www.theguardian.com/books/2010/feb/20/ten-rules-for-writing-fiction-part-one))

12   This is what Carl Newport calls 'Deep Work'. For more on this, and his description of the benefits of structuring your time so that you can do this kind of work, see Newport, 2016, *Deep Work: Rules for Focused Success in a Distracted World*, Piatkus

13   The exact amount of time depends, inter alia, on the type of interruption. David Rock reported one 2005 study, done by the research firm Basex, that 'found that employees spent an average of 11 minutes on a project before being distracted. And after an interruption, it takes them 25 minutes to return to the original task, if they do at all'. See Rock, 2009, *Your Brain at Work: Strategies for Overcoming Distraction, Regaining Focus and Working Smarter All Day Long*, HarperBusiness at p. 47. The study, entitled 'Information Overload: We Have Met the Enemy and He Is Us' is available from www.

basex.com. Another commonly quoted number is that it takes an average of 23 minutes to regain the pre-interruption level of focus and that interruptions also increase stress (see Mark, Gudith and Klocke, 2015, 'The Cost of Interrupted Work: More Speed and Stress', https://www.ics.uci.edu/~gmark/chi08-mark.pdf)

14   See Mortensen and Gardner, 2017, 'The Overcommitted Organization', *Harvard Business Review, op. cit.*

15   See Staw, Standelands and Dutton, 1981, 'Threat rigidity effects in organizational behaviour: a multilevel analysis', *Administrative Science Quarterly*, 501–524; and Jensen, et al., 1994, 'Self-Interest, Altruism, Incentives and Agency Theory', *Journal of Applied Corporate Finance*, 7(2), 40–45

16   When our ancestors needed to escape the immediate danger of the sabre-toothed tiger standing in front of them, being able to describe the situation articulately, or being inclined to collaborate and share the risk, or thinking up brand new ways to escape that had never been tried before, weren't the most successful tactics. Instead, focusing on action rather than analysis, pushing your friend in front of you rather than helping them and going with the tried-and-tested method worked out better on average. *That* was what helped those people survive and so they're the ones who became our ancestors. As a result, the genes we inherited were from the people whose brains shut down those abilities – to communicate, collaborate and be creative – in times of stress

17   Leslie Perlow's memorable phrase for the paucity of time most managers experience – see Perlow, 1999, 'The Time Famine: Toward a Sociology of Work Time', *Administrative Science Quarterly*, 44, 57–81

18   For more general insights on how to say 'no' at work, see Joseph Grenny's 2019 article, 'How To Say "No" At Work Without Making Enemies', *Harvard Business Review*, 5 August 2019

19   The well-known Whitehall studies are probably the best example of longitudinal research that shows the linkage between job-control and stress. Started in the late 1960s, these studies followed 28,000 British civil servants through their careers, investigating how low-status (and therefore low job control) caused higher stress levels and, ultimately, adversely impacted their health. See Marmot, Rose, Shipley and Hamilton, 1978, 'Employment grade and coronary heart disease in British civil servants', *Journal of Epidemiology and Community Health*, 32(4), 244–249; Kuper and Marmot, 2003, 'Job strain, job demands, decision latitude and the risk of coronary heart disease within the Whitehall II study', *Journal of Epidemiology and Community Health*, 57(2), 147–153; and also Vaananen, et al., 2008, 'Lack of Predictability at Work and Risk of Acute Myocardial Infarction: An 18-Year Prospective Study of Industrial Employees', *American Journal of Public Health*, 98(12), 2264–2271. Numerous studies have also linked the concept of low 'job control' – defined as an employee's ability to control how he works and the tasks he works on (see Karasek, 1979, 'Job Demands, Job Decision Latitude, and Mental Strain: Implications for Job Redesign', *Administrative Science Quarterly*, 24, 285–308) – with higher stress and poorer health outcomes. These include the impact on both physical health, such as raised blood pressure (see Rau, Renate and Triemer, 2004, 'Overtime in Relation to Blood Pressure and Mood during Work, Leisure, and Night Time', *Social Indicators Research*, 67, 51–73); and mental health (for example, see de Lange, et al., 2004, 'The Relationships between Work Characteristics and Mental Health: Examining Normal, Reversed and Reciprocal Relationships in a 4-Wave Study', *Work and Stress*, 18, 149–66) More recently, a longitudinal study of 659 employees at a corporate headquarters in the United States, found that having freedom to decide how to work reduced stress. The study compared changes in health and well-being between a cohort of employees who were appraised just on measurable targets, with freedom to decide how to hit those targets, and specifically which hours to work; versus a cohort who stayed on the existing management approach, which closely monitored when, where, and how employees completed their work. The study found that those employees who were free to decide how to meet their targets scored higher on a range of well-being measures, including being less stressed and enjoying better sleep. See Moen, Kelly, Tranby and Huang, 2011, 'Changing Work,

Changing Health: Can Real Work-Time Flexibility Promote Health Behaviors and Well-Being?', *Journal of Health and Social Behavior*, 52(4), 404-429

20 Peter Senge, 2006, *The Fifth Discipline: The Art and Practice of The Learning Organization*, 2nd Ed., Random House, at p. 50

21 Peter Senge, 1990, *ibid.*

22 For more on the 'Do, Measure, Learn' feedback loop, see Eric Reis, 2011, *The Lean Start-Up Model: How Constant Innovation Creates Radically Successful Businesses*, Portfolio Penguin. Eric has shown that this learning loop works provided there is clarity and discipline at each of the stages. Fudging the decision, whether about what was originally targeted or about how successful the outcome was, compromises the quality of the learning loop and so isn't allowed.

23 For more on this, see David Rock's 2007 book, *Quiet Leadership, op. cit.*

Chapter 7: Ask #4: Consistency

1 Martin, 2014, 'The Big Lie of Strategic Planning', *Harvard Business Review, op. cit.*

2 Porter, 1996, 'What is Strategy?', *Harvard Business Review, op. cit.*

3 Gardner and Mortensen, 'The Overcommitted Organization', *Harvard Business Review, op. cit.*

4 Tom Peters and Robert Waterman, 1982, *In Search of Excellence: Lessons from America's Best-Run Companies*, Profile Books

5 Peters and Waterman, 1982, *ibid.* at p. 324

6 Included in Chip and Dan Heath's (2008) *Sticky Messages: Why Some Ideas Take Hold and Others Come Unstuck*, Arrow Books; but originally published in James Carville and Paul Begala's 2003 book, *Buck Up, Suck Up and Come Back to Me When you Foul Up: 12 Winning Secrets from the War Room*, Simon & Schuster

7 Mann and Cadman, 2014, 'Does Being Bored Make Us More Creative?', *Creativity Research Journal*, 26(2), 165–173. See also Mann, 2017, '*The Science of Boredom: The Upsides (and Downsides) of Downtime*', Robinson; and Zomorodi, 2017, '*Bored and Brilliant: How Time Spent Doing Nothing Changes Everything*', Macmillan

8 Although widely attributed to Parker, there is no actual written source for this – but it does sound like her

9 See http://paulgraham.com/startupideas.html, November 2012, 'How To Get Start-Up Ideas'

10 See Rita McGrath, 2019, *Seeing Around Corners*, Houghton Mifflin Harcourt

11 For more on how Gates spent his time, see https://www.cnbc.com/2019/07/26/bill-gates-took-solo-think-weeks-in-a-cabin-in-the-woods.html

12 The depressing reality of many such ideas – including Total Quality Management, Lean and business re-engineering – is that, largely because of how they are implemented, many fail to sustain whatever gains were initially made on their introduction. For more on why such improvements are not institutionalised, see Zeitz, Mittal and McAulay, 1999, 'Distinguishing adoption and entrenchment of management practices: a framework for analysis', *Organization Studies*, 20(5), 741-776, and also Perkmann and Spicer, 2008, 'How are management fashions institutionalised? The role of institutional work', *Human Relations*, 61(6), 811-844. These new practices, or fads, can also result in unintended negative consequences, such as change fatigue and lower morale, in turn reducing the organization's ability to change in the future. For more on the impact of such programmes and why they fail, see Zbaracki, 1998, 'The rhetoric and reality of total quality management', *Administrative Science Quarterly*, 43, 602-636; and Keating, Oliva, Repenning, Rockart and Sterman, 1999, 'Overcoming the Improvement Paradox', *European Management Journal*, 17(2), 120–134

Chapter 8: 'Meaningful' Autonomy

1 As with many inductive research studies, this research produced something different from what I'd originally imagined it would. I'd started out wanting to understand how and why change succeeds in some organizations and not in others. While the research did

answer that question, it also produced something that I hadn't envisaged – a model for implementing successful change that was not only sustainable, but which could be done by managers without the ongoing need for leaders. When I first started presenting this 'extra' finding in research seminars, I found resistance to it among my academic colleagues. They felt this wasn't the main point of the research and advised me to focus on the 'change' story, rather than the 'autonomy' story. They felt that this would make publishing easier, and I'm sure that, for this context, this was probably good advice. But when I came to talk about the research with people who might *use* it, they had a different reaction to these two stories. In all my conversations with both leaders and managers, it's the 'autonomy' story that has been the part of the research that has attracted them most. In fact, they don't see two distinct stories here at all: for both leaders and managers, the 'change' story and the 'autonomy' story are part of the *same* story – i.e. how can we make change happen, and then sustain it, in a way that doesn't require ongoing input from leaders? This, for them, is the prize that this new approach offers because it's the question they've been struggling with for years.

2   This is especially true for companies in the knowledge and services sectors. See James Haskett, Earl Sasser and Leonard Schlesinger, 1997, *The Service Profit Chain*, Free Press

3   Liu, Zhang, Wang and Lee, 2011, 'The effects of autonomy and empowerment on employee turnover: test of a multilevel model in teams', *Journal of Applied Psychology*, 96(6), 1305–1316 at p. 1306

4   See Langfred, 2013, 'To be or not to be autonomous: exploring why employees want more autonomy', *North American Journal of Psychology*, 15(2), 355–366

5   See Trougakos, Hideg, Hayden-Cheng and Beal, 2014, 'Lunch breaks unpacked: the role of autonomy as a moderator of recovery during lunch', *Academy of Management Journal*, 57(2), 405–421

6   See Fernandez and Moldogaziev, 2013, 'Employee Empowerment, Employee Attitudes and Performance: Testing a Causal Model', *Public Administration Review*, 73(3), 490–506

7   Den Hartog and Belschak, 2012, 'When does transformational leadership enhance employee proactive behaviour? The role of autonomy and role breadth self-efficacy', *Journal of Applied Psychology*, 97(1), 194–202 at p. 195

8   Saku Mantere's phrase for this was 'strategic agency' – see Mantere, 2008, 'Role Expectations and Middle Manager Strategic Agency', *Journal of Management Studies*, 45(2), 294–316

9   Spreitzer, 1995, 'Psychological empowerment in the workplace: dimensions, measurement and validation', *Academy of Management Journal*, 38(5), 1442–1465; and Spreitzer, 1996, 'Social structural characteristics of psychological empowerment', *Academy of Management Journal*, 39(2), 483–504

10   Kark, Shamir and Chen, 2003, 'The two faces of transformational leadership: Empowerment and dependency', *Journal of Applied Psychology*, 88(2), 246-255. See also Cheong, Spain, Yammarino and Yun, 2016, 'The two faces of empowering leadership: Enabling and burdening', *The Leadership Quarterly*, 27, 602-616

11   Indeed, this was one of the main benefits that proponents of 'transformational' leadership claimed for it. See Bass, 1990, *op. cit.*

12   Although the concept was first explained by William Sealey Gosset in his 1908 article, 'The Probable Error of a Mean' (see *Biometrika*, 6(1), 1–25), the term 'degrees of freedom' was first coined by the British statistician Ronald Fisher – see Fisher, 1922, 'On the Interpretation of X2 from Contingency Tables, and the Calculation of P', *Journal of the Royal Statistical Society*, 85(1), 87–94. The idea of how this concept could be used to illustrate change readiness in organizations was suggested by Brown and Eisenhardt, 1997, in 'The art of continuous change: linking complexity theory and time-paced evolution in relentlessly shifting organizations', *Administrative Science Quarterly*, 42, 1–34

13   Virginia Woolf in *The Diary of Virginia Woolf, Volume Three, 1925-1930*, Harcourt Brace

14   See Robert Trivers, 2011, 'Don't Believe Everything You Think', *New Scientist*, October 2011, Issue No. 2833

15   Piers Paul Read's book *Alive* (originally published in 1974 and reprinted in 2012 by Arrow Books) details the survivors' ordeal. The book was later made into a film of the same name, released in 1993 and starring Ethan Hawke.

16 Spencer Harrison's 2010 unpublished paper, 'Hope Organizing: The Case of the Andes Flight Disaster', presented at the Academy of Management Conference, Montreal, August 2010. See also Arne Carlson and Tyrone Pitsis, 'Experiencing Hope in Organizational Lives' in Morgan Roberts and Dutton (Eds.), 2009, *Exploring Positive Identities and Organizations: Building a Theoretical and Research Foundation*, Psychology Press

17 Spencer Harrison, direct quote from the 'New Insights into the Workings of Hope in Organizations' PDW Session, Academy of Management Conference, Montreal, 10 August 2010

Chapter 9: A Different Way to Think About Organizations

1 This way of thinking about organizations is based on Giddens' Structuration Theory – albeit a materially simplified version of it. For the original, see Anthony Giddens, 1984, *The Constitution of Society: Outline of the Theory of Structuration*, Polity Press. Structuration theory has been applied to organizations as a way to understand their dynamics – for example, see Ranson, Hinings and Greenwood, 1980, 'The structuring of organizational structures', *Administrative Science Quarterly*, 25, 1–17; Barley and Tolbert, 1997, 'Institutionalization and structuration: studying the links between action and institution', *Organization Studies*, 18(1), 93–117; Jarzabkowski, 2008, 'Shaping strategy as a structuration process', *Academy of Management Journal*, 51(4), 621–650; Pozzebon, 2004, 'The influence of a structurationist view on strategic management research', *Journal of Management Studies*, 41(2), 247–272; Pozzebon and Pinsonneault, 2005, 'Challenges in conducting empirical work using structuration theory: learning from IT research', *Organization Studies*, 26(9), 1353–1376; and by my MIT colleagues JoAnne Yates and Wanda Orlikowski, 1992, 'Genres of Organizational Communication: A Structurational Approach to Studying Communication and Media', *The Academy of Management Review*, 17 (2), 299–326

2 Giddens uses the word 'reified' to convey this idea – see Giddens, 1984, ibid. at p. 25

3 Indeed, the more able managers are, the less comfortable they are likely to be with assuming the risk inherent in making independent decisions where Clarity, Alignment, Focus and Consistency are not present

4 The benefits of being a charismatic rock star have been argued since the early 'Great Man' leadership writing of the 1920s. However, the benefits of quieter, more thoughtful and even introverted leadership are increasingly making an impact on leadership research. See David Rock's 2007 book, *Quiet Leadership, op. cit.*; Susan Cain's 2013 book, *Quiet: The Power of Introverts in a World That Can't Stop Talking*, Penguin; and Ed Schein's 2013 book, *Humble Inquiry: The Gentle Art of Asking Instead of Telling*, Berrett-Koehler Publishers

5 This was Deal and Kennedy's well-known definition of organizational culture, and it perfectly captures the idea that culture is highly dependent on the routines and habits that have accumulated over time so that they have become just accepted – almost invisible – ways of working by the people within the group. See Deal and Kennedy, 1982, *Corporate Cultures: The Rites and Rituals of Corporate Life*, Perseus Books. MIT Professor Ed Shein has a similar definition of organizational culture: 'a pattern of shared basic assumptions that was learned by a group as it solved its problems… that has worked well enough to be considered valid and, therefore, to be taught to new members as the correct way to perceive, think and feel in relation to those problems.' See Schein, 2004, *Organizational Culture and Leadership*, 3rd Edition, Jossey-Bass, at p. 17

6 As Jack Welch once advised, 'Change before you have to.' See Jack Welch and Suzy Welch, 2007, *Jack Welch Speaks: Wit and Wisdom from the World's Greatest Business Leader*, John Wiley & Sons

Index